POWERBOAT
HANDLING
Illustrated

CE
BU

CG•

CB•

International Marine / McGraw-Hill
Camden, Maine • New York • Chicago • San Francisco
• Lisbon • London • Madrid • Mexico City • Milan • New
Delhi • San Juan • Seoul • Singapore • Sydney • Toronto

POWERBOAT HANDLING

Illustrated

How to Make Your Boat Do
Exactly What You Want It to Do

BOB SWEET

The McGraw·Hill Companies

1 2 3 4 5 6 7 8 9 QPD QPD 0 9 8 7 6

Library of Congress Cataloging-in-Publication Data
Sweet, Robert J. (Robert James), 1942–
    Powerboat handling illustrated : how to make your boat do exactly what you want it to do / by Bob Sweet.
        p.   cm.
    Includes index.
    ISBN 0-07-146881-1 (paperback : alk. paper)
    1. Motorboats. 2. Boats and boating. I. Title.
    GV835.S94 2006
    797.1'25—dc22   2006012684

ISBN-13: 978-0-07146881-7
ISBN-10: 0-07-146881-1

Questions regarding the content of this book should be addressed to
International Marine
P.O. Box 220
Camden, ME 04843
internationalmarine.com

Questions regarding the ordering of this book should be addressed to
The McGraw-Hill Companies
Customer Service Department
P.O. Box 547
Blacklick, OH 43004
Retail customers: 1-800-262-4729
Bookstores: 1-800-722-4726

Unless otherwise noted, all illustrations and photos by author.

To my wife, Judy—partner in boating and in life

Contents

Contents

CHAPTER **12** Grounding

Acknowledgments

I've had many opportunities to host seminars and courses with boaters of all skill levels and types of boats. Invariably, no matter what the subject of the seminar, questions arise from the audience about boat handling—even from owners of rather large boats. It became clear to me that there was a dearth of understandable information available to these boaters. It was also apparent that this information needed to be presented in illustrated form.

Undertaking this book required consultation with a number of seasoned skippers and experts, and a lot of reading. The task has been to convert the more arcane technical information into practical, understandable techniques, and to parse that information with the ingrained experiences of seasoned skippers. Experienced mariners appear to have developed their understanding of their boats through years of hands-on trial and error. Even they often seem to have difficulty describing why they do what they do. Hopefully this book will help you bypass, or at least get a jump on, all those years of trial and error.

I would like to acknowledge a group of boaters who reviewed my illustrations and critiqued the maneuvers depicted therein. They include Frank Lingard, Charlie Perkins, and Jerry Daly. Conversations with and observations of skippers Frank Lingard, Bud Tietje, and Peter Moon—all holders of USCG Master's Licenses—were very helpful in formulating the procedures outlined in this book.

I've read and compared a wide range of books related to boats and boat handling along with online resources. A list of books and guides that I feel present good, detailed information on various aspects of the subject is provided at the end of this book for further reading.

A number of manufacturers were very helpful in providing photos and information. Grady-White, Crestliner, Volvo, Mercury Marine, Mustang, Tige, Caravell, Stingray, Regal, Larson, Glacier Bay, World Cat, AfriCat, Danforth, Fortress, Michigan Wheel, Lewmar, and Maptech are prominent in their assistance. I also obtained some excellent photos from the U.S. Coast Guard, U.S. Army, and National Oceanic and Atmospheric Administration (NOAA).

To gain access to various hulls for photographic purposes, I imposed upon a number of marinas and marine stores around Cape Cod with my trusty digital camera.

Last, but not least, I would like to acknowledge the U. S. Power Squadrons and my local Buzzards Bay squadron for providing me with the opportunity to meet with and instruct a host of boaters who have given me insights and motivation to write about boating.

A Harbor Adventure

Handling a boat can be a daunting task. These darn things just don't seem to want to do what we want them to do. It can be particularly frustrating after you see an experienced helmsman glide his craft gracefully into the dock, and you wonder "Why can't I do that?" To add to the stress, when you're at the helm, it seems that the spectators on the dock are really judges observing your every move and scoring your performance.

Imagine that you've just launched your new boat at the ramp in the harbor. Your family is aboard, and you are about to start your first shakedown cruise—a day trip to the island for a picnic, some swimming, and then back to the ramp. The boat's in the water, you've run your blowers and started the engine. The lines are in and stowed, the fenders are stored, your anchor is at the ready. Everyone is wearing a life jacket. You've taken all of the precautions and have charts at hand. You're all set to go.

Now, all you need to do is get through all those moored boats that populate the harbor. Funny, there didn't seem to be this many when you looked from shore, but now it appears that there's a virtual wall of boats in front of you. To make matters worse, there's a gentle breeze that keeps changing direction, and the moored boats keep shifting position.

Threading your way through the maze of boats is going to be a challenge. You decide on a path, keeping to the right-hand side of your lane to leave room for boats that may come from the other direction. Suddenly the boat you're about to leave to your starboard (that's *right* for you landlubbers) begins to move into your path in response to the shifting wind. You steer to port (left), but somehow the stern of your boat seems to be heading closer to the moored boat. You steer farther to port and your stern moves even closer. It appears that you are about to strike the other boat. What a way to start! Your family is about to panic, and your own stress level is soaring. What happened? What are you going to do?

The solution is really quite simple, but it helps to understand how your boat behaves on the water. You've found yourself in a situation that you cannot steer your way out of. At this point, your only alternative is to ease the boat into reverse while steering a bit to starboard. This will bring the bow around to port while you back away from the possible collision. Once you're clear, you can power gently around the moored boat, leaving more clearance.

What will you do in the future? You will need to leave a little more room to starboard and plan your turns earlier. Why? Because unlike cars, boats do not steer from the front. In time you will gain experience, but understanding some of the principles will move you along faster—and with a lot less stress.

Powerboat Handling Illustrated is intended to ease your learning and convert what could be a stressful experience into an enjoyable one. Boat handling is a dynamic, interactive process, and a picture is worth a thousand words, so this book takes a highly visual approach. It divides the subject of boat handling into its logical components and provides the necessary background information for each situation.

Boat handling depends upon an understanding of how boats work, so we'll begin by looking at issues of boat design that affect a vessel's performance and its responses to wind, waves, and current. Then we'll move on to close-quarters maneuvers, which necessitate moving slowly while keeping tabs on the position of every part of your boat with respect to other boats and fixed objects. Successful slow-speed maneuvers—including docking and launch-ramp jockeying—depend less on hull shape than on engine and rudder control. These are probably the most stressful maneuvers for most boaters.

After you are comfortable in and around the docks and harbor, we will go to sea. When running at cruising or planing speeds, hull characteristics play a dominant role in boat handling. You'll learn how trim and throttle affect performance and comfort in a calm sea or a chop. Then we'll investigate rough-weather boating, in which safety, or even survival, becomes the primary objective of boat handling. Finally, we'll look at special situations such as anchoring and going aground.

UNDERSTANDING YOUR BOAT

CHAPTER 1

Flotation Basics

If you're sitting in a parked car, you can bet you won't be going anywhere. Even if the engine is running, you'll be stuck in that same position until you engage the transmission.

A boat, on the other hand, presents a totally different story.

Let's say you're floating in the middle of a harbor. Even if your engine is off, there's no guarantee you'll stay in the same spot. You might bob in a swell, you might be rocked by waves, you might even get pushed great distances by the wind or be carried away by currents. Even if you're at anchor or tied to a dock, your boat can still be pushed around by all sorts of environmental forces.

In this chapter, we're going to focus on your boat at rest. We'll take a look at what makes your boat float, what sorts of motion you might experience while the boat is at rest, and how the boat stays upright. All these forces will affect how your boat handles at speed, so it's important to understand them before you fire up the engine.

WHAT MAKES BOATS FLOAT

You're at a boat ramp at the start of a beautiful day, and you're backing your trailer into the harbor. The boat—still resting in the trailer's cradle —eases deeper and deeper into the water until the stern finally lifts and the boat begins to float. How does this happen? What principles are at work that allow for a vessel constructed of non-buoyant materials such as aluminum, steel, or fiberglass to bob on the water's surface?

The Greek mathematician Archimedes figured it out while taking a bath. As legend has it, Archimedes noticed that when he got in the tub, the water level rose, and he determined that an object in water displaces a volume of water exactly equal to the volume of the object immersed in the water. He further discovered that an object would sink if its weight was greater than the weight of the water it displaced. If the object floated, the weight of the displaced water was exactly the same as the weight of the object. The ratio of an object's weight to its volume is known as density. A chunk of steel, being more dense than water, sinks. A block of wood, being less dense than water, floats.

Materials that are denser than water can still float, but you have to first change their relative densities. For instance, if you roll a 50,000-pound steel ball down a boat ramp, it's going to keep rolling until it hits the sea floor. But, if you can melt, roll, form, and weld 50,000 pounds of steel into a shape that will displace 50,000 or more pounds of water, you've got yourself a floating object. By shaping the steel, you changed the rel-

As a boat is placed in water, it displaces water. If you were to collect and weigh the displaced water, you'd find that it is equal to the weight of the boat.

ative density of the object—its weight per volume. And depending on the shape you've created, you might just have a boat.

STATIC TRIM

The boat's posture at rest is known as its *static trim*. (Things will change at cruising speed. We'll discuss *dynamic trim* in Chapter 7.)

The line of contact between the water's surface and a boat's hull is called the *waterline*. If the boat was well-designed and well-built (and carries a normal load), the boat's waterline at rest will match the *designed waterline (DWL)*: the waterline the designer calculated while drawing the plans. Often, a boat's designed waterline is even painted on the hull.

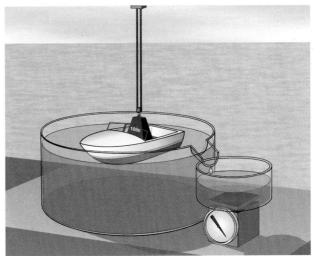

If an object is added to the boat, more water is displaced. The weight of the newly displaced water will equal the weight of the new object.

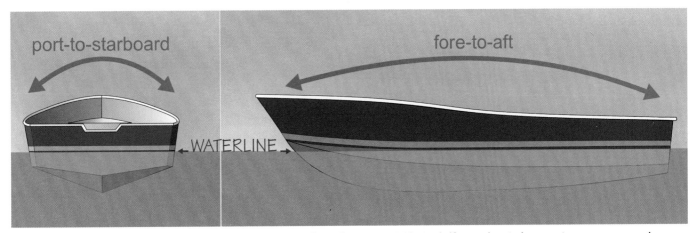

A boat at rest should sit relatively level both fore to aft and port to starboard. If your boat does not, you may need to redistribute weight.

BUILT-IN FLOTATION

Any boat that is less than 20 feet long and sold in the United States will float even when if it's full of water. Why? Because U.S. boatmakers are required to install enough foam flotation to keep a fully loaded boat from sinking.

These guidelines don't apply to boats larger than 20 feet, however. The amount of foam required to counteract the weight of larger boats would detract from usable space aboard. Instead, large boats are designed to block water from intruding into the cabin and bilge by using air spaces to help keep the boat afloat. As long as a sufficient amount of its interior remains unflooded, a boat will maintain a relative density that is lower than water, and it will continue to float. Some especially seaworthy ocean-going boats have watertight bulkheads (internal partitions) that prevent an inrush of water in one section from flooding to another.

The highlighted compartments are filled with foam, making this boat virtually unsinkable. (Courtesy Crestliner)

If the boat's static trim is different from its designed waterline, you should try redistributing weight. In a smaller boat, this can be accomplished simply by moving passengers, spare fuel cans, anchors, or gear. On a larger boat, these actions may have little effect, and it may take some fundamental changes to the boat to restore balance.

MOTION OF A BOAT

Even while your boat is at rest, wind and waves can cause you to move in six different ways.

1. *Roll* describes the side-to-side rocking motion of a boat turning on its long axis—an imaginary line running from bow to stern through the boat.

2. *Pitch* describes the front-to-back rocking motion of a boat turning on its shorter horizontal axis—the port-to-starboard axis.

3. *Yaw* describes the pivoting motion of the boat turning around its vertical axis (i.e., when the bow is pushed to port and the stern goes to starboard, and vice-versa). Most boaters can immediately recognize a boat's roll and pitch, but it's also important to be aware of yaw, because it can push the boat off course.

4. *Heave* describes the up and down motion of a sea lifting and dropping the entire boat.

5. *Slip* describes a boat's sideways movement when pushed by wind or sea, or even its own momentum in a turn.

6. *Surge* describes the motion of a boat being propelled suddenly forward by a passing wave, or the sudden deceleration of the boat slipping backward into the trough behind it.

STAYING UPRIGHT

Stability describes a boat's tendency to stay in, or to return to, its upright position. *Transverse stability* specifically refers to a boat's susceptibility to

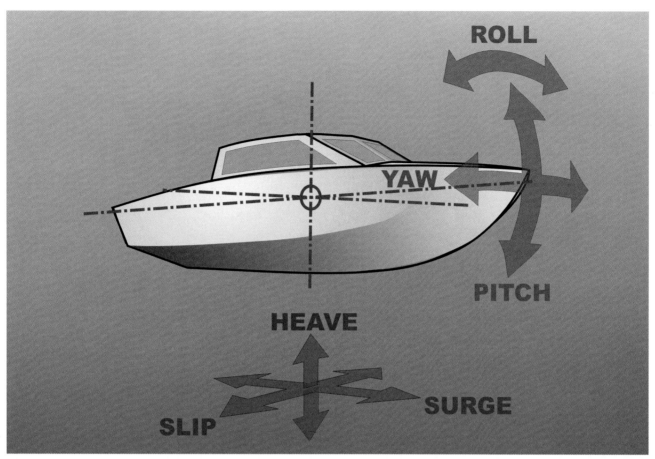

A boat is subject to six types of motion in the water. Three are pivoting motions: A boat rolls *when it rocks side to side.* Pitch *is an up-and-down motion of the bow and stern;* yaw *is a port-to-starboard twisting motion. Three are linear motions:* surge *is a front- or backward motion caused by passing waves;* slip *occurs when wind or wave pushes a boat to the side;* heave *is the up-and-down motion caused by swells.*

rolling motion. (Because a boat is longer than it is wide, transverse stability is usually of more concern than pitch. We'll discuss *longitudinal stability* and *tracking*—a boat's susceptibility to pitching and yawing, respectively—in the following chapter.)

All boats roll; some roll easier than others, and some can return from more severe rolls than others. As such, transverse stability can be broken into two components. *Initial stability* describes a boat's tendency to right itself from small angles of roll, while *ultimate stability* describes the maximum angle of heel a boat can endure before it capsizes. Both of these measures of transverse stability are governed by the locations of a boat's *center of gravity* and *center of buoyancy.*

Center of Gravity

A boat's weight is considered to be centered at one point, its *center of gravity (CG).* If you could connect *(continued on page 8)*

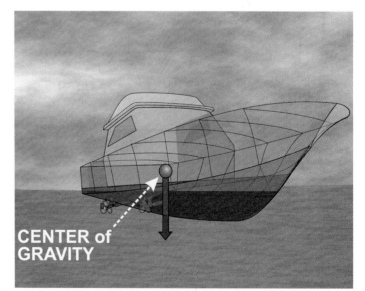

The center of gravity *is a single point within the hull where the boat's entire weight is considered to be focused. If you suspended the boat from this point, it would hang in perfect balance. The location of the center of gravity is critical to the stability of the boat.*

TERMINOLOGY

Boating presents its own unique language. Before we continue, let's make sure we're fluent so we can effectively communicate with our crew on board.

PARTS OF A POWERBOAT

The accompanying illustration shows the names for the main exterior parts of the hull, but here are four terms worthy of mention. *Bow* refers to the front of the boat; *stern,* the rear. *Beam* refers to the width at the boat's widest part. *Quarter* refers to the hull area between the beam to the stern.

DIRECTIONS

Terms for direction or orientation on or around a boat are also important. *Left*, *right*, *front*, and *back* are relative to the observer's point of view, but *port*, *starboard*, *forward*, and *aft* are relative to the boat. *Ahead* (in front of the boat), *astern*

(behind the boat), and *abeam* (to the side of the boat) are also relative to the boat. Using the boat as a reference point allows the crew to unambiguously communicate directions to each other.

Here's a tricky example: Let's say you're sitting on the transom looking forward (toward the bow) through the viewfinder of a camera. Your friend, Dale, is facing you, posing for a picture, but he's standing too close to the camera for you to get a good shot. You ask Dale to "move forward." In this instance, Dale goes forward by stepping backwards.

It's important to note, too, that even though the words *aft* and *forward* are relative to the boat, they're still relative. For example, the pulpit and anchor locker are well forward of the stern, but the anchor locker is aft of the pulpit. In other words, just because an object is described as being *aft* of something else, doesn't necessarily mean that the object is at the stern.

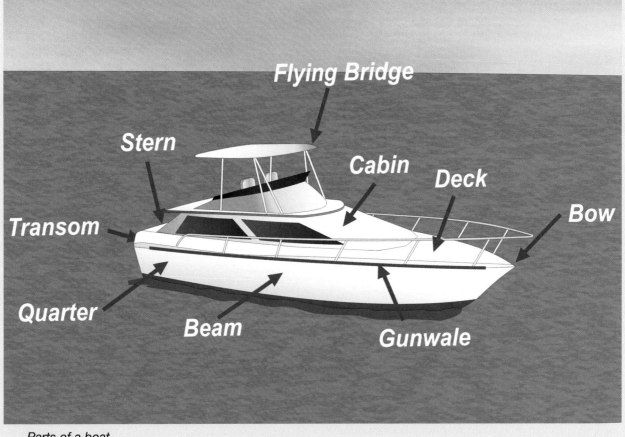

Parts of a boat.

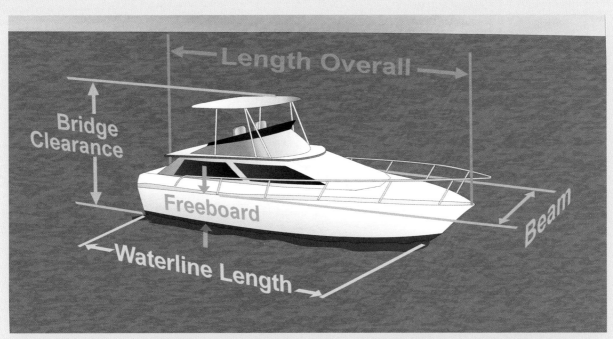

Length overall (LOA) *usually refers to the distance between the hull's forwardmost and aftmost extremes, excluding bolted-on extensions. In the bow this would include a molded anchor platform but not a bowsprit. In the stern it would include a molded swim step but not a sterndrive propeller.* Waterline length (LWL) *indicates the boat's length at the water surface.* Beam *is the maximum width.* Freeboard *is the height of the boat's deck edge above the waterline, typically measured at its lowest spot.* Bridge clearance *is the boat's maximum height above the water level.*

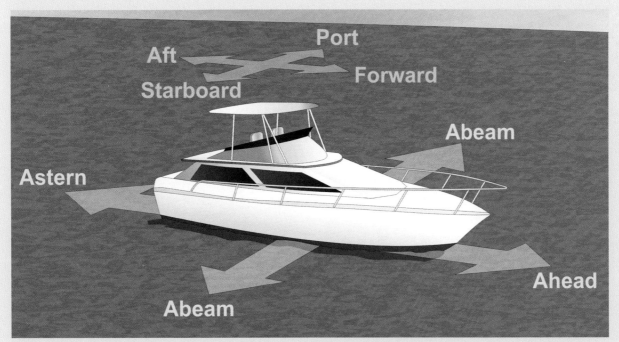

The terms forward *and* aft *are used to indicate locations or directions on the boat.* Ahead *and* astern *are used to indicate locations or directions beyond the boat. Sideways directions are considered* abeam, *with the left side of the boat called* port *and the right side called* starboard.

(continued from page 5)

a cable to the CG and hoist the boat in the air, the boat would dangle in perfect balance, both port to starboard and bow to stern.

The center of gravity has a fairly fixed location on the boat. However, redistributing weight aboard the boat will move the boat's CG to a new location. But, if all the weight aboard the boat is lashed down and your crew stays in one place, the CG will not move, even if the boat is tilted by massive rolls and pitches.

Generally speaking, the lower your boat's CG, the more stable your boat will be. Unfortunately, the higher the boat, the higher the CG will be. Above-deck structures like a cabin or tuna tower will raise the CG, while ballast placed low in the hull will lower it. The CG works as a downward force, pushing the weight of the boat into the water. Fortunately, there's a force pushing back.

Center of Buoyancy

The *center of buoyancy (CB)* is the combined buoyancy of a boat's underwater volume (the portion of the hull underwater) considered to be centered at one point. As we'll discuss below, the CB is the upward force that acts against the center of gravity, and the interaction of the two forces determines a boat's flotation and stability characteristics.

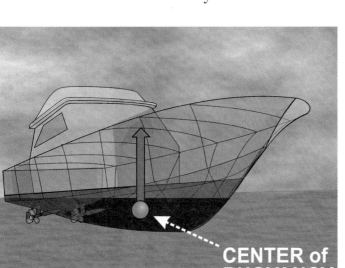

CENTER of BUOYANCY

Buoyancy is the upward force that results when a hull displaces water. This force is considered to be centered at a single point within the submerged portion of the hull: at the geometric center of the volume of displaced water.

Unlike the CG—which is a relatively fixed position—the location of the center of buoyancy moves. As a boat rolls and pitches, the underwater profile of its hull changes, and the location of the CB shifts accordingly.

Interactions of the Centers of Gravity and Buoyancy

Typically, the center of gravity is higher than the center of buoyancy, and when the boat is at rest, it's directly above the center of buoyancy. Thus, they perfectly balance each other and the boat just sits there.

How do the centers of gravity and buoyancy interact? Let's say that a strong gust of wind sweeps over your starboard beam, and your boat begins to heel to port in response. As the boat heels, port-side hull surfaces that were previously dry will slip under water, while a corresponding amount of starboard-side surfaces (that were previously wetted) will lift out. As this happens, the total volume of immersed hull remains the same (the weight has not changed, so the displacement is the same), but your boat's underwater "footprint" changes shape. With this comes a new center of buoyancy; the CB shifts to the geometric center of that new footprint. If your boat is properly designed, the CB will have

CG

CB

With the boat at rest, the center of gravity exerts a downward force (red arrow) directly above the center of buoyancy. This force is countered and balanced by an upward force (green arrow) from the boat's center of buoyancy.

As the boat begins to heel, a previously dry area of the hull slips under the water as a previously wetted surface lifts out of the water, thus changing the hull's underwater shape. The center of buoyancy moves to the center of this new shape. As the upward force of the CB moves to port of the CG's downward force, the two forces no longer directly cancel each other out. This creates a temporary rotational force (yellow arrow)—called righting moment—that turns the boat until the two forces oppose one another again, returning the boat to a level attitude.

As the angle of heel increases, the underwater shape of the hull continues to change, moving the CB even farther toward the lower rail. The strength of the righting moment is even greater than before.

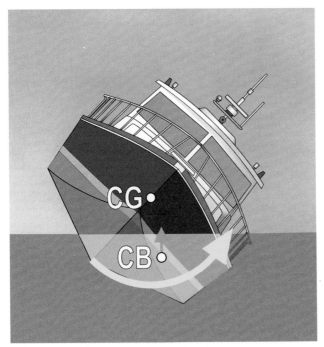

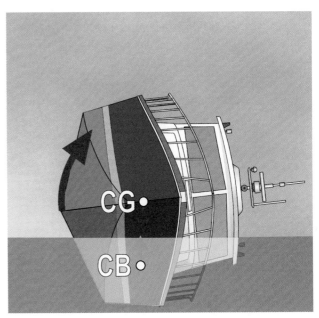

As the boat heels even farther, the changing shape of the submerged portion of the hull has moved the CB inward. The boat still has a favorable righting moment, but less than before.

If the boat heels past its point of ultimate stability, the CB will be on the wrong side of the CG, causing a negative righting moment. This boat is about to capsize. (For this example, we're assuming that water is not getting into the cabin; if it did, the weight of water would become another unfavorable factor.)

moved toward the side of the boat that is slipping downward; in this case, to port. Luckily, the CB's upward force relocates to the place it's most needed.

The boat's center of gravity is still pushing straight down from its fixed location, but the new center of buoyancy has moved out from under the CG. The upward and downward forces still cancel each other, so the boat is no longer rising or falling. However, the two forces are no longer aligned one above the other as they need to be for the boat to be stable. The horizontal shift of the centers of buoyancy and gravity creates a *moment arm*. (A moment arm is a rotational force that causes the boat to roll until the centers of gravity and buoyancy are again aligned.)

The result is that the two forces actually work together to help right the boat. The CB lifts the port side and the CG pushes down the starboard side. The two forces are still equal, but the distance between allows them to act in tandem. This combined force is called the *righting moment*.

But let's say the wind doesn't abate, and boat heels even farther. As the CB continues to migrate outward to port, and the CB and CG grow farther apart, the righting moment continues to increase in strength. In other words, the more the boat rolls, the stronger the righting moment becomes.

But the righting arm will only grow in strength to a point. The angle of heel that results in the highest righting moment is called the *angle of vanishing stability*. Any further heeling produces progressively less righting moment. If the wind grew stronger and the boat continued to roll, the CB will at some point begin to migrate back toward the boat's centerline, closer to the CG. There is still a righting moment, but it is weaker.

If the boat continues to roll even farther, the CB reaches a point were it opposes the CG again, leaving the boat temporarily suspended in the wrong position. In this case, there would be no righting moment—no force to help right the boat. This is the point of *ultimate stability*. Since there is no longer a righting moment, the boat cannot right itself. Any further rolling would cause the CG to move to the outside of the CB, and the resultant force would capsize the boat. Despite how it sounds, the angle of ultimate stability is actually an unstable position; a very small force can cause the boat to either roll toward the upright position, or toward capsizing.

Initial and Ultimate Stability

STABILITY AND FLAT WATER

Boats that strongly resist roll are described as being *stiff* boats; boats that roll easily are *tender*.

A classic example of a stiff boat is a flat-bottomed boat. Flat-bottomed boats resist roll because a small amount of heel will result in a strong righting arm (see accompanying figure).

A round-bottomed boat, on the other hand, is *tender*. A modest amount of heel does not produce the same powerful righting moment, because the center of buoyancy does not move far from the center of gravity.

But the picture changes when we look at ultimate stability. The flat-bottomed boat has great initial stability, but if it tips too far, it will quickly lose its righting moment and become unstable. The round-bottomed boat, on the other hand, may feel tippier, but it has greater ultimate stability. It can heel farther and still have a positive righting moment.

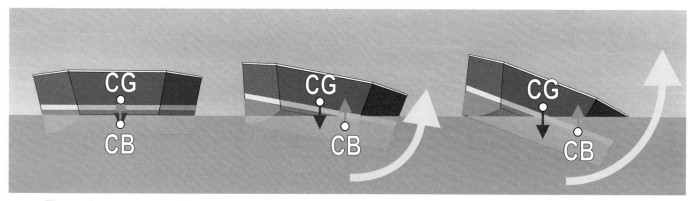

The underwater shape of the hull is critical to the boat's stability. A flat-bottomed boat is a good example of a hull that wants to stay level. Here, a small amount of heel produces a strong righting moment.

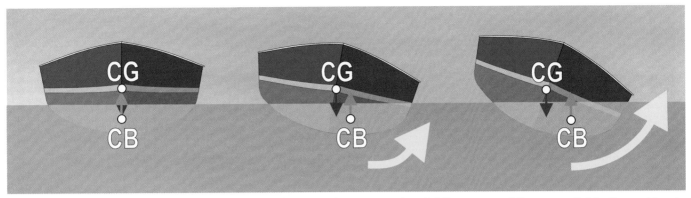

A modest amount of heel on a round-bottomed boat produces a weaker righting moment than on a flat-bottomed boat. The righting moment begins to build, however, as the boat is tipped farther.

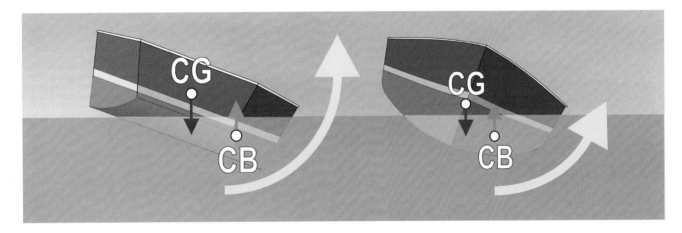

Hull shapes on most powerboats, however, are not so cut and dry; they fall somewhere between a flat-bottomed and round-bottomed boat.

RESPONSE TO SEAS

Earlier, we discussed how wind can cause a boat to heel in the water. A boat's response to undulating seas or waves is similar. In both cases, the boat's footprint will change and the center of buoyancy will shift accordingly. In the latter case, however, it's the rolling action of a wave that influences the boat's footprint. In other words, as a wave rolls underneath a boat, it temporarily wets some hull surfaces while water drains away from other surfaces. How does this affect stability?

Let's say you've been motoring downwind for the better part of a windy afternoon. It's getting late, so it's time to turn around and head for home. Over the course of the day, a moderately steep following sea has developed, and now you have to turn into it. As you're midway through your turn, a large wave rolls toward your beam. What will happen?

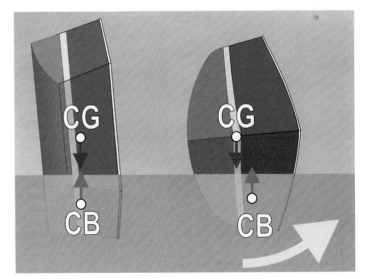

A side-by-side comparison of flat- and round-bottomed boats. Above center: At a moderate angle of heel, the flat-bottomed boat has much greater righting moment than the round-bottomed boat. Above: At a steep angle of heel, the flat-bottomed boat has reached its ultimate stability—any further roll will cause a capsize. The round-bottomed boat, however, still has reserve righting moment. (This assumes that both boats have solid decks and take on no water.)

A passing wave changes the underwater shape of the displaced water, and the response is similar to what you would experience if wind heeled the boat. The boat will respond and tend to align itself to the wave surface.

The bottom of a stiff boat tends to follow the surface of the water. As a wave lifts a flat-bottomed boat, the boat will remain relatively flat on the water's surface—even if that means the boat is lying flat on the near-vertical face of a wave. The boat may then slide sideways into the trough, or even tip over. So despite its high initial stability, a flat-bottomed boat could be rolled over by a strong wave.

A round-bottomed boat will be less affected by waves on the beam; because it doesn't have sharply angled surfaces, waves will tend to roll under and around the hull without tipping it.

RESPONSES TO SHIFTING LOADS

As noted earlier, redistributing weight can change your boat's center of gravity.

Let's say you're going to go fishing on a nearby pond. You'll need to be able to stand up and cast from the boat, so you'll need a hull that can handle sudden shifts in weight. You have a choice

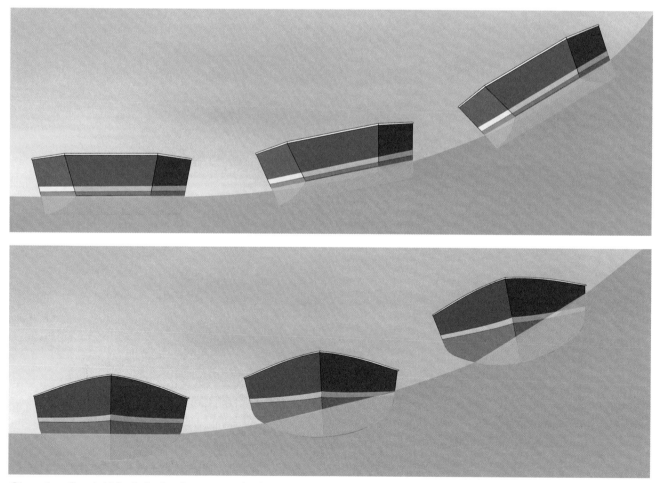

Choosing the right hull design is an exercise in compromises. A stiff boat—although very stable on flat water—can be a liability in rough seas (top). A tender boat—although tippier on flat water—handles seas with greater stability.

Adding weight can move the boat's center of gravity (left). This will cause the boat to heel to an angle where the center of buoyancy once again balances the two forces.

SHIFTING LOAD: WATER IN THE BILGE

Water is heavy, yet its weight shifts easily. This means that water in the bilge—initially a relatively small problem—can quickly compound into a much larger one.

Let's say a gust of wind hits your starboard side. As your boat begins to heel to port, bilge water (that had previously been innocuous) rolls downward. The water begins to collect on the port side of the bilge, and the sudden increase of weight at that location causes the boat to heel even farther. As it heels farther, even more water rolls to port. This causes the CG to move to port

and could substantially decrease, or even eliminate, the strength of the righting moment. If there's enough water in the bilge, the boat could heel to the point where water spills in over the gunwale and your problems compound even further.

Be sure your bilge pump is in good working order and keep the bilge dry. As an additional precaution, if your boat doesn't already have them, you could install baffles in the bilge. Baffles compartmentalize the bilge and hinder the ability of water to move from one part of the bilge to another.

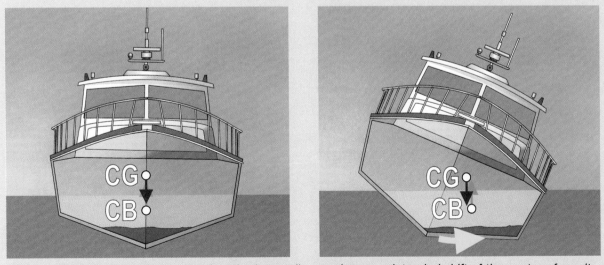

Water in the bilge will roll downward as the boat rolls, causing an unintended shift of the center of gravity, thereby reducing the boat's righting moment.

Shifting weight toward the gunwale of a small boat creates an imbalance that causes the boat to heel. The heeling angle for a flat-bottomed boat is substantially less than for an equivalent round-bottomed boat.

of taking a flat-bottomed jon boat or a round-bottomed canoe. Which makes more sense?

If you stand up in a flat-bottomed boat and move outward toward the gunwales, the boat's CG will shift under your weight, and the boat will begin to heel; however, even a modest amount of heel in a flat-bottomed boat causes a big shift in the CB. The two forces will keep the boat upright.

I'm sure you can guess what would happen if you tried to stand on one side of a canoe.

On any boat, the addition and/or redistribution of weight will move the center of gravity and affect the boat's stability. For example, adding or moving an object higher will raise the center of gravity. And any upward change in the center of gravity will adversely affect the boat's stability.

The degree of effect will depend upon the object's weight and distance from the original center of gravity. Either one will have a similar impact, (i.e., adding more weight or increasing the distance). If you double the weight or double the distance, you'll double the effect. Do both, and you'll have four times the effect.

By the same token, when you're loading your boat, distribute gear as evenly as possible across the boat, both port to starboard and fore and aft.

The height of added weight has a tremendous effect on a boat's stability. The weight on the superstructure (right) is closer to the boat's centerline than the same weight on deck (center), and yet it has a greater adverse impact on righting moment. (The relative strength of the righting moment is represented by the length of the yellow arrow.)

CHAPTER 2

Hull Shape 101

Y ou wouldn't enter an SUV into the Indy 500, nor would you drive a sports car down a muddy, off-road trail. To find the right car, you have to decide what's more important to you: ruggedness or performance.

Boats are no different. Certain boats are better equipped to deal with certain situations than others. Some are fast and nimble, while others are steady and determined. Hull shape—more than any other characteristic—determines how a boat will handle. As we discussed in the last chapter, the shape of the hull is a crucial factor in determining stability, but it also determines a boat's speed, maneuverability, and seaworthiness.

DESIGN FEATURES TO HANDLE THE ELEMENTS

Minimize Pitch

As we discussed in the last chapter, a boat with a completely flat bottom will tend to follow the shape of the waves: it will ride up the face of every oncoming wave, and fall into each successive trough. In other words, it will pitch considerably. What is a better hull shape?

If you want a boat that will pitch less in a sea, a boat with a narrow bow is a good place to start. A sharper, narrower bow allows a boat to cut through waves. Plus, it is less buoyant, so the bow will not be lifted as quickly by each passing wave. This minimizes the resulting pitch; however, as you will soon see, that may not be advantageous in building seas.

Handle Load

In designing the shape of a bow, a boat designer must strike a balance among several factors, including the boat's speed, its weight and weight distribution, interior space, anticipated sea conditions, comfort, and safety.

Because you'll most often be driving your boat forward, the stern does not have to be narrow to minimize pitch. In fact, a broader stern will do a better job of supporting the engine's weight. Beyond that advice, though, the right design for the stern is less cut-and-dry. If the stern is too wide, it could cause the boat to roll sideways following a lateral rolling sea. A flat-bottomed, or nearly flat, stern will help the boat get up on plane easier (as discussed later in this chapter). On the other hand, if it is too flat, it may track poorly (as discussed below) and lead to pounding in choppy seas.

Improve Tracking

Tracking is the boat's ability to stay on course—its ability to resist both yaw and slip. Some boats

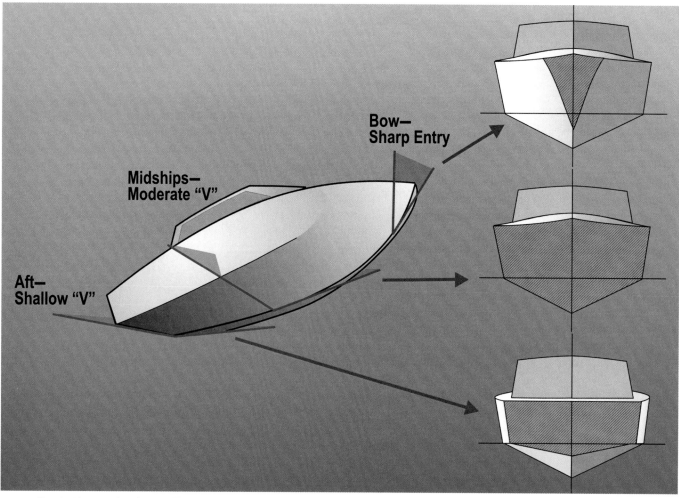

Bow—Sharp Entry

Midships—Moderate "V"

Aft—Shallow "V"

Boats that maintain a uniform shape from bow to stern are generally not versatile (flat-bottomed boats, for example). To make boats compatible with a broader spectrum of sea conditions, designers add varying contours along the hull. Here you can see three cross sections taken from the same boat.

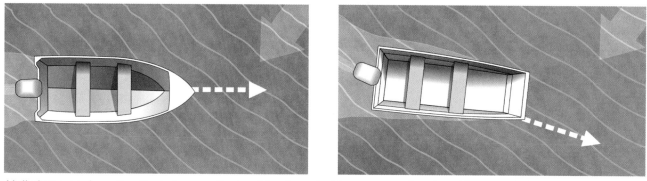

Hull shape profoundly affects how well a boat tracks or holds a course. A pointed bow and sharp keel helps a boat carve a path through the water (left), while a flat bow and bottom allows a boat to be easily diverted by winds or seas (right).

track so well that they resist turning; others track well while going straight but they slip badly in turns; and others have trouble holding a straight course at all. A good boat will hold a straight course, turn readily, and hold that turn with mini-mal slip. An even better boat will do those things in bad weather.

Deeper, longer, narrower hulls generally track better than flatter, shorter, wider ones. Boats with keels and deep-V hulls have substantial *lateral plane*—vertical projected surface running fore-and-aft beneath the waterline. A lot of lateral plane will keep a boat on course, even when waves strike it from the side. Unfortunately, however, the same factors that enhance tracking impede maneuverability (i.e., boats that track well tend to resist turning). A flat-bottomed boat, on the other hand, will turn easily but won't track well. Again, finding the right boat is all about compromise.

Bow and stern shapes also influence tracking. A boat with a sharp, V-shaped bow and a flat stern will tend to grab the water firmly up front, but it will hold less well aft. In a strong cross-breeze, the bow may stay put, but the stern will be pushed downwind. This isn't necessarily a bad thing. Boats steer from the rear, so you can counter the motion from the helm.

A boat that has both a V-shaped bow and stern will track as if it's on rails, but it may be difficult to turn.

Improve Wave Handling

A sharp, narrow bow reduces pitch, but is it best for wave handling? The pointed shape of a bow (as seen from above) allows it to cut into an oncoming wave. This tends to cut a path through the water for the stern to follow. However, while parting the waves, the bow also needs sufficient buoyancy to rise on top of the wave. Otherwise it may dig into taller waves, taking water over the deck, which could swamp the boat. So, you want a bow that will cut through the waves, but only just enough. That's why bow designs for open water, with higher waves, tend to have a flared shape—narrower at the waterline and broader near the deck. A flared shape ensures that the farther the bow is immersed into the water, the more buoyancy is available to push it back up. This means lesser waves are sliced, while higher waves are ridden over. Additionally, as the bow cuts into a wave, flare diverts the water to the side rather than straight up, reducing spray into the boat. Boats are designed with a high bow so they can effectively cut through the majority of waves with only moderate lift required.

That covers the bow, but what about the rest of the boat? A high bow may be practical, but the sides and transom tend to be lower, with the transom generally being the lowest. Waves may come over the gunwales, particularly at their lowest point. The measure of this height is called *freeboard*. Freeboard is the height of hull between the waterline and the gunwale. A boat with one-foot-high gunwales may be at risk in even one-foot seas, if those seas approach the boat where it has only one foot of freeboard. In capable hands, a boat with five feet of freeboard may be able to handle seas of 30 feet or more.

For a boat to handle efficiently, its hull must be in contact with the water rather than allowing water over the topsides. Any water over the side

(continued on page 20)

Boats are designed to take waves on the bow. A pointed bow cuts through smaller, harmless waves, while the bow's flare gives it sufficient buoyancy to rise over larger, more powerful waves. (Courtesy of U.S. Coast Guard)

Another factor in a boat's seaworthiness is freeboard. Freeboard is the height of hull that extends from the waterline to the gunwale. A boat with a lot of freeboard will be better suited to repel water in choppy seas.

HULL SHAPES

This chapter discusses a lot of the pros and cons of different hull shapes in this chapter. Let's review some of the shapes we've discussed, and take a look at a few new ones.

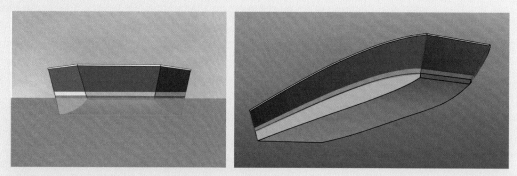

Flat-bottomed boats are designed for sheltered waters and often used by outdoorsmen. They have shallow drafts and can be initially quite stable—thus they are well suited to those who would move around on the boat while fishing or hunting. Typically, flat-bottomed boats are less than 20 feet long.

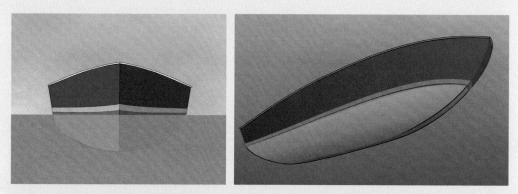

Round-bottomed hulls are found on small rowboats, large offshore trawlers, sailboats, and large seagoing ships. The round hull is considered to be sea friendly and is more likely to roll rather than pound. Rolling can be uncomfortable, however, especially in a beam sea.

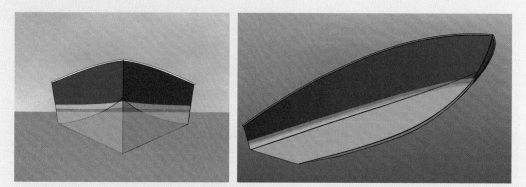

Deep-V hulls are very popular and versatile for several reasons: they plane and respond well to rougher waters offshore; they are faster than round-bottomed boats (though they don't ride as smoothly). The "V" describes the sharp rise, on both sides of the boat, from the keel. The "V" shape slices cleanly through the water, causing the boat to track very well. The deeper the "V" shape, the better it cuts through the waves and resists pounding when addressing waves head-on. But the deeper the "V," the more power is required to get on plane.

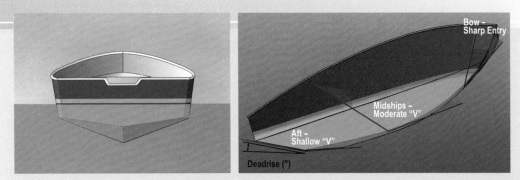

The modified-V hull—with its flatter aft section—strikes a compromise between the tracking and slicing characteristics of the deep-V and the initial stability and lifting characteristics of a flat-bottomed boat. As a modified-V accelerates, the bow rises out of the water, leaving the aft sections to skim along the surface. This substantially reduces power requirements and fuel consumption. The modified-V is the most popular hull type for recreational boaters. It is used on runabouts, cruisers, and many fishing boats.

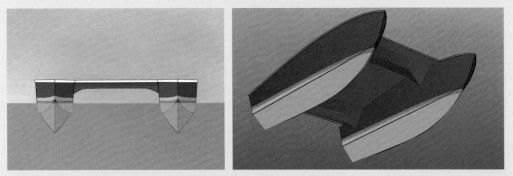

Narrow hulls glide through the water more easily than wide ones. Unfortunately, narrow hulls are also more prone to tipping, because the righting moment can only go so far to one side. Multihulls, like this catamaran, provide the speed and efficiency of narrow hulls with the added stability of a wider beam. Plus, the deck that joins the hulls can provide roomy accommodations in addition to quarters within the hulls themselves. Depending on the shape of the hulls, catamarans can be either displacement or planing hulls. Multihulls do have some disadvantages. They can be difficult to steer, and they tend to follow a rolling beam sea. If waves reach the underside of the joining deck or decks, they will take a pounding. They also have limited ultimate stability: if tipped to near 90°, they will capsize quickly and be virtually impossible to right. And their extreme width makes dockage expensive and difficult to find.

The central portion of a cathedral hull resembles a classic V, but it also has a miniature V-shaped hull on each side—providing the stability of a trimaran without the extreme width. The hull tracks well, and the extra buoyancy from the side hulls provides excellent initial stability, even with shifting loads aboard. When the boat is up on a plane, the deeper central hull provides the primary lift, and the side hulls rise almost completely out of the water. In choppy seas, however, the side hulls cause pounding, throw up a lot of spray, and prevent the water that's been forced up by the central hull from being diverted to the sides. Consequently, cathedral hulls are used most often as fishing and recreational boats, and also as tenders for more sheltered waters.

(continued from page 17)

results in drag as well as added weight, which lowers the boat as well as reducing its stability. That is why open-water boats have decks somewhat higher than the waterline and large scuppers (drains) to shed water quickly from the decks.

The rest of the hull shape plays a large part in the boat's wave-handling capabilities. A boat with a narrow beam relative to its length will slice through the water more efficiently than a beamier boat. A large keel will resist roll. Flat sections will lift the boat out of the water. Hard chines will lift while soft chines will soften the ride. Strakes keep the boat upright. You'll learn more about these features later as we cover different hull types.

Minimize Roll

Now that we've dealt with the pitch of the boat, what about roll? A flat-bottomed boat will track the seas. This applies to roll as well as pitch, so in a beam sea, a flat-bottomed boat will roll with the surface of the water.

A round-bottomed boat will take lateral seas more softly. Unfortunately, the round-bottomed boat will keep rolling long after the wave has passed. To resist roll, vertical keel sections are often added to round hulls. Many ocean-going boats also incorporate stabilizers. One type of stabilizer uses rotating fins mounted below the waterline on both sides of the hull. Electronic sensors detect the roll and adjust the fins to counteract it.

Unlike a round-bottomed boat, V-hulls have hard chines where the sides meet the hull. Assisted by lifting strakes, these hard chines minimize roll by providing more buoyancy on the side of the hull that is being rolled into the water.

Hull Types: Displacement versus Planing

As we covered in the last chapter, all boats displace an amount of water that exactly equals their weight. However, boats with planing hulls will lift and skim along the water's surface when they reach a specific speed. Less of the hull is in the water, so less water is displaced. Boats with displacement hulls have no lifting characteristics and will always displace the same amount of water, even as they move through the water.

Displacement Hulls

Sailboats typically have displacement hulls. Their heavy keels keep them upright against the force of the wind on their sails, and their rounded bottoms give them an easy motion at sea.

Some powerboats, particularly cruising trawlers, also have rounded hulls and are designed to ride in, not on, the water. Under power, these hulls can travel great distances using only a moderate amount of fuel. They generally are more fuel efficient than planing hulls operating in the displacement mode. And they can carry heavy loads of supplies, gear, fuel, and so on.

Round hulls offer a soft ride, gently pushing water aside, whereas the flat, sharp-edged chines on planing hulls tend to bounce around in choppy water. Unfortunately, the rounded hull is more susceptible to rolling motions, particularly when waves approach from the sides—a condition called a *beam sea*.

A beam sea is generally not a problem for sailboats since the steady pressure of wind on the sails mitigates rolling. Powerboats with displacement hulls, on the other hand, are more vulnerable to rolling. For this reason, some ocean-going powerboats add small riding sails to reduce rolling. More often, though, displacement hulls include a large keel with heavy ballast. This improves both roll stability and tracking.

Some trawlers install *roll stabilizers* to reduce rolling. As mentioned earlier, these are powered fins, one on each side of the hull below the waterline. Microprocessor-controlled motors rotate the fins to provide lift on the descending side of the boat to counteract roll. Although quite effective, they are also very expensive, require considerable power, and take up space within the hull.

Semi-Displacement Hulls

Some boaters like the comfort of displacement hulls, but feel limited by their relatively slow speeds. Semi-displacement hulls, on the other hand, have a limited amount of dynamic lift forward that allows them to rise somewhat up on their bow waves and achieve higher speeds than pure displacement hulls. A 40-foot trawler with a semi-displacement hull may have a maximum speed of 16 knots or so—nearly twice that of its pure-displacement counterpart. The downside, however, is very high fuel consumption.

The 43-foot trawler above illustrates the classic design of a displacement hull boat. It has a substantial hull under the waterline and a rounded hull. (Courtesy Nordhavn)

This 57-foot ocean-going trawler illustrates the rounded underwater shape of a displacement hull. The bulb on the bow increases the boat's waterline length and thus its hull speed. (Courtesy Nordhavn)

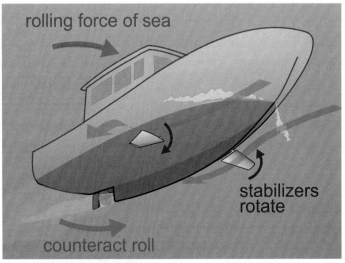

This trawler is outfitted with active roll stabilizers. The fins on the sides of the hull counter-rotate to direct a flow of water up on one side and down on the other to cancel the roll. Electronics sense the boat's roll and adjust the fins accordingly..

DISPLACEMENT HULL SPEED

A boat with a displacement hull has limited speed potential called *displacement hull speed*. Once it reaches that speed, even adding lots of power won't make it go much faster.

Why?

The simple answer is that displacement boats get trapped within their own waves.

The faster a displacement hull goes, the faster its bow wave gets pushed forward. As the bow wave is pushed faster, the trough between the bow wave and the stern wave lengthens. Once the distance between the two waves equals the length of the hull, the boat has reached its theoretical maximum speed, or *hull speed*.

Why can't the engine just keep pushing it faster?

Well, when the boat goes any faster, the distance between the two waves grows and the stern wave falls behind the hull. This widened trough creates a downward slope toward the stern wave, and your boat—already fighting an uphill battle against its own bow wave—will need to work even harder to keep up with its bow wave. If it falls back, the boat will again slow to hull speed.

Boats with very powerful engines can gain a little more speed by climbing farther up the bow wave, but the fuel consumption will skyrocket for a meager speed increase.

It is possible to calculate the hull speed of a boat without ever firing its engine. All you need are a measuring tape and a formula developed in the late nineteenth century by an Englishman named William Froude. First, determine a boat's *length at waterline* (LWL).

Let's say your boat's LWL is 20 feet. If your boat was traveling at its hull speed, the bow and stern waves would be 20 feet apart. Next, apply Froude's formula.

The faster waves move, the farther the waves spread apart. Froude discovered that waves move at a speed that is 1.34 times the square root of the distance between them (in knots). Maximum speed is therefore approximately 1.34 times the square root of the waterline length.

$$1.34 \times \sqrt{\text{LWL}} = \text{hull speed}$$

Applying this formula to your 20-footer gives us 5.99, or 6 knots. A displacement boat with a 25-foot waterline will yield a cruising speed of about 7 knots; a 40-foot trawler, about 9 knots.

The longer the boat, the faster the hull speed. That's why a 500-foot aircraft carrier can move at 30 knots.

With a very powerful engine, the hull speed can be pushed to roughly 1.5 to 2 times the square root of the waterline length (commonly called the speed-to-length ratio, or SLR). Again, the price for this small increase in speed will be a dramatic increase in fuel consumption. Additionally, a larger engine will be heavier—another factor that will make it that much more difficult for the boat to get up on its bow wave.

A semi-displacement hull like this one (shown in two views) can achieve speeds higher than a full-displacement boat, but cannot fully plane. Note the hard chines extending from near the bow all the way to the stern, and the relatively flat hull at the transom. These features help lift the boat somewhat onto its own bow wave.

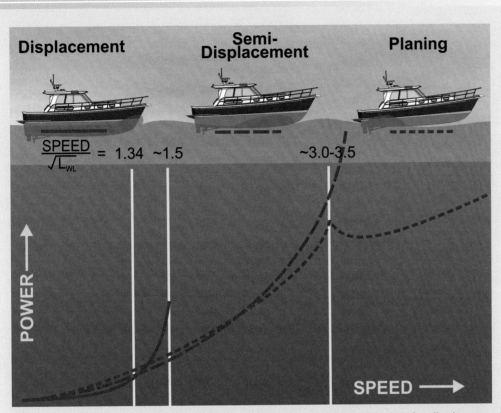

Hull speed limitations and power required. The speed-to-length ratio of a displacement hull is 1.34. This is the SLR at which the boat is nestled between its bow wave and stern wave. Some displacement hull boats (solid red line) can go a little faster, but not much. They typically top out at an SLR of around 1.5. This means a 45-foot displacement hull boat with a 40-foot waterline has a maximum speed of roughly 9.5 knots. Semi-displacement hulls (long red dashes) lift up a bit on their bow waves and can go faster than displacement hulls—SLRs of 3.0 to 3.5. A semi-displacement hull boat with a 40-foot waterline may have a maximum speed of roughly 22 knots. Planing hulls (short red dashes) begin to plane at SLRs where semi-displacement hulls top out.

Semi-displacement hulls commonly have speed-to-length ratios in the 2 to 3.5 range, with some even higher. At the upper end of this range, it could be argued that these boats are actually planing boats.

Planing Hulls

Coastal and inland recreational powerboaters generally prefer more speed than is possible with a displacement hull. Consequently they opt for a planing hull boat. When a boat is riding on its own bow wave, it is *planing*.

To achieve plane, you need a lighter, more powerful boat that has a hull with *dynamic lift*. The hull design incorporates specific characteristics to translate motion through the water into vertical lift. The more effective these lifting surfaces are, the lower the speed a boat needs to achieve to plane. Of course, the boat's weight plays a major role, too. Planing boats are much lighter than similar-sized displacement or semi-displacement boats.

Planing hulls require substantial engine power to achieve planing speed. Once planing, however, the boat's efficiency jumps. Less engine power is required to stay on plane because the amount of its total wetted surface drops substantially and the frictional forces therefore lessen.

However, even taking into account the increased efficiency that comes from being on plane, a planing-hull boat will not be as efficient as a com-

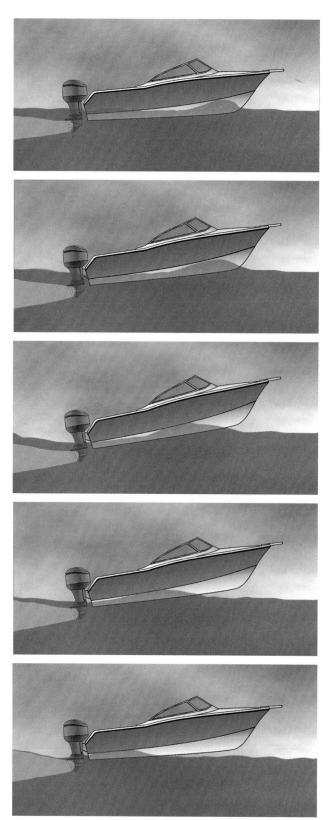

When a boat is on a plane, its bow is out of the water and its bow wave extends from the sides of the hull rather than from the bow. (Photo courtesy Volvo)

parably sized displacement-hull boat. The displacement-hull boat's smaller engine and hull design give it a decided advantage.

In a theoretical sense, your speed is virtually unlimited once you're planing; however, practical considerations such as engine size and weight, sea conditions, and your boat's handling capabilities will ultimately constrain your speed.

HULL SHAPE

A flat-bottomed boat is the ultimate planing hull. Like a skipping stone, it takes very little power to get it on a plane. But, as we've noted already, this shape has many disadvantages, not the least of which is pounding.

Sloping surfaces, such as those found on V-shaped hulls, reduce pounding while also providing lifting surfaces. The amount of lift, however, is reduced by the amount of the slope. Therefore, the more horizontal a hull surface, the more lift it has, but also the worse the pounding it experiences.

To compensate, planing hulls tend to incorporate both flat sections and sloping V sections. Some of the flat sections are placed just below the resting waterline, so they provide lift while the boat is accelerating, but then elevate out of the water after the boat gets onto plane, which minimizes pounding. The modified-V hull is an example, with its deep-V shape forward and flatter surfaces aft. The difference between these varying designs is measured as differences in *deadrise*—the angle between an underwater hull surface and the horizontal plane.

As a boat accelerates, its bow lifts and the boat begins to ascend its bow wave. As the speed increases, the bow wave moves aft with the bow still rising farther out of the water. Once the boat begins to plane, the bow levels out while the aft portion of the hull rides on the bow wave.

This high-speed cruiser is a perfect example of an efficient planing hull boat. Smooth flat surfaces aft help keep it on a plane.

Depending on the hull shape, the deadrise at the transom may change as you move toward the bow. On a deep-V hull, this angle remains the same for much of the hull's length, finally becoming sharper near the bow. On a modified-V, however, the deadrise steadily increases as you move from transom to bow.

LIFTING SURFACES

Planing hull designs incorporate a number of features to improve lift. If you look at the hull of a planing or semi-displacement boat from the bow, you will typically see *hard chines*—sharp angles —where the hull bottom meets the sides. Hard

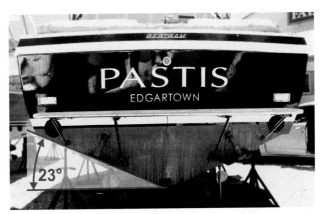

Deep-V hulls will typically have a transom deadrise of 22° or more, while a modified-V will have a deadrise of 20° or less at the transom.

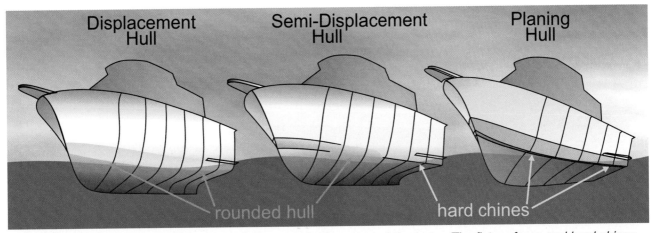

The planing hull on the left is designed to rise up and ride on top of the water. The flat surfaces and hard chines provide lift. The semi-displacement hull in the center is designed to ride partially on the surface. Note the rounded shapes in front that give way to hard chines and slightly flatter sections aft. The displacement hull on the right, with soft chines and rounded surfaces, rides in, not on, the water. (Adapted from Stapleton's Powerboat Bible.*)*

chines provide a better lifting surface than rounded chines.

On the lower surface of the chines, some hulls have *flats*—narrow horizontal surfaces separating the side of the boat from the angled bottom. The advantage of flats is that they provide a substantial degree of lift for their small area, and the wider the flat, the better the lift. Their disadvantage is that they contribute to pounding in waves. However, flats usually curve upward at the bow, so once a boat is on plane, the forward sections are out of the water and no longer contribute to the pounding. On many boats, the flats phase out and virtually disappear by midships, so they don't add to pounding for that part of the hull still in the water.

Reverse chines are flats taken to the extreme.

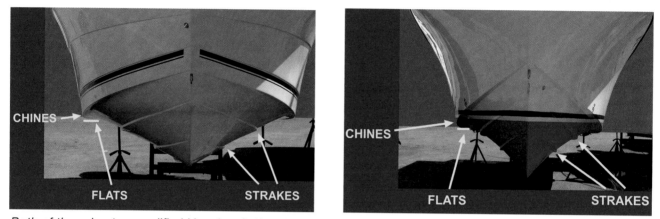

Both of these boats—modified-V cruiser (left) and deep-V fishing boat (right)—exhibit hard chines, chine flats, and strakes. These features contribute to planing performance.

This boat incorporates reverse chines. *These chines actually slope upward in an inboard direction.*

Instead of horizontal surfaces, reverse chines slope upward from the sides of the boat to the sloping hull section. The resultant shallow inverted-V at the chine not only provides good lift, but also improves turning performance

Lifting strakes are tapered triangular surfaces that run lengthwise along the hull bottom—they provide drag as well as lift. (Any surface that increases the wetted surface area will also increase drag.) Depending upon their horizontal size and length, the flat surfaces of strakes also can contribute to pounding. For this reason, designers usually add lifting strakes only to the forward half to two-thirds of the hull. At these lengths, the lifting strakes generally rise completely out of the water when the boat goes into a plane.

Lifting strakes also help prevent a V-bottom malady called *chine walking*. Chine walking occurs on V-bottomed boats with smooth, sloping flat sections. When the boat heels over in a turn, one side of its angled bottom tilts toward the horizontal. Some boats tend to settle onto that surface and stay there, at which point the boat behaves much like a flat-bottomed boat that doesn't want to steer. Lifting strakes help lift the boat back to an upright attitude.

WETTED SURFACE

Once a planing hull breaks free of its bow wave, another factor contributes to improved speed. The amount of *wetted surface*—the area of hull that is in contact with the water—determines the amount of hull friction. Less wetted surface on the hull means less friction; less friction means higher speeds with less energy. When a planing hull breaks out of displacement mode and the bow rides up, over, and beyond the bow wave, the forward hull surfaces are riding out of the water, resulting in a much lower wetted surface area, less friction, and a higher speed.

Hull shapes also determine how much surface area will be wetted while planing. Consider a deep-V hull, for example, which may have deadrise as steep as 30° along its entire length. This shape will place a lot of hull surface area (much of it vertical) in the water even when on a plane. Modified-V hulls seek a compromise, with a deadrise angle near the stern of 18–20°. This low-angle portion of the stern is the only hull surface that remains in the water when planing.

(continued on page 30)

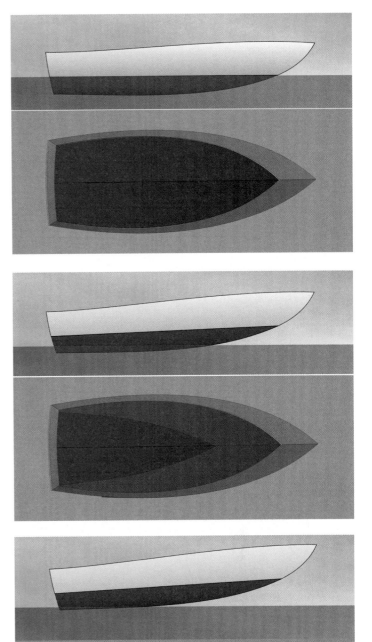

At displacement speeds, the entire hull portion that lies beneath the waterline will be a wetted surface (top). When a boat begins to plane, the forward portion of the hull will lift out of the water (center). At a full plane, you may be riding on a small triangularly shaped section of hull near the stern (bottom). Less wetted surface means less friction and, thus, higher speeds.

BOAT TYPES

We've looked at hull types (displacement, planing, and semi-displacement) and hull shapes (round, flat-bottomed, V-, and so on). Now let's look at boat types.

Inflatable boats were originally intended to be lightweight tenders, but now they are often used as primary boats. Some inflatables can be fully deflated and rolled up for stowage, while others —known as RIBs (rigid inflatable boats)—combine rigid hulls with inflatable tubes to provide great buoyancy, stability, and soft landings. RIBs, like the one pictured, are more durable than roll-ups.

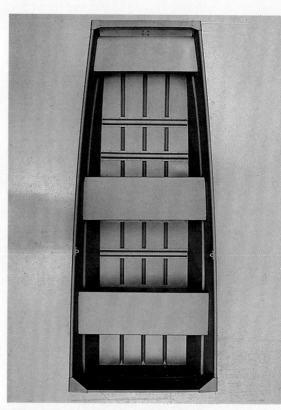

A jon boat is a flat-bottomed boat that is popular with hunters and anglers thanks to its relatively wide beam and high initial stability. Jon boats will plane with low power, but can become unstable at high speeds. They are primarily for use in sheltered waters. (Courtesy Crestliner)

Cruisers are essentially runabouts with added sleeping and eating accommodations. These boats range from about 22 feet to over 50 feet in length. Most cruisers have modified-V hulls. To maximize interior accommodations, the beams are usually wide—typically one-third of the boat's length—and decks are often elevated. The high decks and cabin houses make cruisers susceptible to rolling motions. (Courtesy Mustang)

Runabouts are high-speed open sport boats ranging from 15 to 30 feet in length. They are planing boats, usually with modified-V hulls and small to moderate deadrise at the stern. Runabouts offer speed, maneuverability, tracking, and sufficient buoyancy in the bow to lift over most waves. They will, however, pound in choppy seas. (Courtesy Regal)

Center console boats and walkarounds are designed primarily for fishing. Often based on deep-V planing hulls, these boats tend to be seaworthy and fast; they can be taken considerable distances offshore, where waves can be severe. It's not uncommon to find a 23-foot walkaround venturing in waters where many 30-foot cruisers wouldn't dare to go. (Courtesy Grady-White)

At 50 feet or more, the sportfisherman is larger than center consoles and walkarounds. These fishing boats are fast—cruising speeds of 40 knots are not uncommon. They are intended to take an angler offshore quickly and in comfort. Often employing deep-V hulls, they are very seaworthy. A sportfisherman will also have a substantial beam to help counteract the high center of gravity caused by its "tuna tower."

Providing liveaboard cruising with spacious interior room, trawlers trade speed for comfort, economy, and seaworthiness. Typically, these boats have either displacement or semi-displacement hulls.

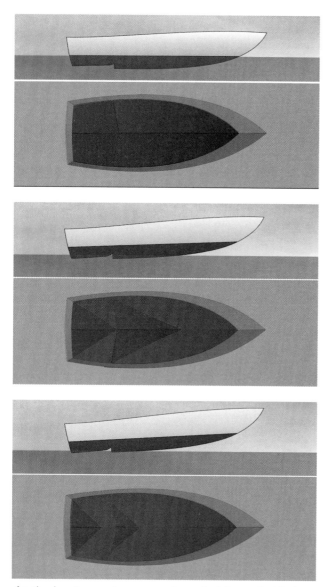

As the boat speeds up, an air pocket forms behind the step, reducing the wetted surface. Some high-speed hull designs incorporate two or three steps.

A step in the hull forms an air pocket under the hull that significantly reduces the wetted surface area and, thus, reduces friction.

(continued from page 27)

A hull feature called *steps* can also reduce wetted surface. On a stepped hull, the bottom surface is broken by an abrupt vertical transition of several inches, from which another long, sloping, relatively flat bottom surface flows toward the rear. Some boats have two or even three steps. Steps extend across the entire width of the hull, providing a flow of air on each side. As the boat accelerates, an air pocket forms within the step and reduces the wetted surface. Each flat section of the hull bottom provides its own lift, and at high speeds, the boat rides on just small sections of the hull bottom at the aft end of each step. This feature also helps the boat get on a plane faster.

PART II

SLOW-SPEED MANEUVERING

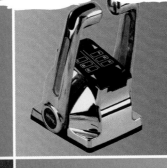

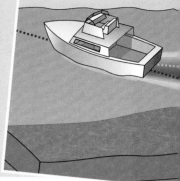

CHAPTER 3

Cars versus Boats

When it comes to steering, a car has a number of advantages over a boat. A few advantages stand out in particular: (1) a car steers from the front; (2) a car's tires help maintain a firm grip to the surface below; (3) cars have brakes; and (4) cars drive on stable surfaces.

Maneuvering a boat is not as easy or predictable as driving a car.

To get a feel for how a boat handles, maneuver a loaded lumber cart between rows of shelves and displays without knocking things over. You need to anticipate where the ends of the load will go and adjust your steering accordingly.

PIVOT POINT

When you turn the steering wheel of a car, the front wheels pivot, the front end of the car moves into the turn, and the tail end of the car follows the path established by the front.

A boat, on the other hand, steers from the rear. When you initiate a turn, the stern swings to one side and reorients the bow in the new direction—kind of like a lumber cart at your local Home Depot or Lowe's store. This can be tricky when you are in close quarters, because you'll need clearance for the stern to swing. (That's why we had such a challenge in our shakedown cruise in the Preface.)

Your stern will dictate how your boat steers, but the bow won't exactly be static while this happens. Your boat pivots while it turns. If looking from overhead, you would see the bow swing into the turn, while the stern swings in the opposite direction. The point around which the boat swings is called the *pivot point*.

While in forward gear, the pivot point for most boats lies along the centerline, about one-quarter to one-third of the boat's waterline length aft of the bow. This means that the bow will turn moderately while the stern will swing wide.

To the frustration of many, however, the pivot point moves to a different location when you go in reverse. On most boats, that new spot will be about

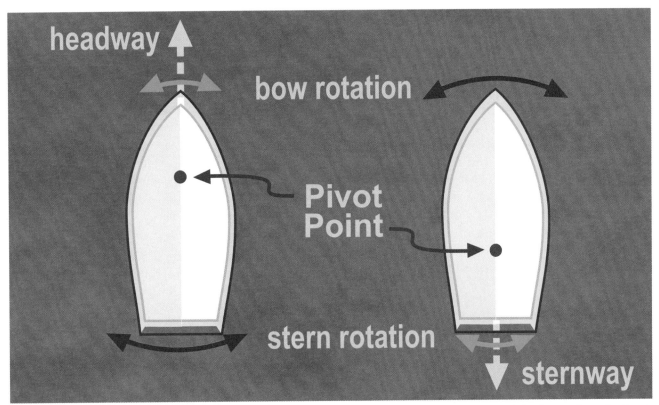

A boat pivots as it turns. The pivot point is ¼ to ⅓ of the waterline length from the front of the boat when the boat is moving forward, and ¼ to ⅓ of the waterline length from the stern when moving in reverse.

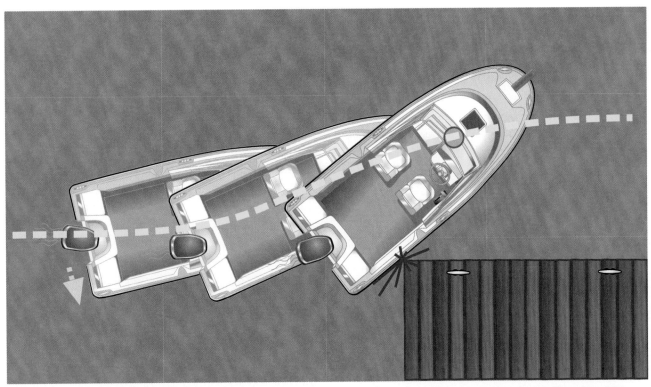

You're traveling down the channel, staying properly toward the right side, when you see a dock off to the right just ahead. You'd like the boat to follow the yellow line. Your natural impulse is to steer left to avoid the dock, but what happens? The boat pivots about a point near the bow and the stern swings wide, striking the very object you were trying to avoid.

one-quarter to one-third of the way forward of the stern. Therefore, when turning in reverse, the bow will swing wide.

The wide swings caused by the pivot point create a potential for danger that doesn't exist for drivers of cars. Car drivers generally only have to worry about their front ends steering clear of obstacles. For instance, if you're making a left-hand turn into your driveway, you don't need to worry about a mailbox that is near the right side of your rear bumper. If you were to somehow make that same turn in a boat, however, the mailbox that is near your stern and on the opposite side of your turn is in jeopardy.

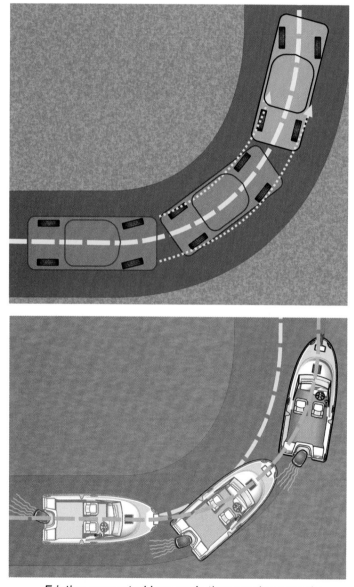

Friction generated by a car's tires moving over the paved road generally provides solid traction. A boat in water, however, produces much less friction, so it tends to slip.

So what should you do? You need to anticipate these situations and slowly ease your boat away from the obstacle before you get too near. Once you approach too near the fixed object, you are doomed—no amount of neat maneuvering in forward gear will help you avoid the collision. Your only recourse is to reverse direction, back away, and regroup.

The same caution applies to both forward and reverse: you have to be mindful of obstacles on the side of the boat opposite the direction you're turning.

The locations of the pivot points vary with the hull form and engine/rudder configuration. In sailboats, the locations of the pivot points are determined, to a great extent, by the deep keel. The same is also often true of trawlers, which tend to have substantial keels. It will take some practice to get the feel for your boat's pivot points.

SLIPPING

When negotiating a turn in a car, the friction between your tires and the road beneath them helps prevent the car from moving sideways, or slipping. The friction between a boat and the water, on the other hand, is considerably less. Every time you turn your boat, you will slip sideways to some extent. Even with full keels, boats are susceptible to slipping.

STOPPING

Stopping is also problematic in water, not only because of the lack of friction but simply because boats don't have brakes.

To stop a boat, you have two options: (1) cut the power and drift to a stop or (2) apply reverse thrust. If you cut the power, the friction between the water and the hull will eventually bring the boat to a stop. In close quarters, however, you'll need more control. Applying a small amount of reverse power will stop the boat much more quickly.

CURRENT AND WIND
Current

Unlike the solid highway beneath a car, the water under your boat is subject to currents. A current is like a moving walkway at an airport: if you stand in one place, the walkway will carry you away. If you

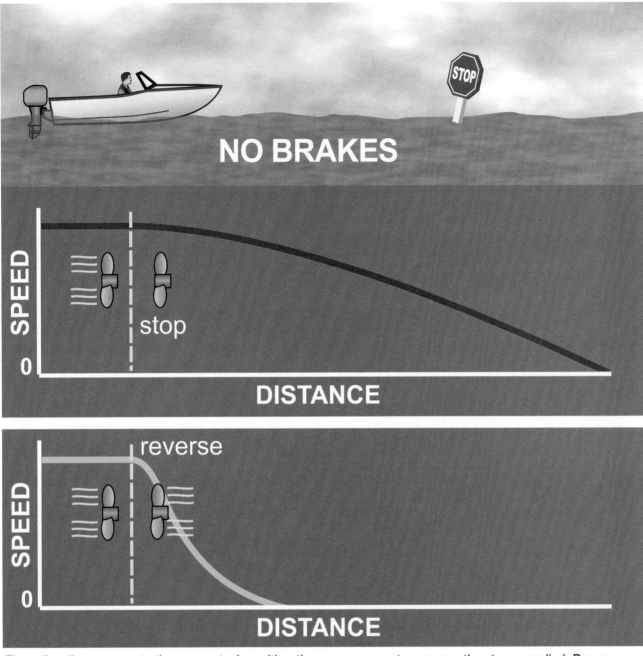

The yellow line represents the moment when either the power was cut or reverse thrust was applied. Reverse thrust will stop a boat more quickly than simply drifting to a stop.

stroll in the same direction the walkway is moving, your speed will increase. If you go against the direction of the walkway, you'll move more slowly, or you might stay in one place, or you might even lose ground.

To put this in the context of boating, let's say you're motoring in the mouth of a river. You're running your engine at a speed that would yield 6 knots if you were motoring on a body of water with no current—say, a lake; however, the current in the river is moving at a brisk 2 knots. How does current affect your speed?

Well, if you travel downstream with the current, your boat speed (6 knots) plus the current speed (2 knots) will combine for an actual speed, or speed over ground, of 8 knots. If you're heading upstream against the current, your speed over ground will be 4 knots (boat speed minus current). A crosscurrent will change both your speed and your course over ground (see figure at the bottom of page 36).

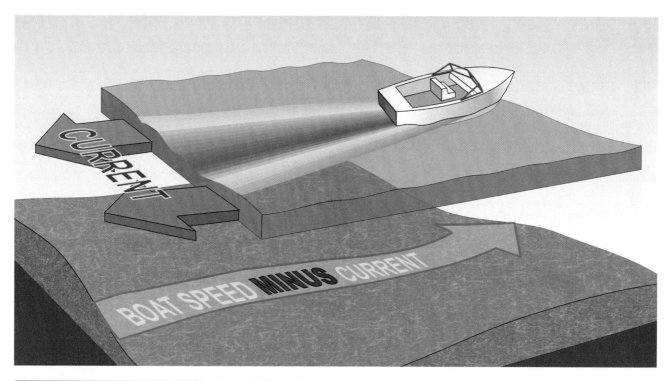

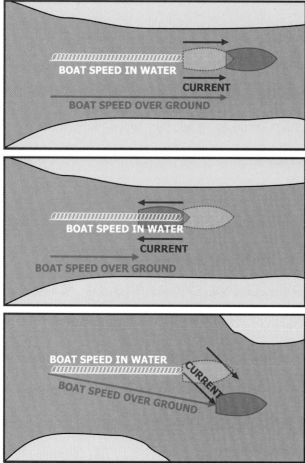

If you are going with the current, your net speed will increase (top). Going against the current will slow your speed (center). A crosscurrent will change both your speed and your course over ground (bottom).

If you're going with the flow, the sudden increase in speed may force you to idle the engine in order to slow down. This, however, means you may have little or no steerage. And if idle speed isn't slow enough, you may need to use reverse gear, which, as you'll learn in Chapter 5, introduces its own steering issues.

If you are powering against the current, you'll experience increased steerage at lower speeds. Even if your speed over ground is zero, you'll be creating enough prop thrust to maintain steerage (again, see Chapter 5.)

Crosscurrents are more troublesome. Not only will they affect your speed, but they may push you sideways into hazards. This could be good if, for instance, a crosscurrent pushes you toward your dock, or it could be bad if you're pushed toward a moored boat.

Because tidal currents and river flows carve paths along constrained waterways, currents flow directly into or out of harbors along the main channels. So, in most cases you will be going nearly directly with or against the current. If, however, you turn to approach a dock, or travel across bays, wide rivers, or open water, you're likely to experience crosscurrents.

In open water, consult current charts to get a sense of how the water will move. For smaller bodies of water like harbors or bays, however, you

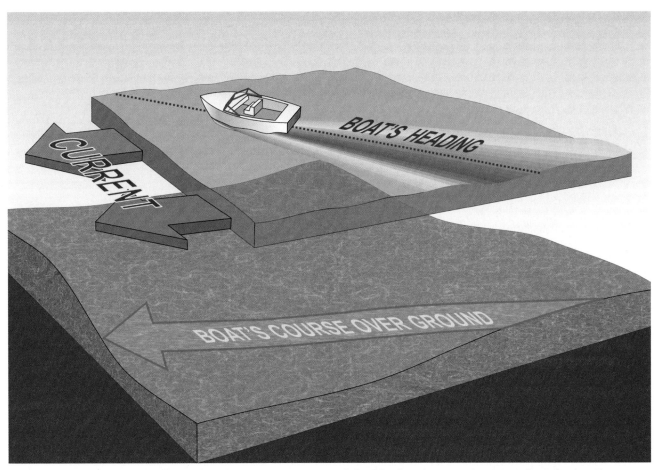

Strong crosscurrents will affect a boat's course over ground. In this situation, you have to adjust the boat's heading to reach your destination. It may feel unnatural to point the bow away from your destination, but it will save you lots of time and energy on open water, and it will be absolutely critical when you're docking in an area with a strong current.

may find fewer printed resources and have to rely more on your wits and observations.

First, if you're on tidal waters, determine whether the tide is coming in or going out. Tide tables or a tide clock can provide this information.

To determine which way the current is flowing, look at moored boats—particularly ones that are similar to yours. Moored boats are particularly useful indicators since they respond to the net effects of wind and current, with current often being the prevailing factor. Very likely, they will be the best indicators of what will happen to your boat. Left to its own devices, your boat will tend to turn and point the same way as the boats swinging to their moorings. If you look around, you will find other telltales, too. The tops of buoys tend to tip toward the oncoming current because their bottoms are being swept under. Ripples form on the upstream sides of buoys, pylons, and other stationary objects. And debris floats with the current.

Remember, your boat will move with the current unless there is sufficient wind to counteract it.

Wind

How will wind affect your boat? Let's go back to your car. On some days, you may feel strong gusts while driving your car; however, only tornado- or hurricane-force winds are likely to push you off the road. A boat, on the other hand, can be pushed off course by a simple breeze.

A boat responds to wind based on (1) its windage and (2) its underwter hull shape. *Windage* is the amount of boat surface, such as the freeboard, cabin, and superstructures, that wind can push on. This amount differs depending upon which side of the boat is presented to the wind. For example, a boat that faces the wind bow-on presents much less windage than a similar-sized boat that lies perpendicular to it.

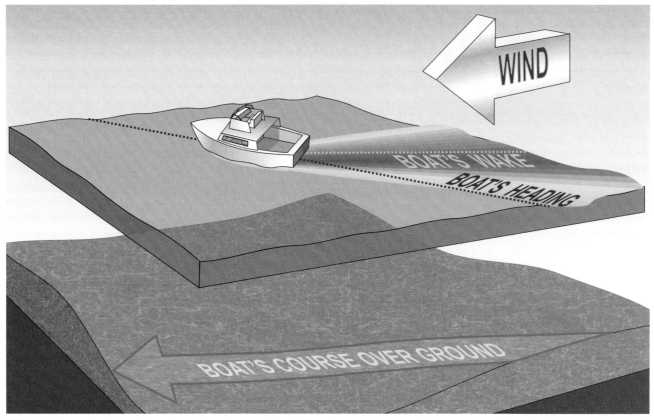

Like current, wind can also alter a boat's speed and direction over ground. Be sure your heading takes these factors into account.

A boat's underwater hull shape can help counteract windage. A boat with a substantial amount of hull in the water, such as a sailboat or trawler, will be less affected by wind than one with a shallow draft.

While under way, wind will have little effect on the stern because the propeller and rudder will help the stern to track through the water. The challenge, however, will lie in controlling your bow. Although the bow's sharp V-shaped entry will tend to hold it in place to some degree, the wind will tend to push the bow downwind. To overcome this, steer into the wind.

In reverse, however, your bow is free to be pushed by the wind. As you will see in Chapter 5, your maneuvering must take this into account.

To determine which way the wind is blowing, look at the flags on other boats or on shore. Trees can also provide clues, although it's not always easy to detect the direction of the wind from their motion.

CHAPTER **4**

A Brief Look at Propellers

Propellers are more complex than you'd think; entire books have been written on the subject. While we won't delve into book-length depth here, we will cover the basic concepts. (If your boat has a jet-drive engine, you can skip this chapter.)

EVALUATING A PROPELLER

When sizing up the correct propeller for your boat, you'll need to consider several factors. The diameter and pitch of the propeller are the most significant specifications, followed by the propeller's slip, lift, and angle of attack. We will cover each of these below. How you plan to use your boat as well as how you load it can also impact your selection. In general, you should consult your boat and engine manufacturer's manuals.

Diameter

As a propeller rotates, the tips of its blades create a circle. The distance across this circle, from blade tip to blade tip, is the propeller's diameter. This measurement must be properly matched to the engine size, since it is the diameter that determines how efficiently the power of the engine is converted into thrust. A large-diameter propeller is capable of moving more water and producing more thrust than a small one at the same rotational speed (measured in revolutions per minute or rpm). But larger isn't always better, and you must consider several factors in choosing the correct propeller:

- Available clearance. The propeller has to fit within the available space under the hull or beneath the waterline.

- Engine size. The propeller must be matched to the engine. Larger propellers need more power. If the propeller is too big for your engine, it will slow down the engine's rpm, and you won't get the thrust the propeller is capable of producing. If the propeller is too small for the engine, you'll lose thrust potential. Plus, in an effort to overcome the lack of power, you may be tempted to over-rev the engine, which could cause damage.

- Potential for cavitation. A propeller that is too small may cause the engine to operate at rpms that exceed the propeller design. If this happens, the water pressure on the forward side of the blade can drop so low that the water actually vaporizes into bubbles. This is called cavitation. It will hinder the propeller from getting a "grip" on the water, a phenomenon we'll discuss later in the chapter.

Pitch

Pitch is the theoretical distance that a propeller moves through water in a single revolution and is related to the angle of the blades. It is analogous to measuring the distance a wood screw would advance into a board in one revolution. So, for example, a blade with a pitch of 24 inches would advance 24 inches, in theory. In the water, however, the actual travel distance is less per revolution because of slippage (see below). The greater the pitch, the farther it will travel with each revolution, but this doesn't mean you always want the propeller with the steepest pitch.

A propeller's pitch must be matched to the boat's ability to move that distance with each revolution. If, for instance, you have a boat with a heavy displacement hull, a propeller with a lot of pitch will be overkill: the propeller will push the boat harder than the bow wave allows, thus putting heavy strain on the engine. Also, a high-pitch propeller will make it difficult to move slowly even at idling speed. You may need to alternate between in-gear and neutral to moderate your speed.

On the other hand, a propeller with too little pitch will move the boat by a much smaller amount per revolution and thus prevent the boat from reaching its potential top speed.

Slip, Lift, and Angle of Attack

Earlier I mentioned that pitch describes the distance a propeller travels through water in one revolution, similar to a screw moving through wood. Water, however, does not provide the same bite as wood. Take a look at the accompanying figure. If you trace the blue line through one revolution, you will see that it does not extend as far as the red line (representing theoretical pitch). The difference between actual and theoretical pitch is called *slip*.

Unlike a screw biting into wood, your propeller needs some help in order to move forward in water. Much like the angle of an airplane wing helps it to develop lift into air, the angle of each propeller blade helps it develop lift through the water. This angle of attack creates a pressure differential between the front and back sides of the blades, which in turn provides the lift that advances the propeller. If the angle of attack is too great, however, the water pressure on the front side can be reduced so much that cavitation results, just as it does when a propeller is underpowered or the leading edge of a propeller blade is damaged. When cavitation occurs, the propeller loses its grip on the water and spins inefficiently. As

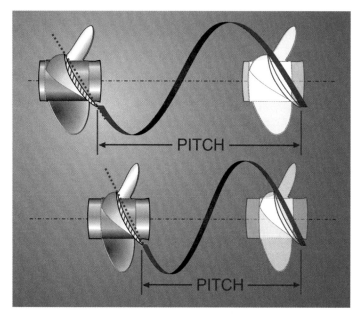

How far the propeller would advance with each rotation (if there were no slip or resistance) is called its pitch (red path). Pitch is specified in inches and determined by the slope of the blade. The flatter the blade, the greater the pitch.

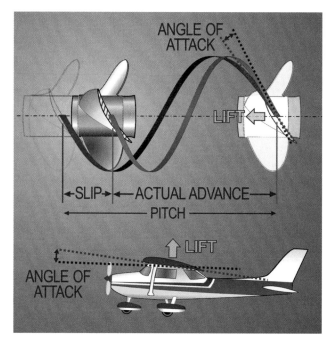

The propeller pitch (red path) shows how the propeller would advance if it were like a screw in wood. If you trace the true progression of the propeller through water, you'll see that it does not advance as far as the pitch would suggest. The difference is called slip. The dotted lines illustrate the angle of attack—a key element in creating lift. (Adapted from Mercury Marine)

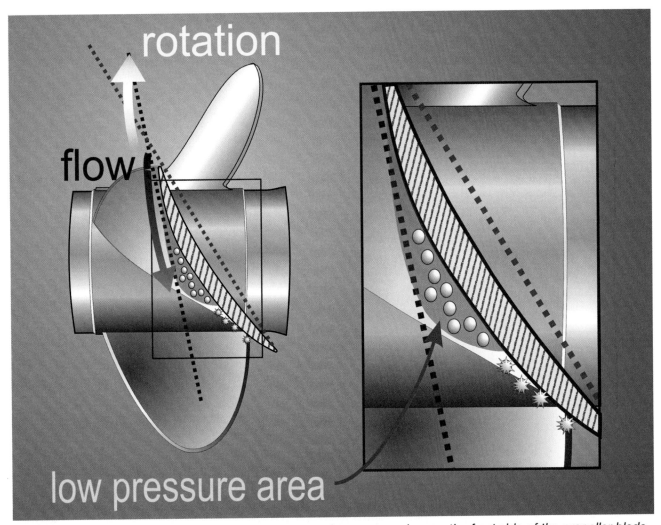

If the angle of attack is too great, it will cause an excessive pressure drop on the front side of the propeller blade. In turn, the water in front of the blade will vaporize, causing cavitation. Cavitation may also occur when a prop is underpowered (which causes overspinning) or if the leading edge of the blade is damaged. The vapor bubbles will collapse back to water when they reach the trailing edge of the blade, where the pressure is higher. As the bubbles collapse, they emit shock waves, which can deteriorate metals and shorten a propeller's life.

the vapor bubbles move toward the trailing end of the blade, the pressure increases. The vapor bubbles condense back to liquid water, releasing enough energy to pit the blade surface.

Propellers are optimized to go forward. Going in reverse is a real compromise for a propeller, since its airfoil is shaped the wrong way to develop good lift in this direction. This often makes props inefficient and sluggish in reverse, adding to your difficulties when going astern. When attempting to slow the boat, you may need to apply a bit more reverse power briefly to make up for this inefficiency.

When selecting a propeller, it's best to follow the guidance of your boat and engine manufacturers.

PROP WALK

Before we take a look at steering systems in the next chapter, it's a good idea to learn about prop walk and how it affects your boat's steering.

When your boat is motoring forward, the propeller is not only producing forward thrust, it is also producing a small amount of side thrust. This side thrust, called *prop walk*, tends to swing the stern outward. Although the propeller's side thrust is much less powerful than its forward thrust, prop walk will have a noticeable effect at slower speeds and can bedevil your close-quarters maneuvering. If you understand it, however, you can use it to your advantage.

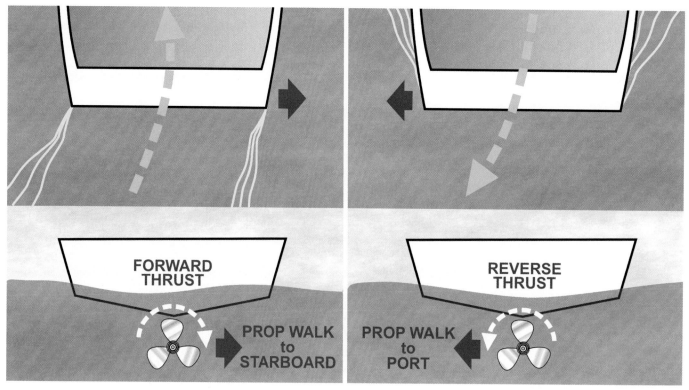

This illustration of a right-handed propeller shows the effect of prop walk. When the propeller pushes the boat forward (left), it also walks the stern to starboard. In reverse gear (right), the stern walks to port.

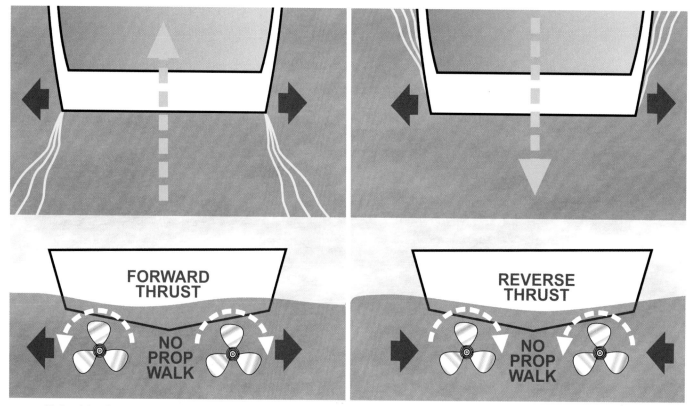

Twin-drive boats usually employ both a right-handed propeller to starboard and a left-handed propeller to port. When twin drives are both in forward or both in reverse, the props turn in opposite directions, causing the prop walk forces to cancel each other. However, if one is in forward and the other in reverse, the prop walks are turning in the same direction, and the forces are added.

Propellers that turn clockwise, or to the right (as seen from astern) when the engine is in forward gear, are called *right-handed propellers*. Propellers that turn counter-clockwise, or to the left, are *left-handed props*. Right-handed props are the most common.

Right-handed props produce a side thrust that pushes the stern to the right (or starboard) while going forward, and to the left (or port) when in reverse. Left-handed props do just the opposite.

At cruising speeds, prop walk has much less impact because a boat's hull shape tends to maintain a straight track through the water. In addition, most outboards and I/O drives have a mini-rudder mounted just above the propeller. This mini-rudder is turned a little to starboard and acts to counteract the prop walk by creating a small side thrust in the opposite direction while cruising in forward gear. This mini-rudder is largely ineffective at slow speeds, however.

Engine Systems That Reduce Prop Walk

To counteract the effect of prop walk, most twin-engine boats have both a right-handed prop and a left-handed prop. When both engines are going either forward or reverse at the same speed, the two propellers turn in opposite directions and their side thrusts are effectively cancelled. On the other hand, running one engine in forward and the other in reverse will double the side thrust effect, which actually can help in turning, as you will soon see.

Some of today's inboard/outboard engines are equipped with both a left-handed prop and a right-handed prop mounted on a coaxial shaft which is designed so that the two props rotate in opposite directions. These contrarotating props eliminate prop walk in a single-engine installation.

Coping with Prop Walk

GOING IN A STRAIGHT LINE Let's assume you have a right-handed prop. While making headway, prop walk will tend to push your stern slightly to starboard. This effect will be more pronounced when you are going slowly, and it will *feel* even more pronounced if there are nearby fixed objects to starboard.

To maintain your course, you may intuitively steer slightly to starboard to counteract the stern's

tendency to swing to starboard. However, you may need to be careful or you could easily overcorrect. Once you begin a turn, even a slight one, the boat will continue turning in that direction even after you straighten the wheel. This is a phenomenon called *angular momentum*. Just as linear momentum will keep you going in a straight line even after you remove the power, angular momentum will keep you going in a turn after you've straightened the rudder. You actually need to counter the steering, but again don't overcorrect too much, or you'll

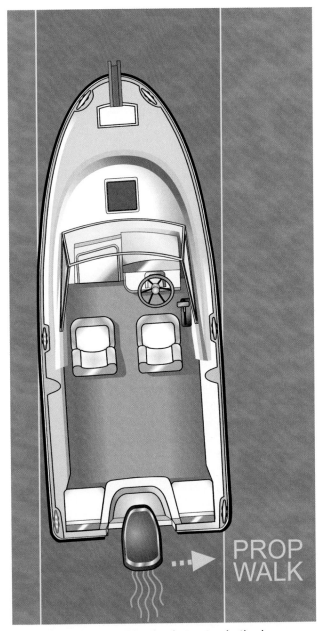

Let's assume your objective is to stay in the lane marked by the yellow lines. Prop walk is pushing your stern slightly to starboard. To compensate, you'll steer slightly to starboard.

Slow-Speed Maneuvering

swing too far the other way. Many boaters, especially new ones, find they are constantly weaving back and forth and having difficulty maintaining a straight-line course.

There are two ways to handle this effect. One way is to return the helm to amidships *before* you reach the desired heading. Or, when you reach the desired heading, briefly turn the wheel in the opposite direction to stop the rotation, then return the helm to amidships. Each boat behaves differently; it may take some time to get used to yours. In the meantime, go slowly and use a gentle touch.

DOCKING As you near a dock, keep in mind how prop walk will affect your approach. If your approach puts the dock on your starboard side, the prop walk will pull your stern toward the dock. If the dock is on your port side, prop walk will push the stern away from it—not necessarily a bad thing.

As you will see in the next chapter, there is a distinct advantage to approaching a dock on the port side of the boat, because ultimately you will have to shift into reverse gear to stop. When you do so, prop walk will cause the stern to nestle nicely against the dock.

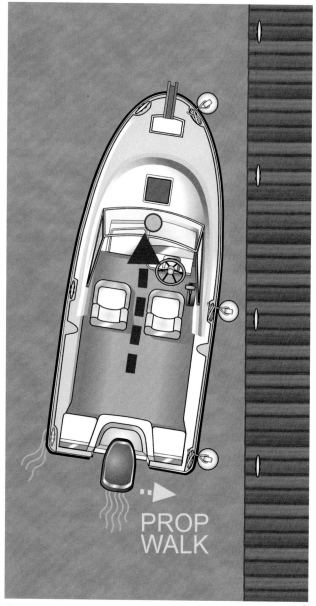

If you approach a starboard-side dock in forward gear, your prop walk will help pull the stern to the dock.

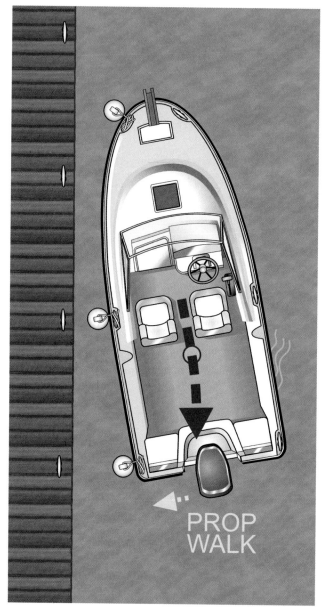

Approaching the dock on your port side, however, gives you a tactical advantage. When you shift into reverse gear to slow your approach, prop walk will cause the stern to turn toward the dock.

CHAPTER 5

Steering Types

Recreational boats use two basic types of steering: rudder and directed thrust. Rudders work in conjunction with inboard engines, and the propeller shaft is held in a fixed direction. They steer the boat by deflecting the propeller's flow of water. Directed-thrust steering, on the other hand, cuts out the middleman: the propellers themselves direct the flow of water. At the end of the chapter, we'll discuss twin engines—a steering type that can utilize either type of steering, but also incorporates some unique tricks of its own.

The type of steering device you have on your boat will have an impact on your slow-speed maneuvering.

RUDDERS AND INBOARD ENGINES

Rudders have had a place on boats for centuries—long before the first engine ever roared to life. They have been used on oared boats and sailboats throughout history, and nowadays they also accompany inboard engines on powerboats.

right hand propeller

prop wash

rudder position

Rudders turn boats by diverting water flow. Here, rudders are positioned behind twin inboard-engine propellers.

45

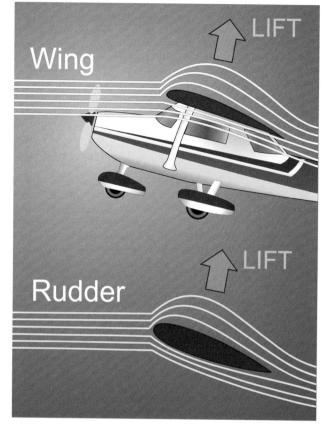

A rudder provides lift much like an airplane wing. The longer path of water over the top of the rudder reduces water pressure, while the compressed flow on the bottom increases pressure. The rudder moves toward the lower pressure.

A rudder is a vertical plane that—on a powerboat—is mounted behind the propeller. When the rudder is *steered amidships* (aligned with the keel), the boat goes straight ahead. When the rudder is turned to one side, water flow from the propeller is diverted and the stern is pushed in the opposite direction, causing the boat to turn.

OK, that explanation is somewhat oversimplified. In actuality, rudders are more like airfoils—they generate lift in the water, much like an airplane's wings in the air. In fact, more turning force comes from the lift created by the flow of water on the outer side of the rudder than the push of water on the inner side. Although a perfectly flat rudder will work, rudders are usually curved in cross section to increase the lifting phenomenon (see the accompanying illustration).

The turning force of a rudder is related to the size of the rudder and the speed of the water passing over it. The faster the water flows over the rudder, the more responsive your boat will be. If there is no water flowing over the rudder, the boat will not turn. This catch-22 can be particularly frustrating when you're docking. You'll need to motor slowly because of all the obstacles, but you'll also need the improved handling that's only available when your boat is moving at higher speeds.

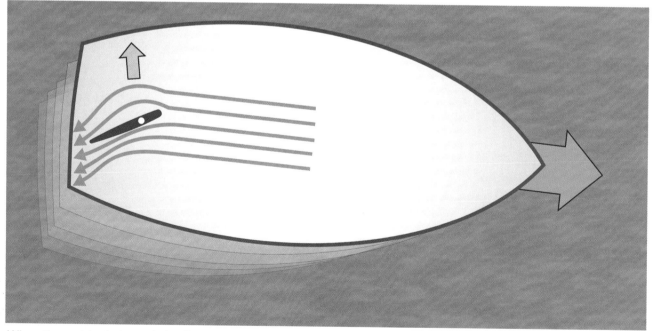

When the rudder is turned, the flow of water deflected to one side pushes the stern in the opposite direction. In addition, the flow of water curving to the rudder's outer side creates lift—a more powerful turning force.

Luckily, there are some ways to get around this.

As soon as a propeller begins to spin, it forces water to flow over the rudder. Even if the boat hasn't begun to move forward, the sudden flow of water, or *prop wash*, will cause the stern to swing to one side. You can use a brief burst of power to turn your boat even if you're not making substantial *headway*, or forward movement.

Reverse is another matter, however. When the engine is in reverse gear, there is no prop wash across the rudder. If the boat is not already moving backward, there will be no flow of water at all over the rudder; hence, no *steerage* (ability to steer). The boat will not steer in reverse until it begins to make enough *sternway* (reverse movement). Control in reverse is further hindered by the flat face the transom presents to the water—not a hydrodynamic boon—and the propeller is optimized for forward, not reverse, gear. Even the keel is relatively flat at the stern. As a result, the boat will not track well and will be sluggish to respond to steering.

Keep in mind that the pivot point will move toward the stern when you're motoring in reverse. This means your bow will swing widely while the stern turns just a little. Be alert to your surroundings.

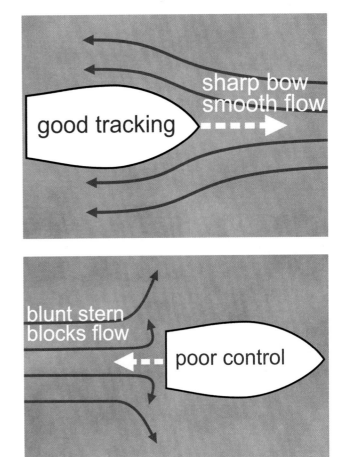

Boats are designed to go forward—the V-shaped bow slices through the water. In reverse, however, the blunt transom tends to plow the surface.

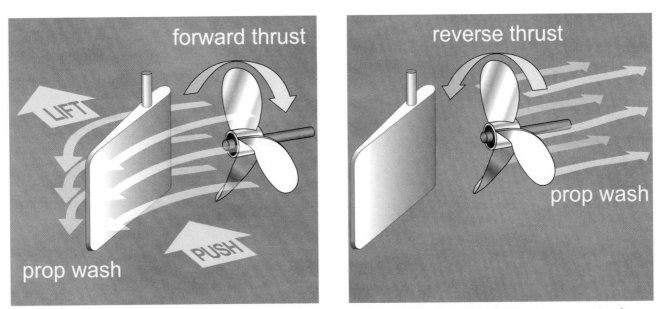

The rudder cannot turn the boat if there's no water flowing over it, but your boat doesn't have to be moving forward to achieve this. A quick burst from the propeller can generate sufficient prop wash to turn the boat in place (left). However, the same technique will not work in reverse gear because the water flow from the propeller is pushed away from the rudder, and not enough water is drawn across the rudder to effectively steer.

ENGINE CONTROLS

There are two basic configurations for engine throttle and gear controls. Most smaller boats use a single, dual-action lever that combines both the gears and the throttle: push the lever forward to shift into forward gear and then to throttle up; pull the lever back to increase speed in reverese; put the lever in the center position for neutral gear and idle throttle speed. The single-lever, dual control is finding increased application on all sizes of boats today, and it is the control I've used in this book's illustrations.

The control configuration often found on larger boats has two separate levers: one for gear and one for throttle. Typically, the gear shift is on the left and the throttle is on the right

Twin engines require a separate control unit for each engine. If the boat is equipped with dual-action levers, there will be a single lever for the starboard engine, and a single lever for port (as shown in the photo). If the boat is equipped with single-action levers, there will be two levers for each engine (not pictured).

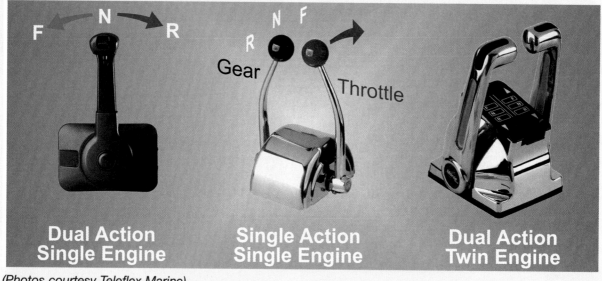

Dual Action Single Engine   **Single Action Single Engine**   **Dual Action Twin Engine**

(Photos courtesy Teleflex Marine)

Maneuvering with an Inboard

TURNING IN FORWARD GEAR Remember the dock we were trying to miss in Chapter 3? In that scenario, we were moving along at near idle speed, and tried to move to port to get around a dock. As we turned to port, however, the stern swung to starboard into the dock. Our mission now is to reposition the stern and safely clear the dock. Let's see how we can use forward gear and low speeds to get out of this dilemma:

1. For this maneuver to work, be sure your bow and forward pivot point are well to port of an imaginary line extending from the edge of the dock (see figure).

2. Turn the rudder hard to starboard.

3. Place the boat in forward gear and apply a brief burst of power. This will kick the stern sharply to port without gaining much headway. Remember that the pivot point is forward so the stern will swing wide to port while the bow moves slightly to starboard. You may need to apply another brief burst of power if the stern does not kick far enough on the first try.

4. Proceed at idle speed until your stern is clear of the dock.

6. Once the boat is clear of the dock and oriented in the desired direction, return the rudder to amidships and proceed.

TURNING IN REVERSE GEAR When backing up, the best way to steer an inboard-powered boat is to first go forward. Bear with me. Here's how:

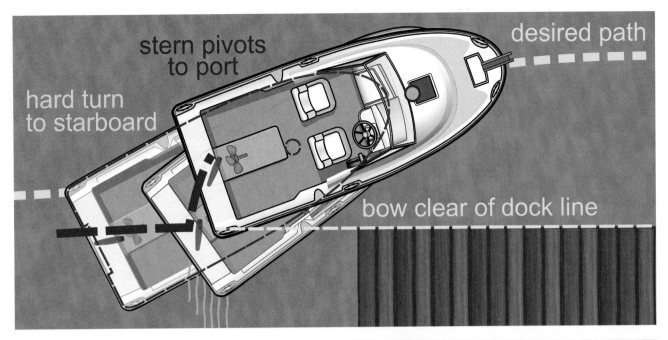

stern pivots to port

desired path

hard turn to starboard

bow clear of dock line

Above: *To avoid striking the dock on the starboard quarter, first, make sure your bow (red dashed line) is to port of the outermost edge of the dock (yellow dashed line). Next, put the rudder hard to starboard and use a burst of power to kick the stern to port. Return the rudder to amidships once your stern has cleared the dock.* Right: *Steering in reverse is a bit of a challenge with an inboard. (A) If you find that you are not properly aligned to your destination, swing the rudder and shift into forward gear. (B) Use a brief burst of power to move the stern in the desired direction. (C) Continue in reverse.*

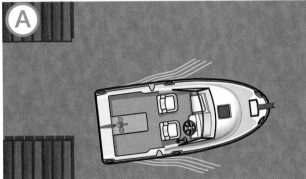

A

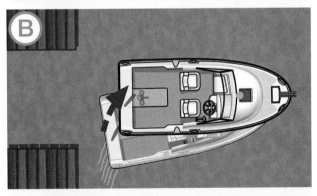

B

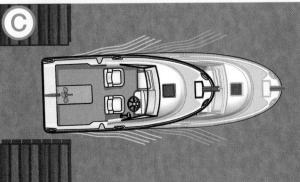

C

1. Put the rudder over to port or starboard and apply a brief burst of power in forward gear— your stern will swing in the opposite direction in response.

2. Once the stern is aligned to your destination, turn the rudder to amidships, shift to reverse gear, and motor backward.

3. If you drift out of alignment, shift to forward gear again and nudge the stern in the proper direction.

4. Shift back to reverse gear and continue.

5. Be sure to account for prop walk when you align the boat (e.g., if you have a right-handed prop, your stern will walk to port as you motor in reverse).

6. If you have sufficient sternway and a large enough rudder, you may be able to direct the stern using the rudder alone. (This is all part of understanding how your boat responds.)

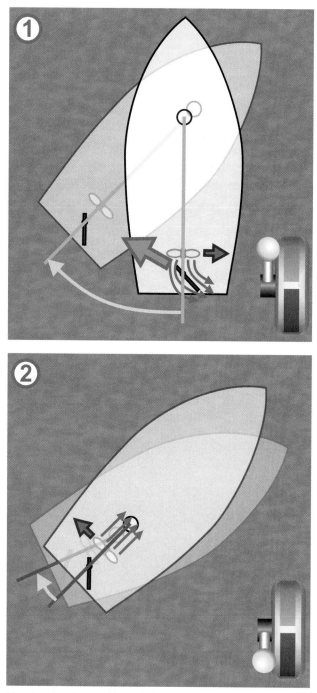

Slow-Speed Maneuvering

TURNING WITHIN A SINGLE BOAT LENGTH In particularly tight quarters, it may be necessary to turn without making appreciable headway or stern-way. This works best in a clockwise direction, as follows:

1. Place the wheel hard to starboard and apply a brief burst of power in forward gear. This will cause the stern to kick to port while rotating around the pivot point near the bow.

2. Shift to reverse gear and give a brief burst of power to halt headway. Prop walk to port will help continue the turn of the boat.

3. When your momentum slows, repeat the above steps.

4. Continue alternating between forward and reverse until you're oriented in the right direction.

This technique is not very effective in a counterclockwise direction. Yes, prop walk in forward gear will push the stern counterclockwise, but the clockwise prop walk in reverse gear will tend to negate your progress.

DIRECTED-THRUST STEERING
Inboard—Outboard and Outboard Propulsion

The majority of powerboats use either outboard or inboard—outboard engines (also called I/Os or sterndrives). Unlike the inboard engine—which has a propeller set at a fixed angle and must rely on a rudder for turning—these engine types steer by pivoting the propeller to the right or left. (Outboards and I/Os can also be tilted up or down to *trim* the boat. We'll cover this in more detail in Chapter 7.) In the case of the outboard, the entire engine pivots, while in the case of the I/O, the "inboard" engine remains in place while the "outboard" sterndrive unit, mounted on the outside of the transom, pivots. With either engine, the propeller wash is directed to the right or left and the water flow—known as *directed thrust*—forces the boat into a turn.

With directed-thrust steering, you'll always have steerage whether you're going forward, backward, fast, or slow. As long as your propeller can turn, so can your boat; you needn't wait for headway or sternway before you can steer. (Steering in reverse, however, is still not quite as effective as going forward.)

Turning in place with an inboard engine. *Assuming you have a right-handed propeller, turning in place with an inboard requires that you turn in a clockwise direction. (1) Place the wheel hard to starboard and leave it there. Start with a burst of forward power; the stern will swing to port. (2) Quickly shift to reverse and give it a brief burst of power to stop your headway; in the meantime, prop walk will continue to turn the boat.*

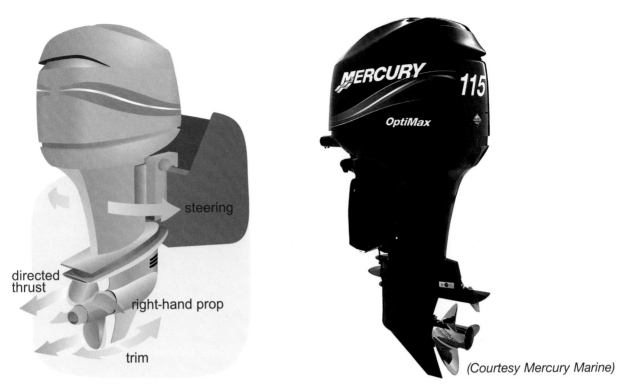

steering

directed
thrust

right-hand prop

trim

(Courtesy Mercury Marine)

Thanks to modern technology, outboard motors are now more reliable, and their popularity has risen accordingly. One of the chief advantages of the outboard is its ability to direct prop wash in any direction—forward and reverse.

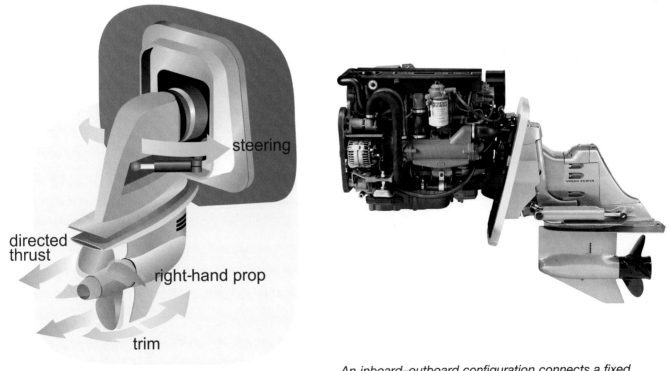

steering

directed
thrust

right-hand prop

trim

The outdrive unit of the inboard/outboard directs the thrust much as the outboard lower unit. It also can be tilted up or down to adjust trim.

An inboard–outboard configuration connects a fixed inboard engine to a steered external prop unit. An I/O offers the power and ruggedness of an inboard with the control of an outboard. (Courtesy Volvo Marine)

BOW THRUSTERS

Handling a boat in close quarters can be a real challenge. The bigger the boat, the more difficult close-quarters maneuvering can be. As a result, bow thrusters have become fairly common on large boats, and they are gaining popularity further down the size range.

A bow thruster is a miniature propeller mounted sideways in a tunnel cut through the bow that, when activated, can push your bow to port or starboard. The tunnel causes a small amount of drag while the boat is under way, but the bow thruster can make docking and other close-quarters maneuvers much easier.

Some larger boats have both bow and stern thrusters, which together can push the boat perfectly sideways.

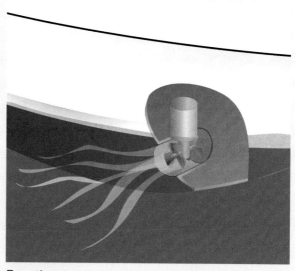

Bow thruster.

On the other hand, boats with rudders do have a noteworthy advantage over directed-thrust steering: A boat in motion can be steered by the rudder even if the engine has been cut. If you have headway and your engine suddenly quits, you'll have a better chance of steering out of the way of trouble with a rudder than with an outboard or I/O. While an outboard or I/O does provide a small amount of steerage due to its underwater profile, it's not nearly as effective as a rudder.

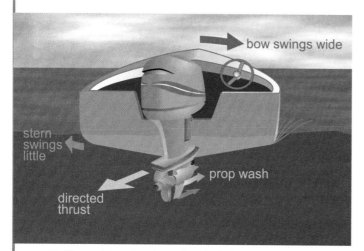

Unlike rudder steering, directed-thrust steering provides decent steerage in reverse. This outboard is in reverse gear and has been steered to port. The boat's stern is being pulled to port while the bow swings wide to starboard.

Jet-Drive Steering

It used to be that jet drives were only found on "jet skis," or *personal watercraft* (PWC), but nowadays they're found on small runabouts and even high-end cruisers.

A jet drive uses an *impeller* rather than a propeller. An impeller is similar to a propeller except that it spins within a tube mounted inside the boat's hull and functions as a high-pressure water pump. The impeller sucks water into the front of the tube through a grate at the bottom of the hull. The water is then forced out the rear of the tube through a nozzle on the transom just below the waterline. The force of the water exiting the tube causes the boat to move forward, much as an unattended garden hose whips around due to the force of the expelled water. Similar to the external portion of an I/O, the jet drive's nozzle can be pivoted to direct the thrust to the left or right.

A jet drive is very effective in forward steering, but it cannot reverse its water flow as a propeller can. Instead it achieves reverse propulsion by dropping a diverter over its nozzle, which redirects the flow of water toward the bow and pushes the boat backward. Unfortunately, this approach doesn't work very well. To compensate, a PWC operator is more likely to spin the boat around in forward gear than to attempt backing.

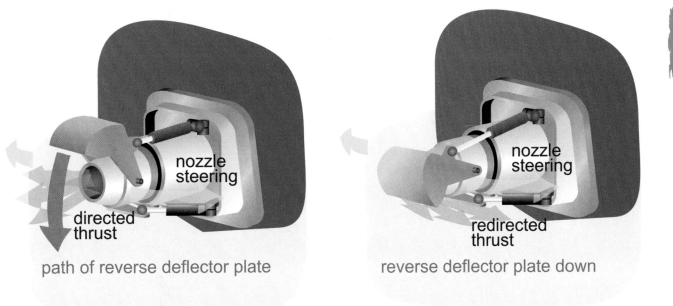

A jet drive propels the boat by expelling a high-pressure water stream through a transom-mounted nozzle like this one. The nozzle can steer the boat by aiming the water flow to port or starboard (left). To move the boat in reverse, a diverter is lowered in front of the water stream, which redirects the water flow forward (right).

But while PWCs will effectively "spin on a dime," this is not the case with larger boats using jet drives. They have no choice but to use reverse thrust when docking and maneuvering. (To help them with maneuvering, most of these boats are also equipped with bow thrusters. See sidebar on page 52.)

Another problem with jet drives is the *complete* absence of steerage without power. If the boat is under way and the engine quits, you'll keep going straight no matter how you turn the wheel. This causes problems (and accidents) for unskilled PWC riders, whose first reaction to an obstacle is often to slam the throttle closed—thereby eliminating their ability to steer around it.

Maneuvering with Directed-Thrust Steering

TURNING IN FORWARD GEAR When you have directed thrust, steering in forward gear is simpler, more immediate, and works well at low and high throttle settings. With the drive mounted farther aft, it provides even more leverage than a rudder to pivot the boat. Turning involves these simple steps:

1. Turn the wheel.

2. Apply throttle in forward gear.

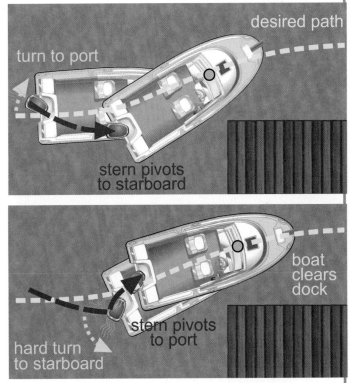

Here's a quick-steer maneuver for directed thrust (similar to what we did earlier with an inboard engine and rudder). As the bow clears the dock, and before the stern strikes, quickly but briefly turn the wheel hard toward the dock and apply a brief burst of power (bottom). The stern will move wide to port to clear the dock. Straighten the wheel a bit and continue at idle speed until you clear the dock.

Slow-Speed Maneuvering

3. Return the wheel to the amidships position as you approach your desired heading. You may need to counter the turn by briefly steering in the opposite direction.

4. Monitor the position of your stern as you execute a turn, particularly in tight quarters.

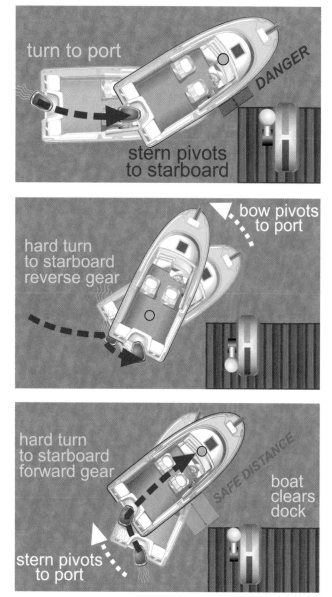

What if you're too close to the dock to continue forward? Try reverse gear. Place the wheel hard to starboard (toward the dock), shift to reverse, and apply a brief burst of power. This will halt your forward progress and swing your bow away from the dock (center). Keeping the wheel hard to starboard, shift into forward gear and use a burst of power to swing the stern to port. With the pivot point now near the bow, this will allow you to clear the dock while turning the boat toward your original course (bottom).

All of this takes some time and distance to execute. Sometimes you may need to reorient the bow's direction more quickly. You can do this by shifting temporarily into reverse gear. For example, if you want the bow to move quickly to port, select reverse gear while steering to starboard. Apply a brief burst of power. Since the pivot point is now nearer the stern, the bow will swing to port without appreciably moving the stern sideways. Then return to forward gear, steering to port to complete your turn.

TURNING IN REVERSE GEAR A boat with directed-thrust steering, when set in reverse gear, will pull the stern in whichever direction the propeller is pointed. Remember: when in reverse, the boat's pivot point will be located toward the stern. As a result, the stern will swing moderately toward your chosen direction while the bow will swing wide in the opposite direction. You need to be aware of any obstructions that the bow may strike.

Meanwhile, you can wind up with the boat

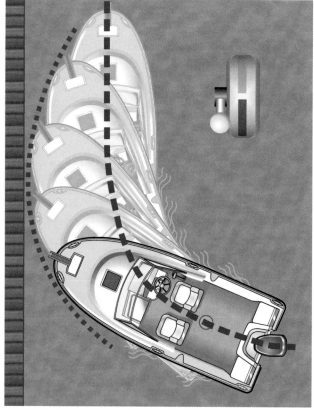

Even with directed thrust, oversteering in reverse can cause problems. In this example, you've attempted to steer sharply away from the dock. With the pivot point near the stern, the bow swings wide and drags alongside the dock.

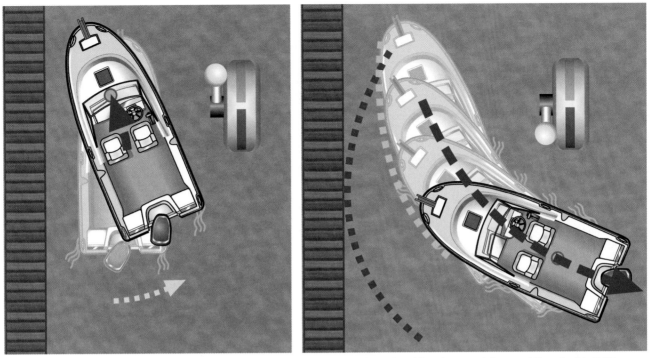

A better way to leave the dock is to begin in forward gear with the wheel hard to port (toward the dock). With the pivot point forward, the stern will swing smartly away from the dock (left). Then shift into reverse gear with the wheel to starboard (right). The path of the bow is now a safe distance away from the dock (blue dashed line) rather than striking it as in the previous figure (red dashed line).

turned the wrong way. For example, while you back the stern to starboard, your bow will swing wide toward port. Now the stern may be where you want it, but the boat is turned sideways and no longer aligned along your intended direction. Since the boat steers from the stern, getting the bow back where you want it can be a challenge.

Here's the best way to steer in reverse when using directed thrust:

■ When in reverse, limit your steering to small corrections.

■ If you need to reposition the stern more, shift into forward gear.

■ Once you have the stern properly aligned, make small corrections to the bow using directed thrust in reverse. Remember, most single-engine boats will tend to back to port due to prop walk.

Let's look at an example. Imagine you are close to a dock to port and you want to pull away sharply, but there are boats ahead and astern limiting your space. If you attempt to simply back away while

steering sharply to starboard, your pivot point will be near the stern, and the bow will likely strike the dock. A better way is to use forward gear to adjust the stern and move it away from the dock. Then apply moderate steering in reverse to pull the boat away without striking the dock.

TURNING WITHIN A SINGLE BOAT LENGTH To turn within a single boat length, use the directed-thrust steering in both forward and reverse. If you have a right-handed propeller, the maneuver will work better if you turn the boat in a clockwise direction. Here's how:

1. Place the wheel hard to starboard and apply a short burst of power in forward gear. The boat will begin turning in a clockwise direction. Because the power burst is brief, you will make little or no headway.

2. Immediately turn the wheel hard to port and apply brief power in reverse. The stern will be drawn to port, continuing the clockwise turn. Prop walk will help the turn. Given the short burst of power, the boat will make little or no sternway while it turns.

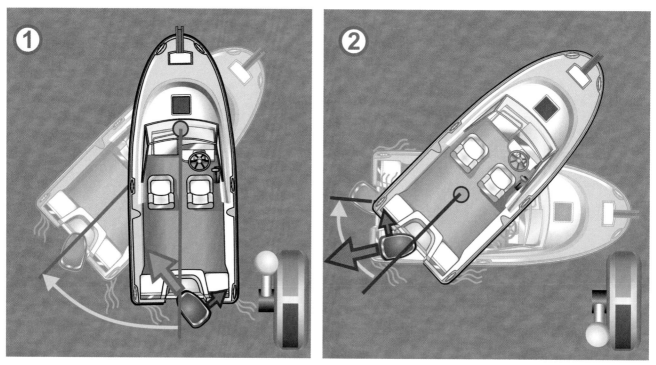

To turn in place with directed-thrust steering, turn the wheel hard to starboard and apply a brief burst of power in forward gear (left). This will begin turning the boat clockwise. Next, turn the wheel hard to port and apply a brief burst of power in reverse (right). This pulls the stern to the left and continues the boat's clockwise rotation. In reverse, prop walk (blue arrows) will work to your advantage.

3. Repeat these steps until you have rotated to the proper direction.

You can make the same turn in a counterclockwise direction, but you'll be fighting against prop walk.

TWIN DRIVES

Twin drives—two independent, side-by-side engines within a single boat—are very effective in close quarters. The most effective twin-drive setup uses two inboard engines, two propellers, and two rudders; however, twin outboards, I/Os, and even jet drives are also effective.

With twin drives, you'll have two throttles and two gear shifts. Each throttle works its respective engine independently from the other and gives you a wide range of options. You'll quickly realize that in close quarters, your steering will be accomplished exclusively using the engines, not the rudders. For instance, you can rev your starboard engine to a higher speed and reduce your port engine to a lower speed. Or, you can shift your star-

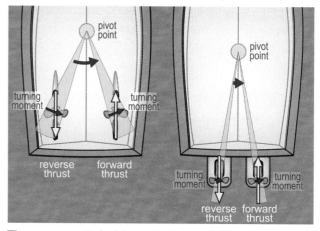

The props on twin inboard engines (left) are spaced farther apart from each other than the props on twin outboards or I/Os (right). Also, inboard props are mounted closer to the pivot point than outboards or I/Os, resulting in better leverage. In the left panel, the ability to turn is represented by the width of the light blue arcs and the lengths of the red arrows. The red arrows illustrate how much energy from the engine thrust is transferred into turning. In the right panel, the red arrows and the blue arcs are substantially smaller. The inboard engines turn at least twice as effectively as outboards with equivalent thrust.

board engine to reverse gear and your port engine to forward. By applying power from each engine in differing amounts and directions, you can steer the boat in close quarters without turning the wheel and without any headway or sternway—advantages unique to this type of engine setup.

The pivot point on boats with twin drives tends to remain fixed when the gears are in opposite directions. On many inboard boats, the pivot point is just aft of midships; on boats with twin outboards, I/Os, and jet drives, the pivot point is located farther aft. When both engines are in the same gear, the pivot point tends to move as with a single-engine boat. For close-quarters maneuvering, using opposite gears with a fixed pivot point is easier than dealing with the pivot point moving forward or aft with

every change of gear (as it does on a single-screw boat).

Twin inboards tend to be more effective for steering than I/Os or outboards.

Prop walk is less of an issue with twin drives. Most twin drives are equipped with both a right-handed prop and a left-handed prop. This means that the prop walk created by one propeller is negated by the opposing prop walk of the other propeller as long as both drives are in the same gear.

Maneuvering with Twin Drives

TURNING IN FORWARD GEAR If you operate both drives in forward gear at unequal speeds, your boat will turn. For example, if the port engine is driven

A twin-drive boat can be steered with the engines alone—ideal for close-quarters maneuvering. If, for example, the port engine is throttled higher than the starboard engine, the boat will turn gently to starboard (left). If only one engine is in gear, the boat will turn more sharply to starboard (right). Note that prop walk actually helps the turn (blue arrows).

Slow-Speed Maneuvering

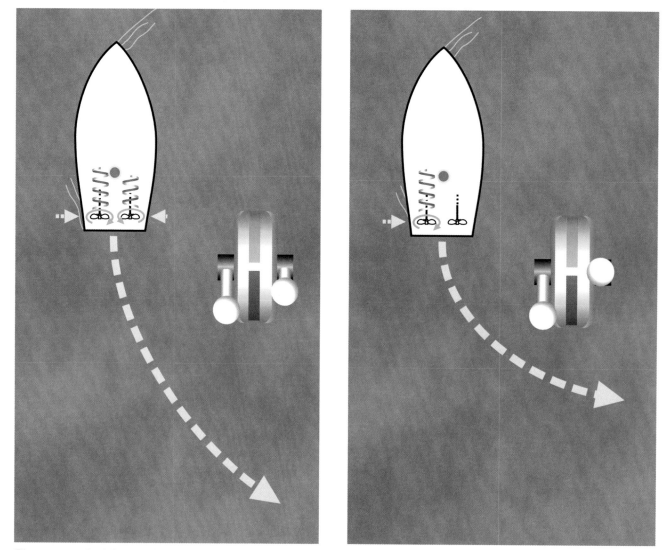

The same principles apply in reverse as in forward gear. Inboard twins add a whole new dimension in maneuverability.

at a higher speed, it will overpower the starboard engine and push the boat to starboard. Alternatively, you can operate on one drive alone, which will cause the boat to turn more sharply.

MANEUVERING IN REVERSE GEAR With twin drives, rotate the boat until you are aligned with your objective. Then simply place both drives in reverse at equal throttle settings and slowly power toward your objective.

If you need to make adjustments, steer a bit to the left or right by controlling the relative throttle settings on the two drives.

TURNING IN PLACE Twin drives are at their best when attempting an in-place turn. Simply place

one drive in forward and the other in reverse—both at low throttle settings. An inboard boat will tend to rotate in place, so you can rotate in either direction with equal ease.

However, making turns with twin I/O drives or outboards is a bit more complicated. Depending upon the configuration of the engines and your specific hull, you may find that the pivot point moves somewhat farther aft of midships, which will cause the bow to sweep around the stern. Also, for the reasons explained earlier, the turning efficiency with outboards or I/Os may fall far short of the effectiveness of twin inboards. Consequently, you may need a great deal of maneuvering space. You may also need to interrupt your turn periodically by switching both drives to reverse

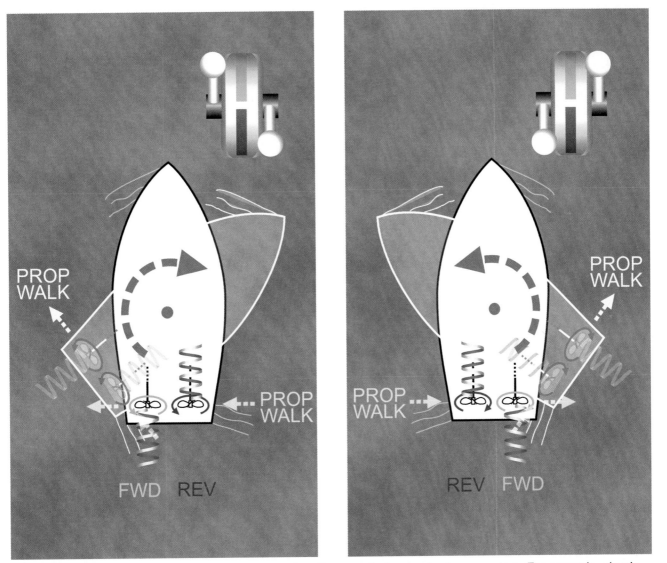

Twin engine inboards have a distinct advantage when it comes to turning in close quarters. For example, simply place the port drive in forward gear, and the starboard drive in reverse gear. The boat will turn clockwise about a pivot point slightly aft of midships (left). Perform the opposite maneuver to achieve a counterclockwise turn (right). These techniques are perfect for turning to align the boat with a slip or doing a 180° turn to reverse direction in a tight spot.

and backing up to your original location. From there, you can continue your rotation.

In some cases, with closely spaced twin outboards, for example, you will not be able to get the boat to rotate using drives alone. If this is how your boat is configured, you'll need to use the technique for a single drive, which was described above.

CHAPTER 6

Departing and Docking

The conditions under which you will be departing or docking will have one constant—they will never be the same. Wind, current, and boat traffic will always be changing, and you will need to know the best maneuver for the prevailing conditions. Sometimes wind will be the dominant factor, sometimes current. Sometimes, the dock will be empty except for your boat; sometimes you may have boats ahead and astern. Departing and docking can be highly stressful moments within an otherwise relaxing activity. To limit that stress, follow these simple guidelines:

■ Ignore the onlookers: as you depart or dock, you may feel that all eyes are on you; to the best of your ability, ignore everyone but the ones who will be helping you at the dock.

■ Assess your environment: watch how your boat reacts to the currents and wind or check moored boats to see which way they are pointing. Look for flags or other clues to identify the wind strength and direction, and look at buoys or pilings to see how the current is running.

■ Plan your approach and make sure all lines and fenders are at the ready. Also plan what you will do if something goes awry.

■ Explain your intentions to the crew: assign them specific tasks; tell them what you expect and how you will communicate instructions.

Departing and docking are both stressful situations, but docking is definitely the more stressful of the two. Docking is akin to a controlled collision, or similar to landing an airplane. You must encounter a fixed object, but you want to do so softly, without inflicting damage. At the same time, environmental conditions such as current, wind, and waves make your job more complicated. Below are some commonsense guidelines, which, when used along with the situation-specific instructions in this chapter, will help make that job easier. The following apply to all docking conditions and propulsion systems:

■ Survey the dock: look for moving boats and traffic, available dock hands, and the locations of cleats or pilings.

■ Visualize your approach: Which side is better? Should you make a forward or backward approach to the dock? What lines do you intend to use? Who needs to do what?

■ Determine if you need help: if possible, call on your radio and arrange for assistance.

■ Take the approach slowly: docking is no place

for speed. (Remember—you're going for a controlled collision.) Relax and focus.

■ Use only the power necessary to move the boat and maintain control. Shifting between idle speed in gear and drifting in neutral is one way to slow your movement. Apply very brief bursts of power to help with steering, then shift to neutral afterward to limit your speed.

■ Plan an exit strategy: if things don't go according to plan, back out and try again rather than continue with a flawed approach. Also consider approaching from another direction or selecting another dock.

■ Plan for a no-escape situation: if you get into a situation from which escape is difficult, use spring lines with dock hands or fellow boaters on the dock to help keep you in control.

The following sections will present step-by-step instructions for docking and departing under different situations of wind, current, dockages, and propulsion systems.

As we discussed earlier, there are subtle differences in how drive/steering systems perform at slow speeds. For that reason, the scenarios for departing and docking are presented by type of drive; we'll look at inboards first, then directed-thrust drives, and conclude with twin drives.

SINGLE INBOARD ENGINE
Departing Maneuvers

In these scenarios, you'll be departing from a port-side dock with a single inboard engine. As we discussed earlier, your rudder will be largely ineffective in reverse; therefore, the bulk of your steering maneuvers will be executed in forward gear. Plus, reverse gear will cause your stern to walk to port—toward the dock—exactly the spot you're trying to avoid.

DEPARTING FROM A DOCK

No Wind or Current You may want a fender at the bow. The maneuver proceeds as follows:

1. Place a fender to protect the dockside bow (if there isn't one there already); remove all lines.

2. Apply a brief burst of power in forward gear

As you approach the dock, look for telltales. Look at the wind direction: flags are a good indicator. Look at the current: patterns in the water around buoys or pilings are dead giveaways. Most of all, look at moored boats in the vicinity, especially ones like yours, to see which way they are pointed. If there are few telltales in your vicinity, put your engine or engines in neutral and observe how conditions affect your boat.

while you steer the boat toward the dock. The prop wash will push the stern outward while the bow is pressed against the dock—that's why you want the fender. (If you're obstructed ahead, go to step 4.)

3. Shift to neutral and drift until the stern swings clearly away from the dock. Go to step 5.

4. If there is a boat ahead limiting your space, do the same maneuver with an after bow spring line. The spring line will constrain your forward motion while also helping to pin the bow against the dock, thus causing the stern to swing outward. Now go to step 5.

5. Power in reverse to move the boat away from the dock. Initially, you will have no steerage, so place your rudder in the neutral position.

6. As you gain sternway, turn the rudder toward the dock. This will turn the boat to be more parallel with the dock.

7. When you are far enough away to begin a forward turn, shift into forward gear, steer away from the dock, and power away.

Wind or Current on Your Bow With a little help, nature will take its course in helping you with this maneuver:

(continued on page 64)

DOCKLINES

When tying up to a dock, your objective is to impose loose but effective control on the boat's motion, using at least four lines to tie up your boat: one bow line, one stern line, and two spring lines.

Hint: Some of the maneuvers discussed in this chapter involve powering forward or back against a spring line. If you're departing a dock with the aid of a spring line, double the line around the dock cleat, post, or ring, controlling both ends on the boat. As you leave the dock, simply release one end and pull in the other to recover the line.

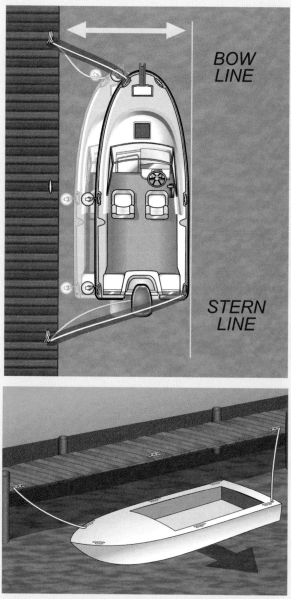

BOW LINE

STERN LINE

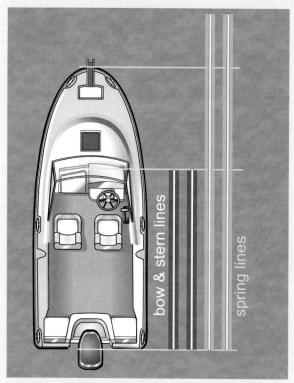

bow & stern lines

spring lines

Relative lengths of docklines. *Bow and stern lines should be about ⅔ the length of the boat; the two spring lines about 1¼ times the length of the boat.*

Bow and stern lines keep your boat next to the dock. Tie the bow line to a cleat forward of the bow, not directly abeam of it. Tie the stern line to the boat's stern cleat on the side away from the dock and lead it to a dock cleat farther astern. You don't want to tie the boat snugly to the dock; a little bit of play in the lines allows the boat to float independently and absorb boat wakes and swells and reduces the chances that the lines will snap.

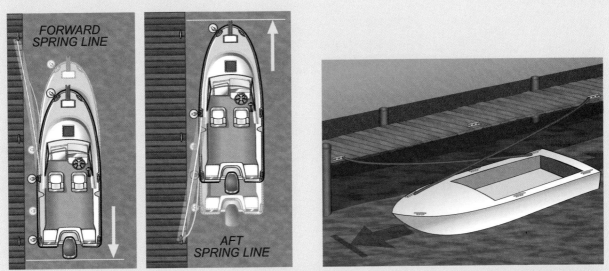

The after bow spring line (red) constrains forward motion; the forward quarter spring line (blue) constrains aftward motion. The after bow spring line generally extends from the bow to a dock cleat toward the stern. The forward quarter spring line generally extends from the dockside stern cleat to a dock cleat nearer the bow. Depending on your boat's hardware and the cleats available on the dock, you may choose to tie spring lines from midships cleats. Spring lines can be tied more tightly than a bow or stern line because they're longer and have more "spring."

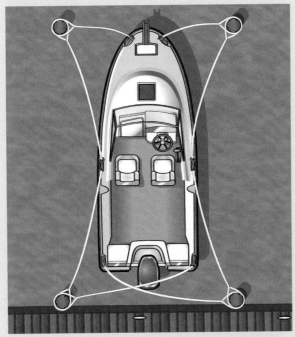

When tying to pilings, it's generally wise to use two full sets of lines—bow, stern and two spring lines—one set on each side of the boat. Leave them with sufficient scope to allow the boat to almost reach, but not strike, the opposite piling. In tidal waters, make the lines sufficiently long to allow the boat to rise and fall.

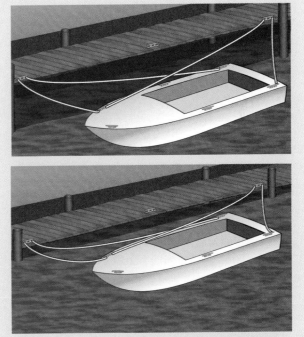

Docks come in two varieties: fixed and floating. If you encounter a fixed dock in a tidal area, be sure to make the lines long enough to handle the rising and falling of the tides. If you tie up at high tide (top), be sure to leave enough slack on the lines to accommodate a falling tide (above). The same is true if you tie to pilings.

Slow-Speed Maneuvering

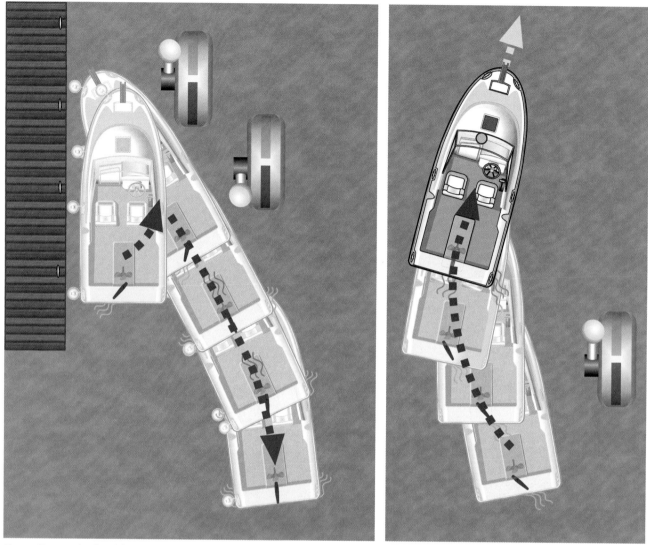

Departing a dock with no wind or current. *Remember, inboards don't steer well in reverse. Start by going forward with the wheel toward the dock. When the stern swings out, shift to reverse (left panel). When you're well clear of the dock, shift to forward and depart (right).*

(continued from page 61)

1. Remove all lines except a forward quarter spring line. (Don't release the bow line until your engine is warmed and you are ready to depart. Otherwise, your bow might swing out before you are ready.)

2. Have a dockhand or crew member use a boat hook to give the bow a nudge away from the dock—the wind or current will then carry the bow away from the dock. Just be sure you are ready to remove the last spring line.

3. Once the bow has swung away from the dock and you've retrieved the last remaining line, power away in forward gear.

If the boat is too heavy to push away from the dock by hand, or the maneuver above does not work, you will need to use your engine to help:

1. Remove all lines except a forward quarter spring line.

2. With a fender near the stern, apply a brief burst of reverse power with the wheel turned hard toward the dock. This will cause the bow to move away from the dock.

3. Turn away from the dock in forward gear. Your bow will swing out nicely (helped by the wind).

4. As soon as the bow moves away, straighten the wheel.

5. Remove your spring line and power away, turning more to starboard as necessary as the stern clears the dock.

Wind or Current on Your Stern With this maneuver, you will want to remove all but an after bow spring line. Don't remove the stern line until you are ready to begin the maneuver, or your departure may be determined by the wind or current, not you.

1. Use a gentle push to get the stern moving away from the dock. Because the spring line is preventing the boat from going forward, the stern should swing out.

2. If the stern does not swing out on its own, turn the wheel hard toward the dock and apply a brief burst of power in forward gear. (Again, the spring line will help restrain the bow while the stern swings wide.)

3. When the stern is sufficiently clear, back straight away, and remove the spring line when clear of the dock.

4. Power away in forward gear.

Wind or Current on the Dock This is the most challenging departure, since the wind or current wants to pin you to the dock. The technique is similar to that used with no wind or current, except that you will need to swing the stern farther out to enable you to back more directly into the wind or current. Here's how:

1. Remove all but an after bow spring line. Make sure you have a fender near the bow on the dock side.

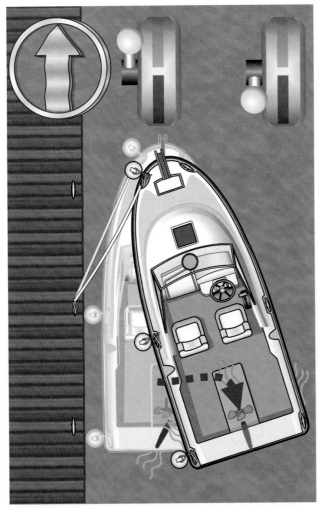 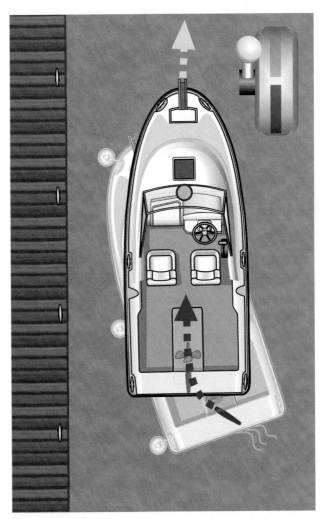

Departing with wind on your stern. *Using an after bow spring line, let the stern swing out in the wind, then power in reverse and pull away from the dock. Then apply forward power (right).*

Slow-Speed Maneuvering

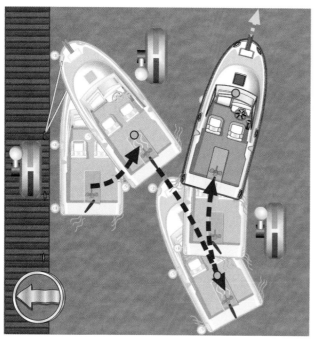

Departing with wind on the dock. *Power forward against an after bow spring line, steering toward the dock. When the stern swings out sufficiently, back away. Then power forward.*

2. Apply a gentle amount of power in forward gear and steer to port (toward the dock). The spring line will constrain the bow and push the stern away from the dock.

3. Once the stern has moved sufficiently clear of the dock and is pointed well into the wind or current, shift to reverse gear.

4. You will have little steerage, so place the wheel amidships.

5. Power straight back in reverse until the boat is sufficiently clear of the dock.

6. Shift into forward gear and turn the rudder toward the wind. The bow will turn.

7. Power clear of the dock.

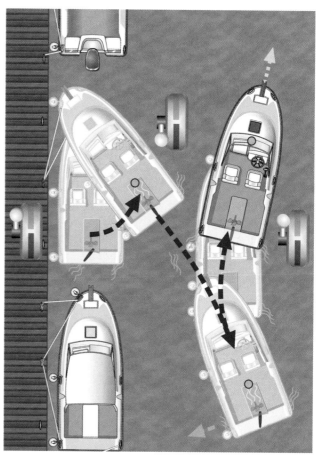

Departing between boats. *This technique works with all engine configurations. Secure an after bow spring line and power forward with the wheel toward the dock. Swing the stern clear of the boat behind and back away.*

This maneuver will also work if you want to depart but have boats ahead and astern of you. Since it also works for outboards and I/Os, it's considered the universal technique for getting out of a tight spot on the dock.

DEPARTING A SLIP When departing a slip, in all likelihood, you will be entering a channel or waterway with traffic. Be alert. It's also a good idea to

DEPARTING FROM THE STARBOARD SIDE

So far, these instructions have focused on departing from the port side. What if you're departing from a starboard-side dock? The procedures are mostly just mirror images of the ones described above. There are, however, principal differences: in reverse, the prop walk will pull your stern away from a starboard-side dock, and in forward, prop walk will push your stern toward the dock.

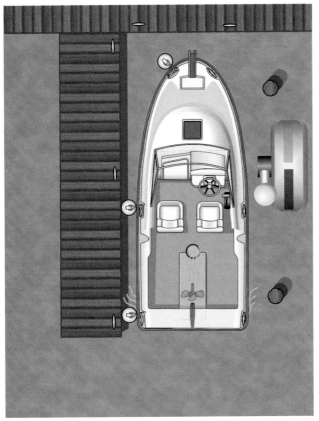

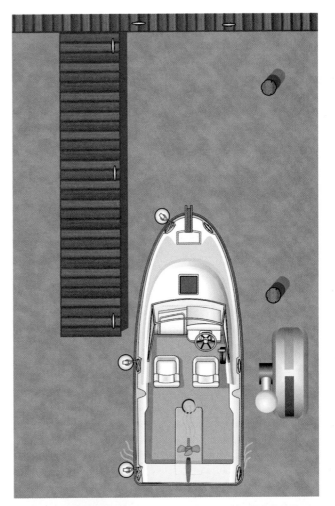

Departing a slip bow-in. *This is as easy as departing from a side dock. Remove the lines as you are ready to depart, sound a long blast to alert other boaters, and power gently from the slip in reverse gear.*

sound a prolonged blast (four seconds or more) on your horn to signal your departure. A response of five or more short, one-second blasts indicates that another boat is approaching; wait before departing.

Bow-In Bow-in is very common and makes for easy docking (described later). Departing is not quite as easy, but not difficult.

1. Release the lines and push the boat away from the side pier.

2. Place the engine in reverse gear and slowly power out into the open waterway.

3. When you are clear of the pier and pilings, and you have enough sternway for steerage, begin a turn to power away from the slip.

Bow-In with a Crosswind or Crosscurrent Departing a slip with a crosswind can be a challenge because the wind or current is pushing you to the other side of the slip, or in many cases,

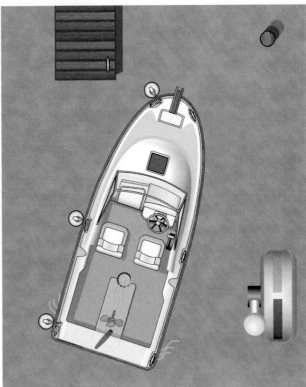

Slow-Speed Maneuvering

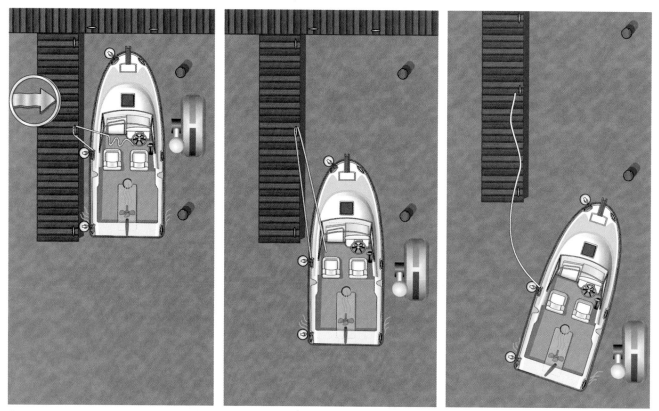

Departing a slip bow-in with a crosswind. *This is a challenging situation. Use a looped spring line to help you hold position against the windward side pier as you depart (left and center). After clearing the slip, let the line go and recover it from the boat cleat (right).*

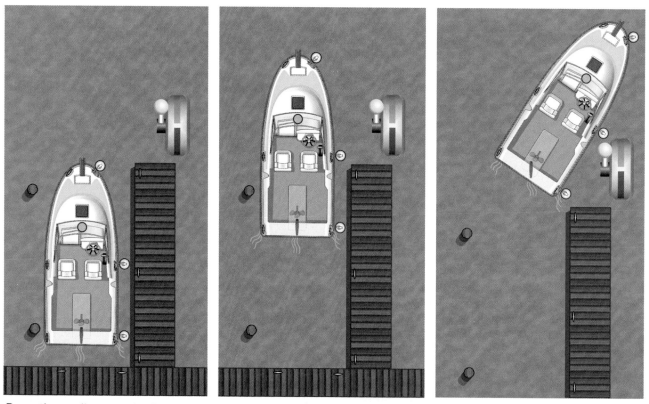

Departing a slip: stern-in. Remove the lines and push the boat from the side pier (left), then power gently from the slip in forward gear (center and right).

toward another boat as well. Or it might be pushing you into your side pier. The latter is easily handled by fending the boat away from the pier with boat hooks as you depart.

1. Loop a line from your midships cleat around the corresponding cleat on the dock and back into the boat.

2. Release all other lines and use the looped line to hold your position.

3. Gently power away from the slip in reverse gear, paying out the line as you go and keeping it taut enough to keep you from being blown into the lee dock.

4. As you clear the slip, release the end of the line you are holding (it will unwrap from the dock cleat), recover the line from the ship's cleat, and coil it.

5. Shift into forward gear when you clear the slip.

Stern-In Being docked stern-in a slip is often the preferred method, particularly if access to the boat is from the stern. As you will see later, docking is a bit more of a challenge, but departing is quite easy.

1. Release the lines and push the boat away from the side pier.

2. Place the engine in forward gear and slowly power out into the open waterway.

3. When you are clear of the pier and pilings, begin a turn to power away from the slip.

Docking Maneuvers

Some say the single-engine inboard is the most difficult boat to handle. I believe that with good technique and some experience, you can get it to do almost anything you want it to. Again, we'll use port-side docking as our basic scenario.

DOCKING ON A PIER

No Wind or Current As noted earlier, docking in the absence of wind and current is an ideal, yet rare, situation. Here are the steps if you should be so lucky:

1. Deploy fenders fore and aft, and have these

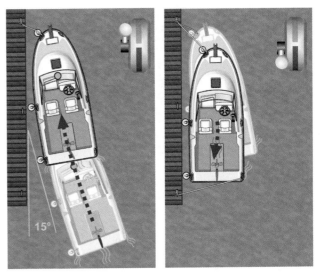

Docking with no wind. *Approach the dock at 15°. Next, turn slightly to starboard—your momentum will continue to take you toward the dock. Apply light power in reverse when you come in contact with the dock to slow your progress and to walk the stern to port. Tie the bow line first, then tie the remaining docklines.*

docklines ready: bow line, stern line, two spring lines. Brief your crew.

2. Approach the dock slowly at a shallow angle of about 15° (assuming there are no boats in the way; otherwise you will need a steeper angle). Turn the wheel to amidships and use minimal power in forward gear. (If another boat is at the dock, you will need a different approach. We'll cover this scenario shortly.)

3. As you near the dock, turn slightly to starboard to bring the boat almost parallel with the dock. Momentum should continue to carry your boat toward the dock.

4. As the boat comes in contact with the dock, apply light power in reverse gear. The prop walk will pull your stern toward the dock.

5. Tie the bow line first, followed by the rest of the lines.

Into the Wind Docking into the current or wind gives you maximum control and is the best approach. When motoring into the wind or current you'll need more power to overcome the environmental conditions that are slowing your approach. More power means more prop wash; and more prop wash means better steerage with your inboard's-rudder. Plus, with the wind on your nose, you'll

(continued on page 72)

TWO IMPORTANT KNOTS

The two principal knots used to secure a line to a boat, dock, or piling are a cleat hitch and a bowline. With these two knots you can accomplish most of what is described in this book. (If you want a more in-depth study of knots, there are many excellent books on the subject [see the appendix].)

Let's start with a bit of terminology. You will need to know two terms regarding the lines: *standing part* and *bitter end*. The standing part is the part of the line that is under load. The bitter end is the part of the line that you are working with (i.e., the loose end you're using to make the knot).

KNOT 1: THE CLEAT HITCH

The cleat hitch provides a very secure attachment to the cleat. If a line is under a heavy load, the cleat can be a lifesaver. By simply looping a line around the base of the cleat, you can transfer the load from your body to the cleat—which may save you from being pulled overboard or off the dock.

Note: If, after you've tied the hitch, you see that a section of line is on top and parallel with the cleat, you've turned the last loop the wrong way. Back it off and try again. If you leave this knot the wrong way, you might not be able to untie it once it's under load, and you'll have to cut it.

The cleat hitch. *First, take a full turn around the base of the cleat. This relieves the load while you tie the rest of the knot. Then pass the line diagonally across the top of the cleat and under the opposite horn. Then pass the line once more across the top of the cleat, but make this an underhand loop in the end of the line (i.e., pass the bitter end under the standing part) with the bitter end pointing toward the cleat. Pass this loop over the second horn, then pull the bitter end until the knot tightens. (There's no need to add any additional loops—they will only slow you down when you're untying to depart.) The finished cleat hitch will show two parallel parts running diagonally across the top of the cleat beneath a single part crossing diagonally in the other direction. (Courtesy United States Power Squadrons)*

KNOT 2: THE BOWLINE

The bowline is a versatile knot that forms a non-slip loop in a line. The bowline takes a little more practice than the cleat hitch, but it's worth the effort.

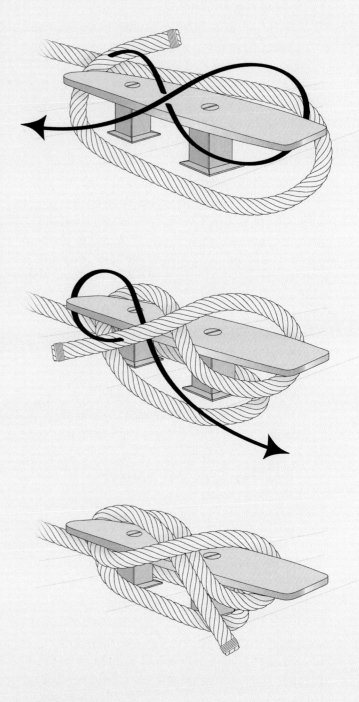

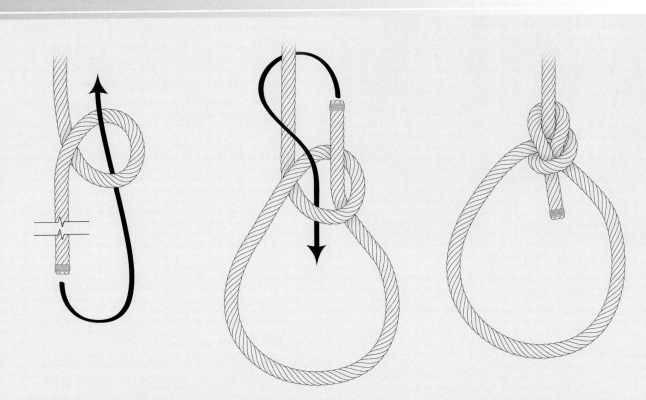

The bowline. *Form a small overhand loop on the line. (This loop will form the base of the bowline, so be sure the overhand loop is far enough away from the bitter end to accommodate your finished loop.) The overhand loop is made by turning the bitter end over the standing part of the line. Next, pass the bitter end up through the overhand loop from underneath. Pull a short section of line through the tiny loop, and pass it under the standing part. Then pass the bitter end back through the small loop. To tighten the knot, grasp the bitter end against the loop in one hand, grasp the standing part in the other hand, and pull. Once tied, the bowline can be passed over the top of a piling. (Courtesy United States Power Squadrons)*

Putting the bowline to work. *Although you can attach a bowline to a cleat by simply placing it over the cleat, it isn't very secure. If the cleat has an open base, there's a better way to attach it. Collapse the bowline loop and pass it through the cleat's open base. Once it's through, open the loop and stretch it over the cleat's horns. Pull the standing end back through the base until the line draws tight. This method of attachment is quite secure.*

Slow-Speed Maneuvering

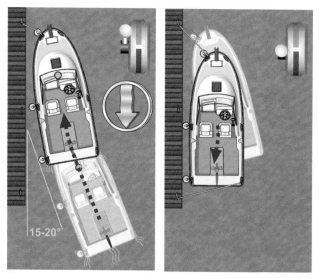

Docking into the wind. *In this situation, a slightly steeper approach is needed; this will prevent the wind or current from pushing your bow away from the dock. Once you come in contact with the dock, tie the bow line first.*

(continued from page 69)
have an effective braking system at your disposal. If you're coming in too hot, throttle down and let the wind slow you.

1. Approach from an angle of about 15 to 20°. A larger angle minimizes the chances that your bow will be blown away from the dock; however, this angle could allow the bow to be pushed toward the dock prematurely. Adjust your angle for the best control.

2. As you near the dock, turn the wheel very slightly to starboard; you still want the bow to touch first. (If the stern touches first, the bow could be spun around by a strong wind or current. If so, you'd have little choice but to depart the dock and try again.)

3. As you come in contact with the dock, have a crew member step off the boat and quickly tie the bow line. If the current or wind is pushing you backwards while your crew is working the lines, continue to apply very light forward thrust with the wheel straight ahead. Or, if the wind abates and you're still making forward progress, apply a touch of reverse power. This will also help pull the stern in with prop walk.

4. Once the bow line is secured to the dock, the current or wind will naturally push the stern toward the dock.

5. If you are docking without crew, as your bow touches the dock, use a boat hook to loop a line from your midships boat cleat to a midships dock cleat. Pull this line to draw the boat against the dock and secure your position. Then tie the bow line. Under no circumstances should a single-hander step off the boat with the engine engaged.

With the Wind or Current Docking with the wind or current presents two evils. First, your steerage will be adversely affected; second, the conditions may push you toward the dock faster than you'd like.

1. Approach at a shallow angle, as little as 10° if space permits.

2. As you approach the dock, apply power in reverse gear to halt your progress and hold your position. Your propeller side thrust will help pull you in.

3. You will have little steerage in reverse unless there is a strong current from astern. If you cannot move the stern effectively toward the dock with prop walk, shift into forward gear and apply a very brief burst of power with the wheel hard to starboard, then shift immediately into reverse to halt forward progress.

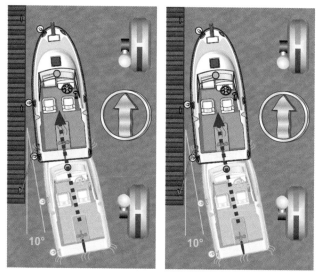

Docking with the wind. *Approach at a shallow angle; you'll want your stern to be as close to the dock as possible when you stop. Steerage will be your biggest challenge, especially if you have a following current. As you near the dock, place an after quarter spring line on a dock cleat and, if necessary, apply reverse gear to halt forward progress. Tie the remaining lines.*

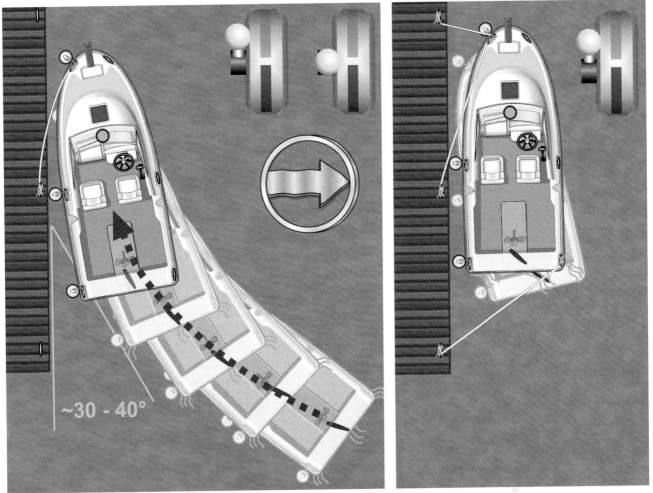

~30 - 40°

Docking with wind off the dock. *Approach at a steep angle to cut through the wind. Flare the boat such that you arrive almost parallel with the dock. Toss an after bow spring line to a dockhand or put a crew member ashore with a line in hand. Once secured, power forward with starboard helm to pull the boat to the dock.*

4. Don't worry about your bow: the wind or current will help push it in once your stern is secured.

5. When your stern quarter makes contact with the dock, have a dockhand or crew member tie an after quarter spring line to hold your position, then tie the bow line.

6. Cut your engine and tie the remaining lines. I recommend that you add a stern line (simply a spring line led aft from a cleat aft of amidships) from the outside cleat.

7. If you're single-handed, use a boat hook to loop a line from your midships boat cleat to a midships dock cleat to temporarily maintain position. If you don't have a midships boat cleat, consider using the port-side stern cleat instead.

Wind or Current off the Dock Docking with wind or current off the dock is challenging. Here the instructions have been broken down into three situations.

With a Dockhand. Given the adverse conditions, time is critical. Once your boat comes in contact with the dock, it won't be long before the wind or current pushes you away from it. A dockhand can be most useful in this situation.

1. Deploy fenders quite far forward, since your port bow will be the first part of the boat to reach the dock.

2. Make a sharp approach of 30 to 40° to provide adequate headway toward the dock against the wind or current.

3. *Flare* your landing with the dock (i.e., turn your boat so that the port bow, not the very front of the boat, touches the dock).

Slow-Speed Maneuvering

4. If you need to halt forward motion, shift briefly into reverse, then back into neutral.

5. As the boat slows or stops at the dock, have a crew member toss an after bow spring line to the dockhand, who will secure it toward the aft end of your intended berth.

6. Once the line is secured, apply forward power, turning hard to starboard. The prop wash across the rudder will force the stern toward the dock and pin it there. Your boat will nestle against the dock while the remaining lines are secured.

With a Crew Member. If you don't have the assistance of a dockhand, you can place a crew member on the dock. If she can step from the bow of your boat directly onto the dock, use the same approach described above. If not, she may need to step from a spot more amidships. To do that, you will need to make contact with the dock almost parallel with it.

1. Make your approach a little steeper and with a bit more throttle; flare before the bow touches the dock so you turn parallel to the dock; your momentum will carry you the rest of the way.

2. You may be in this position for only a short time before the current or wind pushes you off, so make sure your crew member is ready to step (not jump) off at the right moment.

3. Next, your crew member steps onto the dock and secures the after bow spring line.

4. Use forward throttle with starboard rudder to hold the boat to the dock while the crew member secures the other lines.

Single-Handed. If you are handling your boat alone, securing an after bow spring line while you make momentary contact with the dock will be impractical. Instead, place a loop around the midships dock cleat from your midships boat cleat to hold your

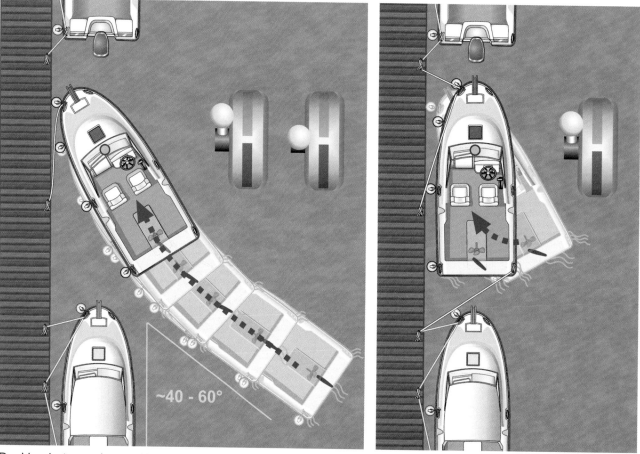

Docking between boats. *Now that you have mastered the technique of docking with wind off the dock, docking between boats will be a snap. It is basically the same maneuver. Arrive at a steep angle to clear the boat behind. Toss an after bow spring line or flare nearly parallel with the dock and put a crew member ashore with the line. Powering forward against the spring line keeps the boat against the dock.*

boat in place until you can secure other lines.

Obviously, your strategy will be tailored to the strength of the wind or current off the dock. The stronger the force, the sharper your approach and the more throttle you need to apply. But in no case do you want to encounter the dock bow-on. Instead, limit contact to the forward quarter or beam with good fenders in place.

Docking in a Slip—Bow-In

No Wind or Current A typical slip for bow-in docking consists of a single finger pier connected at right angles to a main pier. The finger pier may be on either the port or starboard side. A port-side pier is easier due to prop walk. Entering this slip is akin to any port-side docking maneuver with one limitation—you are constrained by how far forward the boat can advance before it strikes the main pier.

1. Enter the slip at a slight angle to the finger pier. This angle will be shallow due to the limited width of the slip.

2. Point your bow to the point where the finger pier intersects with the main pier; you are aiming your port bow toward the dock.

3. As you near the dock, gently apply reverse power to stop your forward progress. The prop walk to port will work in your favor, bringing the stern close to the dock.

4. Have a dockhand tie the bow first, then the stern, or have a crew member step off as the stern settles against the dock. If you are single-handed, cut the engine and step off yourself with line in hand.

If you're docking at a starboard-side pier, approach the dock at a slight angle. When you reach the entrance, halt your progress with reverse gear and a bit of starboard wheel. Then put in forward again and slowly enter the slip with the bow pointed at the intersection of the finger pier and the main pier. As you approach, prop walk will push the stern to starboard (i.e., toward the pier). A slower approach will require less reverse thrust when stopping, and thus less adverse prop walk to port.

Docking in a Slip—Stern-In

Stern-in is a popular approach to a slip. It usually affords easier access

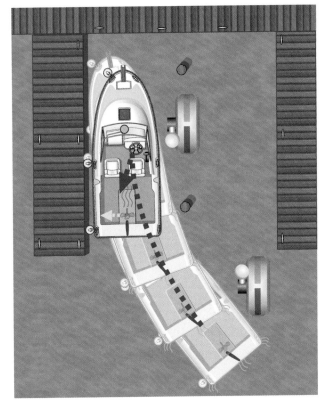

Docking in a slip bow-in. *Come into the slip as if you were approaching a portside dock. Apply reverse gear; prop walk will bring the stern to the dock.*

for crew and gear and may be the only practical dockage if the finger pier is shorter than the boat. In the absence of wind or current, it can be done with some degree of ease, but it takes some practice.

No Wind or Current Typically, you'll approach the slip perpendicularly before turning parallel to the finger pier and backing in.

1. Deploy fenders and make docklines ready before you begin the maneuver.

2. Begin turning away from the slip before you reach the entrance. This will align the boat to the slip.

3. Adjust for expected prop walk. For a starboard-side landing, line up your boat so its transom slightly overlaps the finger pier, as in the illustration.

4. Shift into reverse and proceed.

5. As you back up, the stern will move progressively and slowly to port. If you need to correct for this, shift into forward gear and apply a brief

Slow-Speed Maneuvering

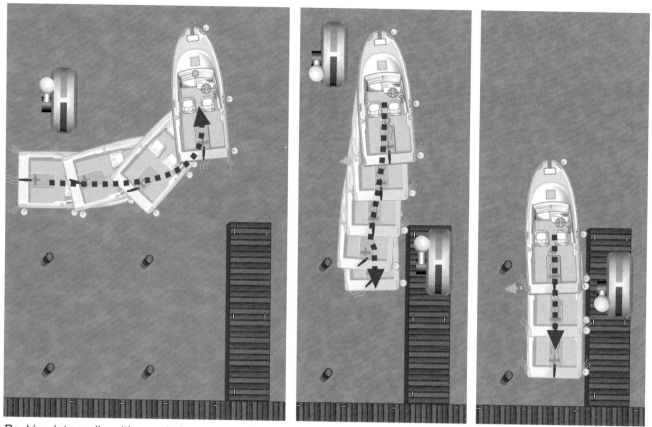

Backing into a slip with no wind or current. *Before you reach the slip, execute a turn that is just short of 90°. If prop walk moves the stern away from the side pier as you back in, briefly shift into forward gear with your wheel to port to kick the stern over, and then proceed in reverse.*

burst of power with the wheel hard to port. This will move the stern back to starboard.

6. Proceed into the slip.

7. As you approach the end of the slip, apply light power in forward gear to halt your progress. The prop side thrust will help move your stern toward a starboard-side dock. If you are approaching a port-side finger pier, use less forward power to minimize adverse prop walk.

8. Have a dockhand tie either the bow or stern to secure the boat. If using a crew member, have him wait until he can step from the stern with a line in hand.

Backing into a Slip against the Wind or Current If wind or current is pushing against the boat, you'll need to get an after spring line in place as soon as possible to keep the boat from being driven out of the slip.

1. Enter the slip normally, but with the after spring line at the ready.

2. Attach the spring line to your boat's midships cleat prior to backing in, and have a loop ready at the other end.

3. Upon entering the slip, use a boat hook to place the loop over the cleat at the inside end of the slip or a piling. This will constrain the boat from being blown or swept away as well as help keep it close to the side pier.

4. Tie up and cut the engine.

Backing into a Slip with the Wind or Current If wind or current is pushing the boat directly into the slip, you'll want to tie a forward spring line in place as soon as possible to keep your boat from colliding with the main pier.

1. Enter the slip normally, but with the forward spring line at the ready.

2. Attach the forward spring line to your boat's midships cleat prior to backing in, and loop the other end.

3. Upon entering the slip, use a boat hook to place the loop of the spring line over a dock cleat or a piling. Make sure the spring line is short enough to keep you from hitting the main pier behind you. When the spring line draws tight and halts your progress, the combination of wind and power will hold you tight against the side pier.

4. Tie up and cut the engine.

Docking in a Slip with Wind or Current on the Side Pier If conditions drive you toward the side pier, simply back into the slip as you would with no wind, but leave a little extra room between the boat and the side pier, then let nature take its course.

Docking in a Slip with Wind or Current off the Side Pier If the wind or current is pushing you away from the side pier, you're in for a challenge. For starters, your angle of approach is limited when entering a slip; this will make it difficult to compensate for the effects of wind and current.

The bow will be the biggest challenge here, so it's best to approach the slip entrance with your bow pointing to the wind. If your docking maneuver begins to go awry—if the wind catches your bow and pushes it downwind away from the entrance—pull out, regroup, and try again.

The following example uses a starboard-side pier, but the process for docking at a port-side pier is basically the same.

1. Begin this maneuver from as close to the slip entrance as possible. This will shorten the time required to back into the slip and lessen the amount of time the forward quarter will be exposed to the full brunt of the wind or current. That said, you should position yourself slightly upwind or upcurrent from the slip entrance to allow yourself a little room to drift backwards.

2. Put the engine in reverse gear and start backing toward the slip entrance. As you do, the bow will swing downwind. Anticipate the rotation and drift so that the boat just clears the end of the side pier as you enter the slip while keeping roughly parallel to the pier.

3. Deploy a forward midships spring line with a loop in the end. Place the loop over a cleat or piling near the entrance.

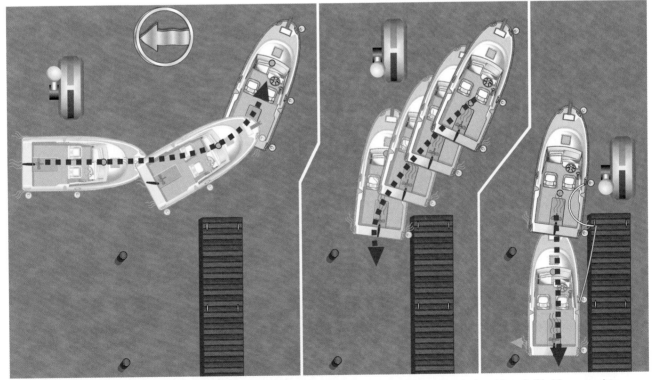

Backing into a slip with wind off the side pier. *Turn upwind or upcurrent and begin backing (left). You need to anticipate how far the boat will slide sideways as you approach the outer end of the slip (center). As the stern clears the end of the side pier, tie a forward midships spring line over the outermost cleat. Back in, and let the midships spring line hold your position while you deploy the remaining lines (right).*

4. Back somewhat briskly into the slip before the wind has a chance to push you away. The spring line will help limit your downwind drift as well as prevent you from backing into the main pier.

5. Continue to apply power in reverse; the spring line will hold the boat against the side pier.

6. Tie off the stern and reign in the bow.

DIRECTED-THRUST STEERING: OUTBOARDS, I/OS, AND JET DRIVES

Outboards and I/O drives provide directed thrust, and thus more options for close-quarters maneuvering than inboard drives. The principal advantage is their ability to provide directed thrust in reverse, which can help steer the boat; whereas, an inboard would have very limited control. This ability opens up some additional techniques unavailable to owners of inboard propulsion. It should be noted, however, that virtually any maneuver that works for an inboard will work for an outboard or I/O, although the opposite may not be true.

Jet drives also are directed thrust; however, they're less maneuverable in reverse than their outboard and I/O counterparts. Consequently, many boatowners with jet drives should use the inboard techniques described in the previous section. In all cases, the specifics will depend on your boat. Understand the principles, then try them out to see what works best for your boat.

Departing Maneuvers

DEPARTING FROM A DOCK The ability of outboards and I/O drives to steer while backing provides new options for departing over those described for inboards. You will learn ways to depart in reverse and in forward gear. Which technique you apply depends upon your comfort level, the room you have at the dock, and the prevailing conditions.

No Wind or Current

Method 1. An excellent technique for departing from the dock with an outboard or I/O is to back away.

1. Apply light power in reverse while turning the wheel away from the dock (in this case to star-

board). This will use the directed thrust of the engine to pull your stern away from the dock.

2. The pivoting of the boat will cause the bow to be pressed against the dock, so make sure you have fenders in place.

3. As soon as you are free of the dock, stop, shift into forward gear, and power away.

This is also a handy method to use if you have a boat docked close ahead of you but no boat behind you.

If you find you have boats ahead and astern, use the method described under Inboard Drives: Departing from a Dock: Wind or Current on the Dock (pages 65–66). As noted earlier, this method works for all boats and is the universal maneuver for getting out of tight spots on a dock.

Method 2. Here is an alternative technique that is as effective and potentially needs less space fore and aft:

1. Beginning in forward gear, apply a brief burst of power with the wheel turned hard over toward the dock (in this case to port).

   The bow will be pinned against the dock, so make sure that you have adequate fenders in place. Meanwhile, the stern will kick out rather smartly while the bow remains in place. The prop walk in this case will help push the stern out from a port-side dock.

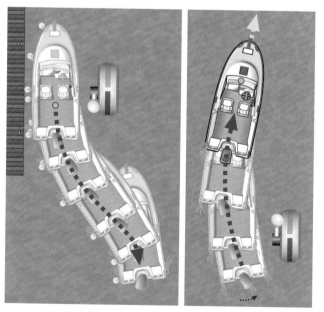

Departing a dock: Method 1. *If you have an outboard, you can use it in reverse to pull away from the dock.*

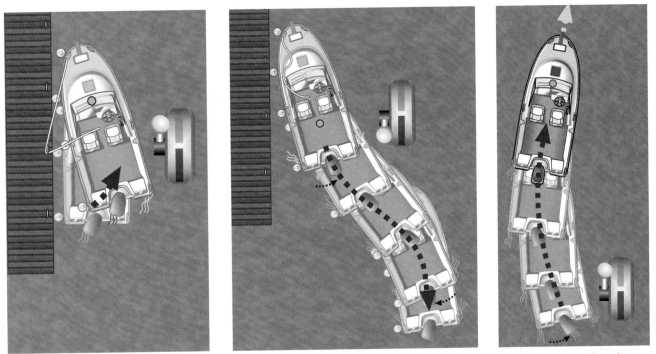

Departing a dock: Method 2. *Start in forward gear, steering toward the dock. This brings the stern out sharply. Then back away. This takes less dock space to perform.*

2. Turn the wheel slightly away from the dock (to starboard in this case) and power away gently in reverse.

3. When sufficiently clear of the dock, continue with gentle power in reverse and turn the wheel toward the dock (to port). The bow will swing away from the dock, taking advantage of the pivot point near the stern.

4. When the bow is pointing sufficiently away from the dock, shift into forward gear and depart.

AN EASY WAY TO OPERATE IN REVERSE

Going in reverse can be confusing, so try this: reorient yourself so the controls make sense. Turn around and face the rear. Hold the top of the wheel behind your back. If you move the wheel to the right, the stern will go right. If you have a single-lever control with neutral in the middle, advancing the lever toward your front accelerates the boat in the direction you are facing (astern), while pushing it away from the direction you're facing makes the boat go that way (forward).

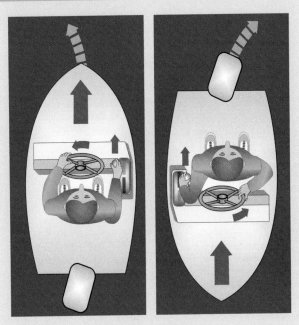

Slow-Speed Maneuvering

Into the Wind or Current This condition may be the easiest for departure because the wind or current will do some of the work for you:

1. Release all of the lines except the forward quarter spring line. (If you release the forward lines too soon, the boat may swing out and you will be committed to a departure whether you're ready or not. The spring line helps to hold you in place.)

2. The bow will swing out in response to the wind or the current.

3. Apply gentle forward power. The stern will also swing out due to prop walk. Release the spring line and you'll begin to make headway.

4. Balance your use of power: use just enough power to overcome the effects of the wind or current until you are well clear of the dock. Too much power limits your ability to adjust to

changing conditions or other boats passing by. In close quarters always use the minimum power needed for control.

With the Wind or Current If the wind or current is running with you, you must change your strategy.

1. Prevent the boat from moving forward with the after bow spring line; release it last. The natural effects of the wind or current will also restrain the bow from swinging away from the dock. You will use your stern to get away.

2. Apply a little power in reverse. The prop walk will try to move you toward the dock, so steer your outboard or I/O a little to starboard.

   This and the wind or current will cause the stern to swing out, but the bow will be pinned to the dock. Make sure you have adequate fenders to protect the bow.

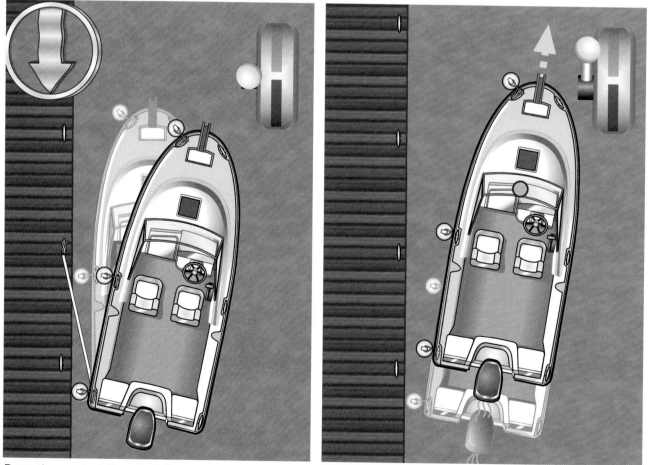

Departing against the wind. *If you are faced with a wind coming along directly toward you, use a forward spring line from the stern as your last line. Let the wind push the bow off, and away you go.*

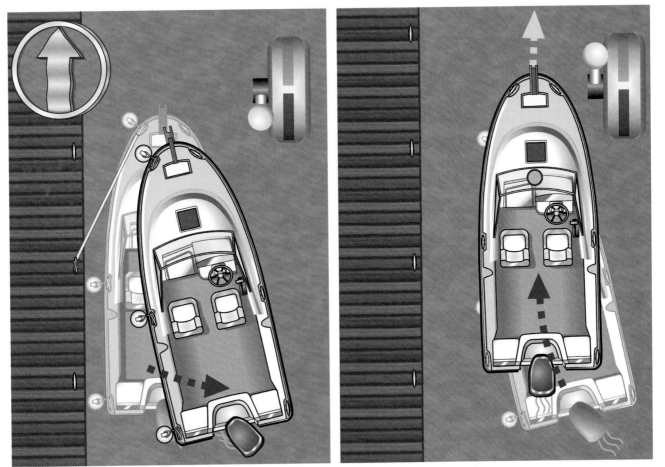

Departing with the wind. *If the wind is coming from behind you, use an after bow spring line as your last line on the dock. A little reverse throttle will counteract the wind and cause the stern to swing out. Once you've pulled away from the dock, you can shift into forward gear and depart.*

3. Still in reverse, apply more power so that the spring line tension is reduced.

4. If you have a dockhand, have him release and toss the spring line at this point. If you have a crew member on the dock, have her bring the line aboard if entry near the bow (which is still next to the dock) is possible. If not, loop the after bow spring line around the cleat on the dock and manage it from the boat.

5. Continue powering backward away from the dock until you are clear enough to change gear into forward to power away.

With Wind or Current on the Dock This is the most difficult departure scenario because the wind or current is trying to pin you onto the dock. Also you will need to get your boat some distance from the dock before you execute a turn because the wind or current will push you back toward the dock—quickly reducing your room to maneuver.

1. Untie all but the after bow spring line and ensure that you have adequate fenders on the bow.

2. Power forward and steer toward the dock to push the stern away from the dock. The bow will be pushed against the dock while the stern swings wide.

3. Power in reverse into the wind and release the after bow spring line.

4. Continue backward, steering into the wind until your bow is well clear of the dock. At this point, and still in reverse, turn the boat by steering to port to swing the boat more parallel with the dock.

5. With the boat now parallel to and clear of the dock, shift into forward gear and steer to starboard and away from the dock. The stronger the wind or current, the farther you will need to back away before shifting gears; otherwise, you may be pressed back onto the dock.

DEPARTING FROM THE STARBOARD SIDE

So far, these instructions have focused on departing from the port side. But what if you're departing from a starboard-side dock? The procedures are mostly just mirror images of the ones described, but there are differences: in reverse, the prop walk will pull your stern away from a starboard-side dock, and in forward, prop walk will push your stern toward the dock.

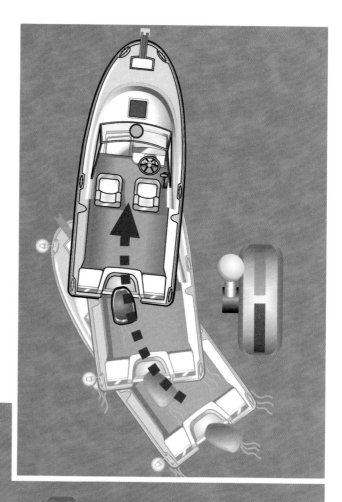

Departing with wind on the dock. *Wind on the dock can be difficult to overcome. Use an after bow spring line and power forward with the wheel toward the dock. That will pull the stern out smartly. When far enough out so that you won't be pinned back, release the line and power away in reverse.*

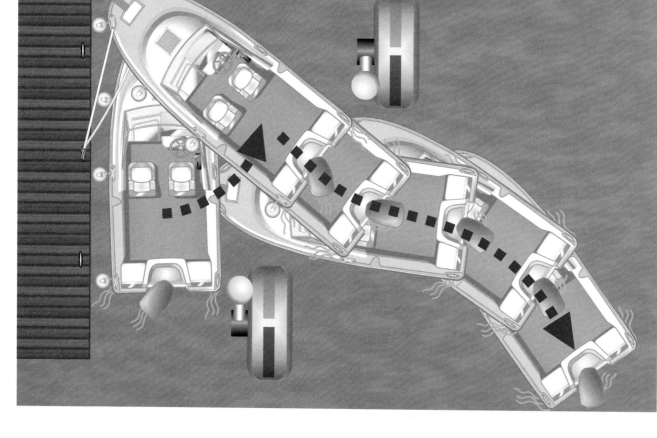

DEPARTING FROM A SLIP When departing a slip, in all likelihood, you will be entering a channel or waterway with traffic. Be alert. It's also a good idea to sound a prolonged blast (four seconds or more) on your horn to signal your departure. A response of five or more short, one-second blasts indicates that another boat is approaching; wait before departing.

If you are docked alongside a finger pier and there's no wind or current, the procedures for departure will be similar to those described above. If, however, you are exposed to a crosscurrent or crosswind, your departure can be complicated. Remember, your steerage comes from the stern. You can counteract a reasonable degree of wind or current at the stern, but your bow will be pushed aside.

If your dockage is bow-in and the wind or current is off the side dock, you may need to constrain the bow as you depart. You can do that with a line from amidships looped around a cleat on the dock. Back out slowly while paying out the line, then turn parallel to the wind or current as you depart from

the slip and retrieve your line. As soon as all is under control, power away.

Similarly, if your dockage is stern-in, you again should consider a bow line looped around a cleat on the side dock. Unhook the line from the dock cleat as you pass by. At this point your boat should be nominally clear of the slip. If you cannot unhook the line, be prepared to pull it in quickly from one end so it does not foul your propeller.

Docking Maneuvers

DOCKING ON A PIER

No Current or Wind We'll start with the simple case of no wind or current, although it is unusual for the environment to be this friendly. (It often seems that wind strength increases the closer you get to the dock.)

1. Put fenders out on the port side, both fore and aft, and have your bow line, stern line, and spring lines ready. Brief the crew.

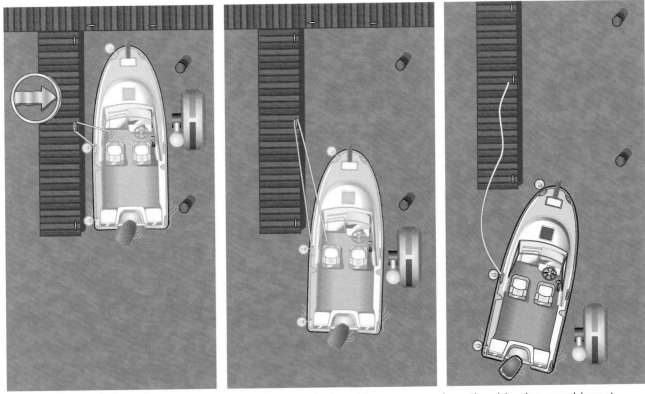

Departing a slip in a crosswind: bow-in. *With a crosswind pushing you away from the side pier, your biggest challenge is to avoid downwind pilings or boats. Here's a technique to stay close to the pier: Loop a line back into the boat from your midships cleat to a nearby cleat on the dock. As you back away, pay out the line, maintaining some tension to constrain the boat against sideways motion. Release the line when free of the slip and retrieve it quickly from the water to avoid fouling the prop.*

Slow-Speed Maneuvering

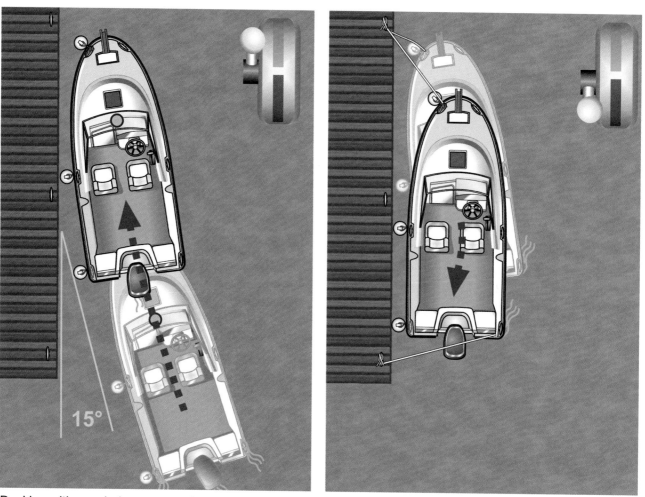

Docking with no wind or current. *Approach at about 15°. Pull up to the dock and hand a bow line to the dockhand, or have a crew member step ashore with the line and tie it to a cleat. Then shift to reverse; the prop will walk the stern to port, thus completing the maneuver.*

2. Approach the dock at a relatively shallow angle—15° is ideal.

3. Keep the helm straight ahead, and use minimal power in forward gear (just enough to maintain steerage). You can shift between forward gear at idle speed and neutral to minimize your speed, using forward gear only when you need steerage.

4. As you near the dock, turn slightly to starboard to bring your boat almost parallel to the dock; your momentum will bring you alongside it.

5. As you make contact with the dock, apply light power in reverse to halt your forward progress. The prop walk will pull the stern toward the dock. (This is the reason why port-side docking is preferred.)

6. Pass a bow line ashore to a dockhand, or have a crew member step ashore with the line and secure it ahead of the bow.

7. Kill the engine, and tie up the remaining lines. If you are alone, be sure to cut the power before you step on the dock.

Wind or Current on the Dock Wind or current aimed toward the dock presents the easiest of all docking situations:

1. Have the lines ready and fenders deployed.

2. Pull the boat parallel to the dock but a few feet away.

3. Let the wind or current push the boat sideways until you make contact with the dock.

4. Step off with the lines and secure the boat.

If the wind or current is very strong, you will need to prevent damage to the boat. In this case, approach closer to the dock before you let the wind carry you; this will prevent your boat from building up too much sideways momentum.

Against the Wind or Current Docking into the current or wind gives you maximum control and is the best approach. When motoring into the wind or current, you'll need more power to overcome the environmental conditions that are slowing your approach. More power means better maneuverability. Plus, with the wind on your nose, you'll have an effective braking system at your disposal. If you're coming in too hot, throttle down and let the wind slow you.

1. Approach the dock from a shallow angle of about 15 to 20°.

2. As you near the dock, turn slightly to starboard but keep the attitude such that the forward quarter will touch first. (If the stern touches first with the bow out, the wind or current could spin the bow out and around, and you'd have to regroup and try your approach again.)

3. Tie the bow line first.

4. Once the bow line is attached, the wind or current will naturally push the boat against the dock. Use a touch of reverse power if necessary to help walk the stern in.

5. Use a dockhand to tie up, or have a crew member step off your boat as it touches the dock. If you are single-handed, use a boat hook to loop a line from your midships boat cleat around a midships dock cleat. Use this line to pull yourself in and temporarily secure your position, then tie permanent dock lines starting with the bow.

Under no circumstances should you step off the boat with the propeller turning unless there is

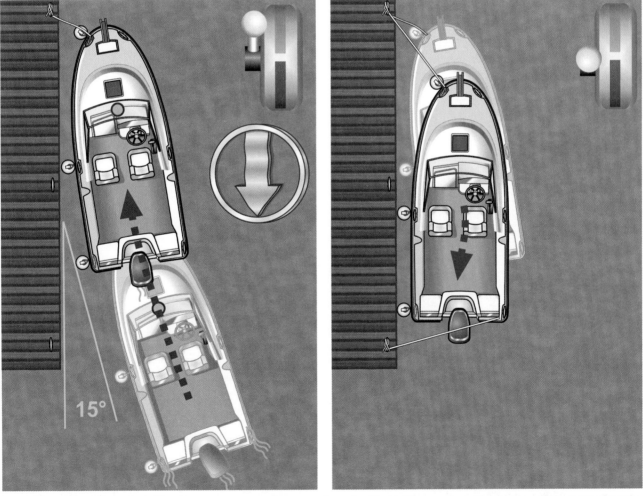

Docking against the wind. *Use the same procedure as when docking with no wind, but apply a little more throttle to overcome the wind (or current). Make sure you tie a bow line promptly to hold the boat.*

Slow-Speed Maneuvering

someone at the helm. The best way to ensure this is to stop the engine before stepping off.

With the Current or Wind Docking with the wind or current presents two evils. First, your steerage will be adversely affected; second, the conditions may push you toward the dock faster than you'd like.

If docking with the wind, you may be able to minimize your windage by staying stern-to the wind. If you turn broadside to the wind, you'll present more windage, and your speed downwind will increase. A following wind will tend to push you faster through the water, so your steering may not be adversely affected as it would be in a current, but this increased speed may become a factor you'll need to take into account.

Whichever situation you face, wind or current from behind will make you go faster than you might have intended. Your objective will be to halt your forward progress and hold the boat stationary when you reach the dock.

1. Approach the dock from a shallow angle—as little as 10° if space permits.

2. Put fenders out at your bow, stern, and amidships on the port side.

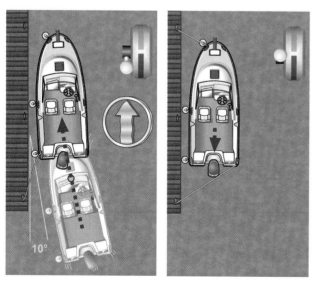

Docking with the wind. *Your biggest challenge will be to maintain steerage, especially if you have a following current. Use reverse gear when you reach the dock and turn the wheel to port. This will pull your stern in. Halt the boat with an after quarter spring line. Tie the stern line before the bow line.*

3. As you approach the dock, apply power in reverse gear to halt your progress and hold your position. Steer a little to port to let the engine pull your stern toward the dock. For port-side docking, the prop walk from reverse gear will also help bring your stern in. Don't worry about your bow; the wind or current will push it against the dock.

4. When your stern quarter makes contact with the dock, have a dockhand or crew member tie an after quarter spring line to hold your position.

5. Cut your engine and tie the remaining lines.

6. If you are single-handed, use a boat hook to loop a line from your midships boat cleat to the midships dock cleat. Use this line to pull yourself in and temporarily secure your position, then tie permanent docklines, starting with the stern. If you don't have a midships boat cleat, consider using the port-side stern cleat instead.

Current or Wind off the Dock Docking with wind or current off the dock is challenging. Here the situation has been divided into three scenarios.

With a Dockhand. Given the adverse conditions, time is critical; your boat is likely to drift away from the dock if you don't tie it down quickly. This is a situation when a dockhand can be most useful.

1. Deploy lines and fenders. You'll want to deploy fenders quite far forward.

2. Approach the dock with slow but steady headway, then turn slightly to starboard to be more parallel to the dock.

3. As the bow touches, have a crew member hand or toss a coiled bow line to the dockhand. The dockhand promptly secures the bow line.

4. With the bow line secured, shift into reverse and apply power, turning the wheel toward the dock. The directed thrust of the outboard or I/O will pull the stern to the dock, while the bow line keeps the bow in place.

5. Continue to apply power as needed to hold position while a crew member passes a stern line to the dockhand.

6. With these two lines secured, shift into neutral and shut down the engine.

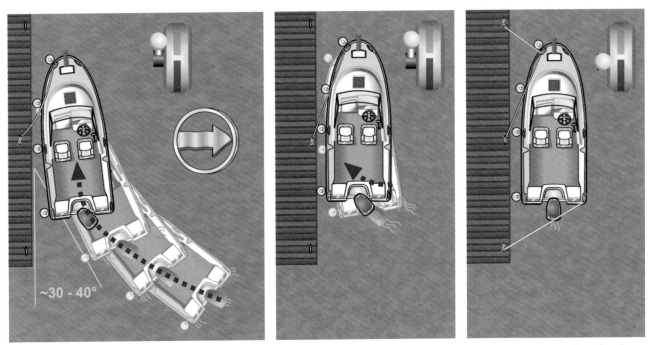

Docking with wind off the dock. *Approach at a steep angle of 40° or so. Touch the dock and secure the after bow spring line. Then apply forward power with neutral or starboard rudder to pull the stern in.*

With a Crew Member. In the absence of a dockhand, have a crew member step onto the dock. If you have an open bow and a crew member can step ashore safely from it, use the dockhand-assisted maneuver above. If it is difficult for him to step from the bow, you'll need a different strategy. Place the side of the boat against the dock so that your crew member can step off safely, and follow these steps:

1. Approach the dock at an angle of 30 to 40°. Use a bit more power than in the approach above—you're building some momentum.

2. At about one-half boat length from the dock, quickly swing the wheel hard to starboard. This will kick the stern toward the dock. Momentum will carry the boat parallel with and up to the dock, but it will hold this position only briefly, until the wind or current moves you away. (As you approach the dock, be prepared to apply a brief burst of power in reverse if it appears you will strike the dock too hard or if you continue to move alongside the dock once you're parallel to it.)

3. As soon as the boat touches, have your crew member secure the after bow spring line to a midship dock cleat (or any suitable cleat aft of the bow).

4. With the line secured, straighten the wheel or even steer away from the dock and apply a little power in forward gear. This will keep the boat close to the dock while the crew member ties the remaining lines in place.

Single-Handed. Occasionally, as a single-hander, you'll arrive at a port with no dockhand in sight. In this case you'll need to bring the beam of the boat alongside the dock as you did with the crew member–assisted maneuver. The steps are as follows:

1. As you approach the dock, find a dock cleat that will be about amidships when you touch.

2. Secure a dock line to your boat's midships cleat and have it coiled at the ready. Also have bow and stern lines ready.

3. Deploy fenders far forward, aft, and amidships. Have a boat hook at the ready.

4. As the boat touches the dock next to the dock cleat, place the engine in neutral.

5. Work quickly, using a boat hook, and loop the midship line around the dock cleat. As soon as the loop is in place, wrap the end of the line back around your midship boat cleat and secure it.

Slow-Speed Maneuvering

6. With the midship line firmly secured, step ashore and cleat the usual docklines. (The looped midship line is not necessarily secure so don't rely on it for very long. If the loop comes free, your boat could leave without you.)

DOCKING BETWEEN BOATS A dock can be a busy place. You may not have the luxury of an entire dock to yourself. Instead, you may need to pull in ahead of, behind, or between other boats.

If you are docking behind another boat, your first priority is to tie an after bow spring line to prevent a collision with the other boat. You can use the same technique shown on page 74 for virtually all wind conditions.

If you are docking ahead of another boat, or between boats ahead and astern, you will use a variation of the same technique, as outlined here:

1. To clear the other boats, you'll approach the dock at a relatively steep angle—as much as 40 to 60°. Use no more power than is necessary to maintain steerage; shift into neutral as much as possible.

3. Aim the bow slightly forward of the midpoint of the available space.

4. Begin a turn to starboard to present your port bow to the dock.

5. With your target now about two-thirds of the way forward in the available space, make sure the stern will clear the boat astern.

6. As the port bow makes contact with the dock, shift into neutral, and hand an after bow spring line to a dockhand, or have a crew member step off with the line and secure it to a cleat on the dock aft of the bow.

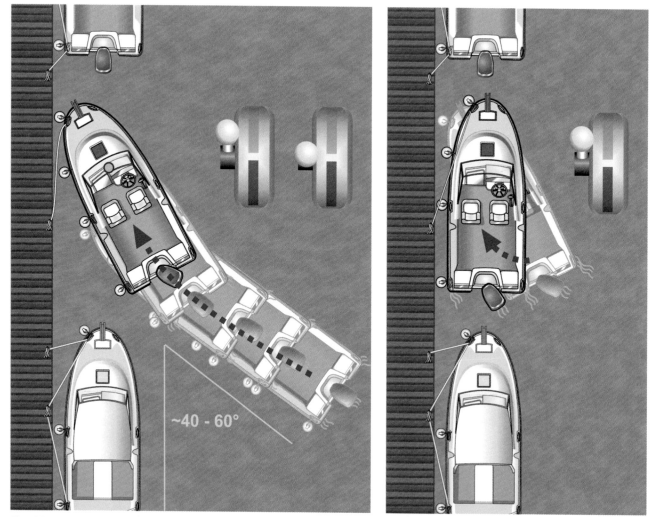

~40 - 60°

Docking between boats. *Bring the boat in at a sharp angle. Aim for a spot about ⅔ of the length of the clear dock forward of the rearward boat. Flare (i.e., turn just before you hit the dock) and secure an after bow spring line.*

7. Turn the wheel to starboard and shift into forward gear.

8. Apply gentle power until the stern settles against the dock. The spring line will constrain your boat from reaching the docked boat ahead.

9. Tie the remaining docklines. If necessary, run the engine at idle speed to keep the boat tight against the lines.

If you are single-handed, loop a line from your midships cleat over a dock cleat midway between the two docked boats. Then shift into neutral and get other lines in place.

DOCKING IN A SLIP—BOW-IN

No Wind or Current Docking an outboard or sterndrive in a slip is a straightforward process, performed much as you would at any parallel dock.

1. Approach at a slight angle so that your momentum will help carry you up to the finger pier. Your approach angle will need to be shallow to fit within the space available.

2. Aim for the corner of the slip between the finger pier and the main dock, then flare on final approach by turning slightly to starboard.

3. Proceed at idle speed in forward or even neutral.

4. Shift to reverse when your bow or forward fender has touched the side dock.

5. In reverse, the prop walk will bring the stern alongside the dock for a parallel landing.

6. Hand a line to a dockhand or have a crew member step off with a line.

Crosswind or Current If there's crosswind or current, you'll need to use lines to hold your position.

1. Enter the slip as with no wind or current, but before you are fully in, hand an after spring line to a dockhand, or have a crew member step onto the dock with the line.

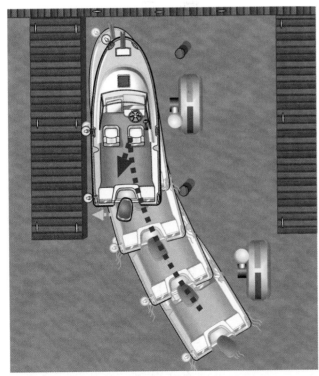

Entering a slip with no wind or current. *This is just like approaching a dock, except that you must stop before you strike the end of the slip. Use prop walk in reverse to pull in the stern.*

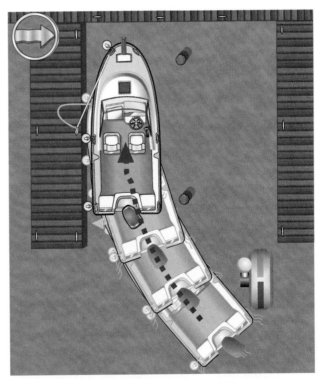

Entering a slip with wind or current off the dock. *Wind or current off the finger pier is a challenge. Have a crew member step onto the pier with an after bow spring line and secure the line to a dock cleat amidships. Now light power in forward gear will pin you to the dock. An alternative is to attach a spring line to your midships cleat, then pass it over the outermost cleat on the pier.*

Slow-Speed Maneuvering

2. The dockhand or crew member cleats the line on the dock to stop the boat's forward motion and prevent the boat from hitting the back of the slip.

3. Turn the wheel hard over to starboard, and apply a gentle forward thrust against the spring line to force the stern of the boat against the dock while the remaining lines are secured.

Docking in a Slip—Stern-In Stern-in is a popular way to tie up in a slip. It usually affords easier access for crew and gear and may be the only logical approach if the finger pier is shorter than the boat. In the absence of wind or current, it can be done with some degree of ease, but it takes some practice.

No Wind or Current Typically, you will make a perpendicular approach to the slip and turn before backing in.

1. As the bow passes by the slip, execute a sharp but slow-speed turn away from the slip.

2. When you have turned at least 45° and the stern is facing the finger pier, shift into reverse gear and power in. Keep in mind that with outboard or I/O propulsion, you have the ability to steer the boat; use this ability to align the boat to the entrance such that you'll only need to make minor adjustments once you've entered the slip.

3. The prop walk will be to port, so as you are

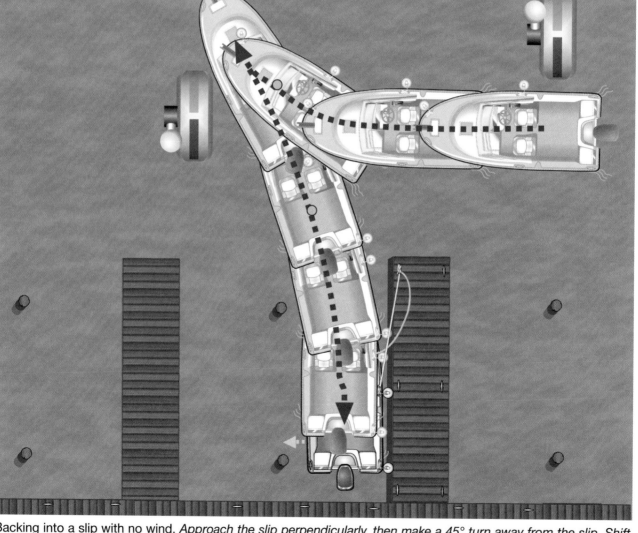

Backing into a slip with no wind. *Approach the slip perpendicularly, then make a 45° turn away from the slip. Shift to reverse and approach the side pier at a slight angle, much as you would if going forward. Aim slightly to your left (looking rearward) because prop walk will move the stern to your right.*

looking rearward, the stern of the boat will want to move to the right—away from the finger pier. Counteract this by steering a bit to the left of your target (looking rearward). The prop walk will help turn the boat parallel to the dock.

4. If you get too far away from the side pier, shift briefly to forward gear while steering very slightly toward the side pier. The thrust from the prop, aided by prop walk, will push the stern toward the dock. Proceed from here in reverse.

5. As you approach the end of the slip, apply light power in forward gear to halt your progress. Alternatively, you can attach a forward spring line (attached to your midships cleat) to the dock as you pass by. The spring line will halt your progress and keep you from striking the main dock. It will also pull the boat against the side pier.

6. Have a dockhand tie either the bow or stern line to secure the boat. If using a crew member, have him or her wait until he can step from the stern with a line in hand.

Wind or Current Directly in or out of the Slip These conditions will not have a major impact on your docking strategy. If necessary, you may need to use power or lines to constrain the boat.

If the wind or current is driving into the slip, get a forward spring line in place as soon as possible so that your boat is not driven into the main dock.

If the driving force is away from the slip, use a aft spring line to keep the boat in place until you're tied up.

Wind or Current across the Slip A crosswind or crosscurrent can be either a help or a hindrance, depending upon whether it is pushing you to the side pier or pulling you away. If the wind or current is driving you onto the finger pier, all you have to do is enter the slip, leaving a little extra room, and let nature take its course. However, if the wind or current is pushing you away from the pier, you have a challenge on your hands.

Let's assume the side pier is on the starboard side (to your left looking aft), and the driving force is from your left to right. This is the worst possible scenario, since prop walk will move the stern from left to right at the same time that the boat is being driven that way by the wind or current. Even worse

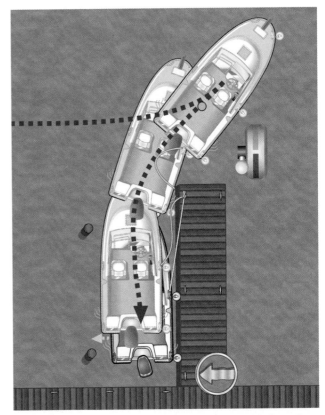

Backing into a slip in a crosswind. *Approach into the wind or current and turn just after you pass the slip, leaving enough room for downwind or downcurrent drift as you back in. Aim slightly to your left (looking aft) to counteract prop walk. Attach a forward spring line as you pass by the end of the dock.*

is the fact that the bow is even freer to move, since the pivot point is near the stern. What can you do?

Because you have an outboard or I/O drive, you have some control over the direction of thrust, so you can steer the boat in reverse.

1. Steer the bow into the wind or current and proceed slightly past the slip. Remember: as soon as you stop, the wind or current will begin pushing you back, so be sure to leave enough room to allow for this. (It's a good idea to stop your boat and observe the drift conditions prior to approaching the dock.)

2. The pivot point will be near the stern, so the bow is free to swing. Anticipate this by beginning with the bow somewhat to windward. Use your directed thrust to steer and straighten the boat.

3. Complete a sweeping turn with only a touch of helm to starboard. This will bring the bow around such that it's nearly parallel with the

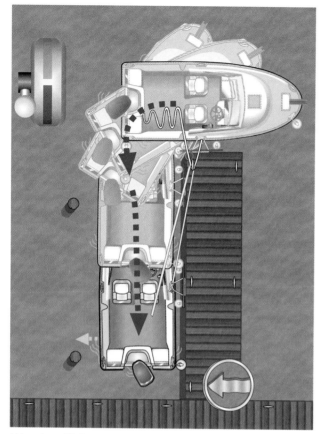

Warping. If the wind is just too strong to simply back into a slip, consider warping. Bring the boat to the end of the side pier and loop a line from the midships cleat to the dock cleat at the end of the pier. Using the pier as a fulcrum and the line to hold you against it, spin around the corner of the pier using reverse gear. Slowly pay out the line as you back into the slip, until you can use it as a spring line.

dock. Remember, prop walk will push your stern to port, so steer a little left (facing aft) to compensate; the stern should just barely clear the end of the slip.

4. Prepare a forward spring line and attach it to the midships cleat on the boat. As you pass by the end of the side pier, pass a line to a waiting dockhand, have a crew member step on the dock with the line, or loop the line over the cleat using a boat hook.

5. Continue to steer the stern toward the dock; the bow will continue to turn downwind. You should be nearly parallel with the side pier by now. As you enter the slip, the spring line will become taut and help pull you toward the side pier while preventing you from colliding with the back end of the slip.

6. Stay in reverse with your engine at low power and steer your engine slightly to starboard to help hold the boat against the pier. Tie the remaining docklines.

If your docking maneuver begins to go awry, pull out, regroup, and try again. If you get into a slip with the bow turned too far away from the side pier, it will be very difficult to correct. In this situation, it is the bow that will present your greatest challenge, not the stern.

Warping If the wind is particularly strong, you may have difficulty with the approach above. In this case, a more secure approach to use is *warping*, which is the art of using lines and fulcrums to move your boat. This maneuver requires the use a fender board (see accompanying illustration) to protect the boat's topsides.

1. Align the boat with its bow into the wind or current and closely approach the end of the side pier (or piling). Place a fender board at your beam to protect the boat.

2. When you come abeam to the end of the finger pier, loop a line (which you've tied to your midships cleat) around a cleat or piling, then bring the bitter end back onto the boat. Use your engine to help hold you in position.

3. Holding the line taut, power in reverse gear, steer into the turn, and use the dock as a fulcrum to pivot your boat into the slip.

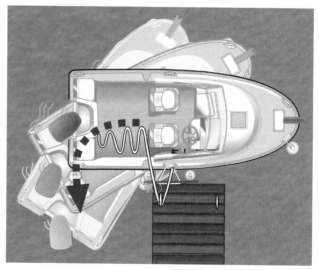

Warping: a close-up.

4. Continue powering in reverse (lightly) and pay out the line as you enter the dock, keeping it taut so you stay close to the pier.

5. Continue in reverse, steering to starboard and using the directed thrust to hold the stern to the dock.

6. When you are in the slip, tie off the spring line and continue light power until the remaining lines are secured.

TWIN DRIVES

In addition to providing the security and peace of mind that comes with having a backup engine while at sea, twin engines also provide a substantial advantage over single engines in close-quarters maneuvering. The basic maneuvers with twin or dual engines were described in Chapter 5, Steering Types. This section puts those maneuvers to work in specific situations. To a large extent, you will steer by varying the power applied through your forward and reverse gears, rather than with your wheel. This provides more precise control in both directions.

The figures in this section show twin inboard drives. As also described in Chapter 5, dual inboards generally provide more maneuverability than twin I/Os or outboards due to the locations of the propellers; however, the same principles apply to dual outboards and sterndrives.

If you have twin outboards or I/Os you may find that the dual drives are ineffective or limited for these maneuvers. In that case, use the two drives in tandem in the same gear, and the techniques for a single outboard or I/O should work.

Departing Maneuvers

Having twin drives can make departures quite easy. Under most conditions you can use the turning power of one drive in forward gear and the other in reverse to spin the bow away from the dock.

DEPARTING FROM A DOCK

No Wind or Current Below are the steps for a port-side dock departure, but the same technique, performed in reverse, works for a starboard-side departure.

A fender board is easily made from two fenders and a length of board. It's a good way to increase the protection between your hull and the dock.

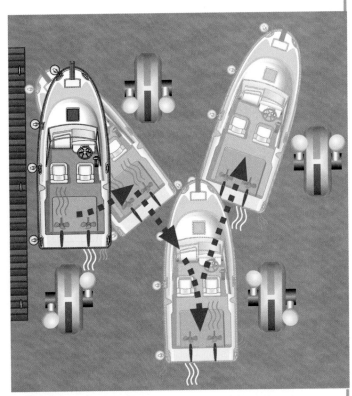

Departing with no wind. Place the outside engine in reverse and the dockside engine in forward gear, swing away from the dock, and go.

Slow-Speed Maneuvering

1. Make sure you have adequate fenders on the port quarter.

2. With the helm straight ahead, shift the dockside (port) drive into reverse gear and gently throttle.

3. Shift the starboard drive into forward gear. The stern of the boat will swing outward.

4. When your path is clear, shift both drives into reverse gear and back away until you are clear to depart in forward gear.

Against the Wind or Current This situation closely resembles the scenario with no wind or current, but here you may want to use a forward spring line to help you get out.

1. Make sure you have adequate fenders on the port quarter.

2. Untie all lines but the bow line and forward quarter spring line. You may want to loop the forward spring line around the dockside cleat for easy retrieval. When you are ready to depart, release the bow line.

3. With the helm straight ahead, shift the dockside

drive into forward gear and gently throttle.

4. Shift the starboard drive into reverse gear. The bow of the boat will swing outward.

5. When your path is clear, shift both drives into forward gear, retrieve the forward spring line, and depart.

With the Wind or Current Twin drives provide a great deal of flexibility in departing with a following wind or current.

1. Make sure you have adequate fenders on the port bow.

2. Untie all lines but the stern line and after bow spring line. You may want to loop the after spring line around the dockside cleat for easy retrieval.

3. With the helm straight ahead, shift the dockside drive into reverse gear and gently apply throttle. This should hold you against the wind or current so you can remove the stern line and possibly the spring line.

4. Shift the starboard drive into forward gear. The stern of the boat will swing outward.

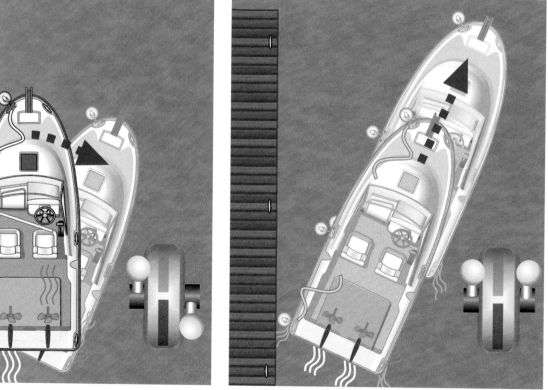

Departing against the wind. *This scenario is much like the last one; however, you may need to incorporate a forward spring line into your strategy.*

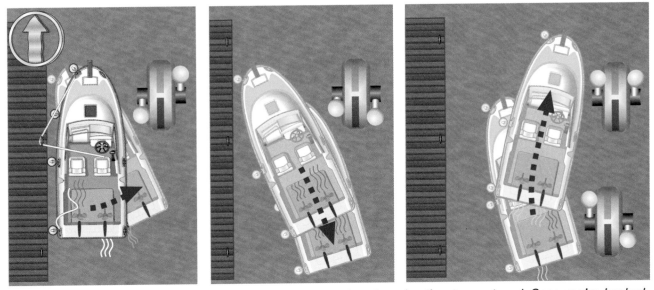

Departing with the wind. *In this scenario you'll use your engines to swing the stern outward. Once you've backed into a clear pathway, you're free to depart.*

5. As the stern moves away from the dock, shift the starboard engine to reverse. Apply a bit more power to the port engine than the starboard engine; the boat will move away from the dock at an angle.

6. When your path is clear, shift both drives into forward gear and power away.

Wind or Current on the Dock This is the most challenging departure since the wind or current wants to pin you to the dock, but the twin drives provide considerable help. There are two approaches to departing in these conditions. The first approach is to use the same technique as you used for no wind or current (see above).

If, however, the wind or current is too strong, you can use the following technique.

1. Remove all but an after bow spring line. Make sure you have a fender near the bow on the dock side.

2. Apply a gentle amount of forward power to the starboard engine and reverse on the port engine. The spring line will constrain the bow. This will rotate the boat about the spring line; the stern will swing away from the dock while the bow is pressed against the dock.

3. Once the stern has moved sufficiently clear of the dock and the stern is pointed well into the wind or current, shift both drives into

reverse gear. Using the two drives with different throttle settings will enable you to steer in reverse.

4. When the boat is sufficiently clear of the dock, shift both drives into forward gear and power away.

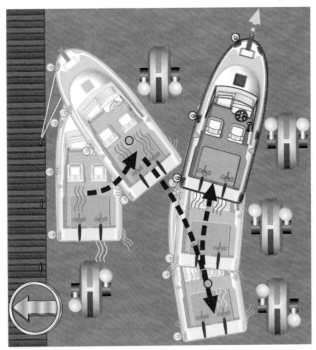

Departing with wind on the dock. *Power forward against an after bow spring line, steering toward the dock. Once your stern is facing toward the wind you can release the spring line and back away from the dock. When your path is clear, power away.*

DEPARTING FROM THE STARBOARD SIDE

If you are departing from a starboard-side dock, the procedures for twin drives are the mirror images of the ones described above. Since you have two engines with counter-rotating props, the prop walk directions are also mirror images of the port-side maneuvers.

This departure maneuver will also work if you're docked between tightly spaced boats. Since it also works for outboards and I/Os, it's considered the universal technique for getting out of a tight spot on the dock.

DEPARTING FROM A SLIP

When departing a slip, in all likelihood, you will be entering a channel or waterway with traffic. Be alert. It's also a good idea to sound a prolonged blast (four seconds or more) on your horn to signal your departure. A response of five or more short, one-second blasts indicates that another boat is approaching; wait before departing.

If you are docked in a slip alongside a finger pier and there's no wind or current, the procedures for departure will be similar to those described above. (See also the Departing from a Slip instructions in the Single Inboard Engine: Departing section [pages 66–69].) If, however, you are exposed to a crosscurrent or crosswind, your departure can be complicated. Remember, your steerage comes from the stern. You can counteract a reasonable degree of wind or current at the stern, but your bow will be pushed aside.

In a Crosswind or Crosscurrent Departing a slip with a crosswind can be a challenge because the wind or current is pushing you into the other side of the slip, or, in many cases, another boat. Or it might push you onto your side pier. The latter is easily handled by fending the boat away

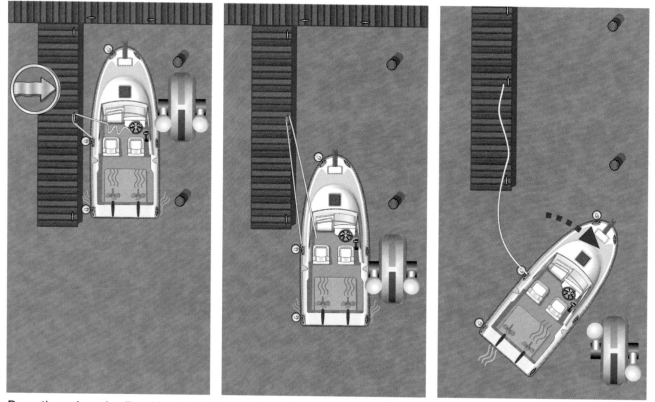

Departing a bow-in slip with wind off the dock. *In this situation you'll use a line to keep your boat from being blown into the pilings on the other side of the slip. Pay out the line as you back out, then retrieve the line once you've exited the slip.*

from the pier with boat hooks as you depart. The wind off the side pier presents more of a challenge:

1. Loop a line from your midships cleat around the corresponding cleat on the dock, then back to the boat.

2. Release all other docklines and use the looped line to hold your position.

3. Shift both engines into reverse gear and gently power away from the slip. Pay out the line as you go, keeping it taut enough to help you hold position.

4. As you clear the slip, let the line go (it will unwrap from the dock cleat), recover the line from the ship's cleat, and coil it.

5. Shift one of the engines into forward gear to begin the turn and power away.

Docking Maneuvers

DOCKING ON A PIER

No Wind or Current The following is a port-side docking.

1. Deploy fenders on the port side fore and aft, and have a bow line, stern line, and two spring lines ready. Brief the crew.

2. Approach the dock, alternating between forward gear and neutral, at an angle of about 15°.

3. Hold the rudders straight ahead and use minimal power.

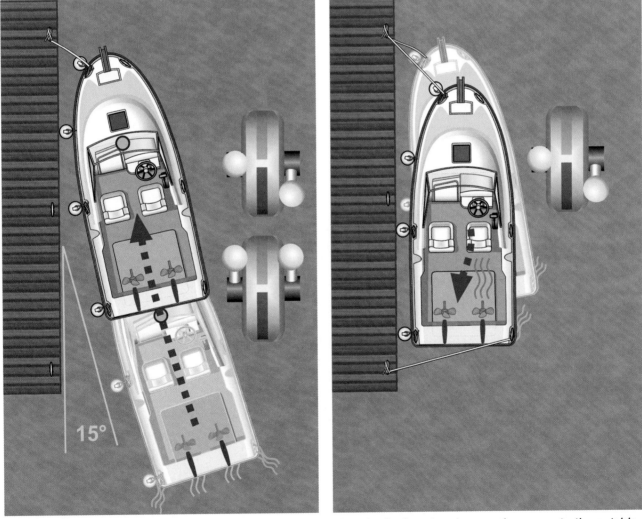

Docking with no wind. *Approach at a shallow angle if possible. As the bow touches, apply reverse to the outside drive to pull the stern in.*

Slow-Speed Maneuvering

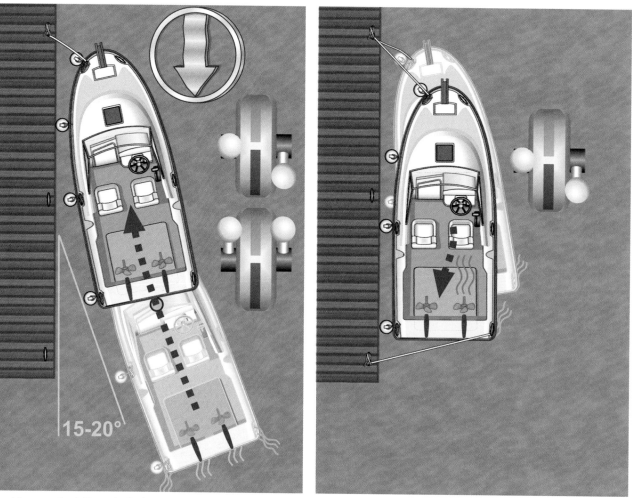

15-20°

Docking against the wind. *Approach the dock slowly at a 15–20° angle. When the bow touches, tie a bow line, and place the outside drive in reverse to pull the stern in.*

4. As you near the dock, shift both drives to neutral, then put the starboard drive gently into reverse. The prop walk will work to your advantage by bringing the stern toward the dock. This will both slow your forward progress and turn the boat parallel with the dock. Your momentum will carry the boat up to the dock.

5. Hand a bow line to a dockhand and continue with the outside engine in reverse to force the boat up against the dock.

6. Secure the remaining lines.

AGAINST THE WIND OR CURRENT

The ideal docking approach is into the current or wind. This permits you to use slightly greater power to improve maneuverability and control, while the environmental conditions keep you from advancing too quickly. This is true for all but quite strong winds, when the wind might take control of

the bow and push it downwind—but we'll cover that later.

1. Approach from a shallow angle of 15 or 20°.

2. Keep both engines in forward gear. The amount of power you apply depends on the conditions, but shifting in and out of neutral will help slow your speed.

3. Just before you touch the dock, shift the dockside (port) engine into neutral and the starboard engine into reverse. The prop walk will work to your advantage by bringing the stern toward the dock. This will both slow your approach and turn you more parallel with the dock.

4. Maneuver so that the bow touches first. If the stern touches first with the bow out, a strong wind or current could spin the bow out and around, and you would have to regroup and try again.

5. Tie the bow line first. As soon as the bow line is secured, the wind or current will tend to push you back and against the dock. If you want to speed up this process, continue applying reverse power on the starboard engine.

6. Secure the stern and spring lines.

Under no circumstances should you step off the boat with the engine engaged unless there is someone at the helm.

With the Wind or Current Docking with the wind or current is a challenge. Wind or current at your back can make you go faster than you might have intended; however, twin drives provide more steerage control than a single drive. Your objective here is to halt your forward progress and hold position when you reach the dock.

1. Make your approach at a shallow angle—as little as 10°.

2. As you approach the dock, apply power in reverse gear to halt your progress and hold your position. If you apply more reverse power to the outside (starboard) drive than the inside drive, prop walk will turn the boat parallel to the dock.

3. Have a dockhand or crew member secure the boat with a stern line, then tie the remaining docklines.

With the flexibility afforded by twin drives, you will find docking and maneuvering with a following wind or current can be quite easy. Since the bow is downwind or downcurrent, there is no risk of being blown around; the boat will simply align itself with the wind or current.

You can maneuver the stern by applying dif-

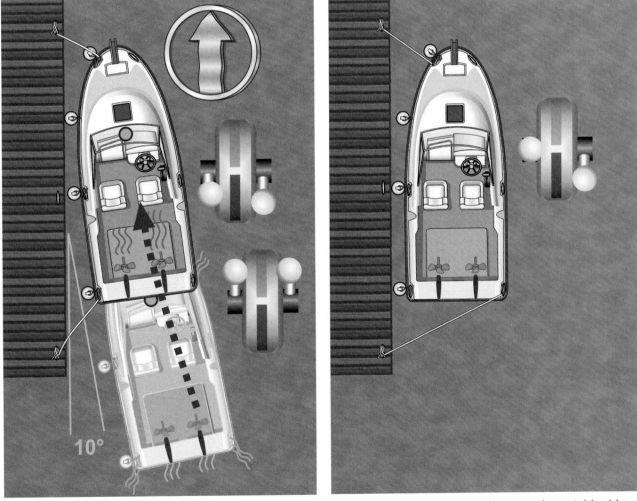

Docking with the wind. *When you are parallel to the dock, apply slightly more reverse thrust to the outside drive than the inside drive. The boat will walk toward the dock.*

TWIN DRIVES: DOCKING

Slow-Speed Maneuvering

ferent amounts of power in reverse gear and almost walk the boat sideways, even in a strong current. More reverse power to the outside drive will move the boat toward the dock; more reverse power to the inside drive will move the boat away from it.

Wind or Current off the Dock Docking with wind or current off the dock is challenging. Luckily, your twin engines will give you an added measure of control.

1. Deploy fenders quite far forward, since your port bow will contact the dock first. Have an after spring bow line ready—if you don't tie up quickly your boat is likely to drift away from the dock.

2. To counter the effects of the wind or current, make a sharp approach of 30 to 40° or more. This angle will provide you with adequate

momentum toward the dock in the face of wind or current.

3. Approach the dock with slow but steady headway.

4. Just before you make contact with the dock, begin a sweeping turn by applying more forward power to the dockside drive than the outside drive. This is known as *flaring* the boat.

5. When you're nearly parallel with the dock, place the inside drive into neutral while shifting the outside drive into reverse. The reverse gear will slow your forward movement. (A parallel docking makes it easier to hand a line to a dockhand or have a crew member step to the dock.)

6. Secure the after bow spring line to a dock cleat roughly amidships.

7. Apply light forward power to the dockside drive while shifting the outside drive into neutral. This

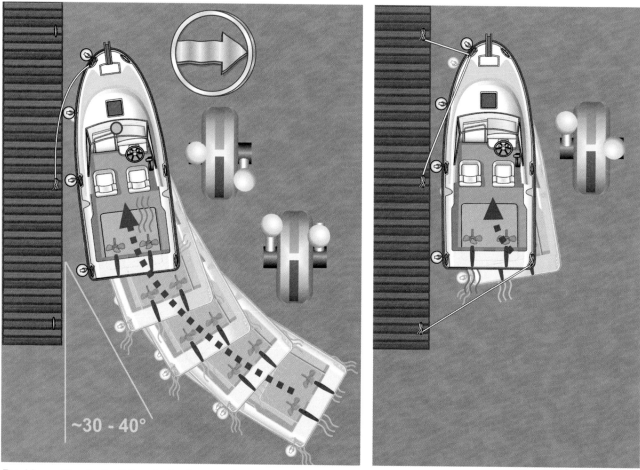

~30 - 40°

Docking with wind off the dock. *Approach at an angle steep enough to overcome the wind or current. Flare toward the dock using reverse gear on the outside drive. Secure an after bow spring line, then power forward with the inside drive to pin the stern to the dock while the remaining docklines are secured.*

will push the boat up tight against the dock, using the leverage of the spring line while the remaining lines are secured.

If you are single-handed, securing an after bow spring line while you make momentary contact with the dock will be very difficult. Instead, place a loop around the midships dock cleat from your midships boat cleat until you can secure other lines.

Tailor your strategy to accommodate the strength of the wind or current off the dock. The stronger the effect, the sharper your approach and the more throttle you need to apply. But in no case do you want to encounter the dock bow-on. Aim for the forward quarter or beam-on, and be sure your fenders are well placed.

DOCKING IN A SLIP

Bow-In—No Wind or Current The typical slip for bow-in docking consists of a single side pier, or finger pier, connected at right angles to a main pier, which forms the back of the slip.

The finger piers may be on either the port or starboard side. Docking to a port-side pier is easier for single inboard drives, since they back to port. With twins, neither side has any advantage, since you can apply prop walk in either direction, depending on which engine you use. In this example, however, we'll stick to a port-side docking. Entering a slip is akin to any docking maneuver, with two limitations: (1) the length of the slip limits how far forward the boat can go, and (2) the width of the slip limits your angle of approach.

1. Enter the slip at a slight angle to the finger pier.

2. Point your bow to the intersection of the main and side piers, turning slightly to starboard to align the boat to the finger pier as you approach.

3. Execute this turn in forward gear, using slightly more power with the port engine than with the starboard. Make liberal use of neutral to slow your advance. You may make the final turn with the starboard engine in neutral and just a touch of power in forward gear on the port drive.

4. As you near the inner end of the slip, gently apply reverse power to stop your forward progress. In this case, give the starboard engine

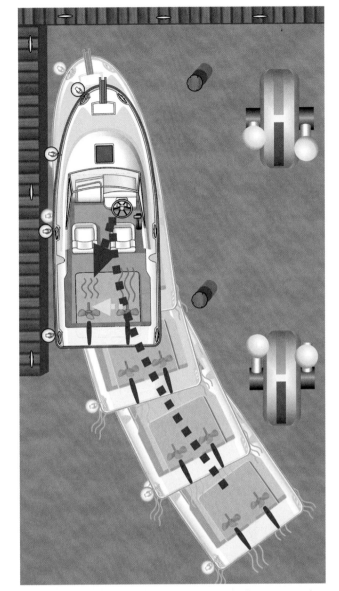

This maneuver is basically the same as the approach to a dock. Use reverse to avoid striking the main dock at the end of the slip.

a little more throttle than the port engine. This will allow prop walk to rotate the stern toward the dock. While the prop walk from the port engine is away from the dock, the greater throttle on the starboard engine means its prop walk will be a little stronger, and in the proper direction. If you are moving slowly enough, you may be able to stop the boat with port drive in neutral and just a touch of reverse power on the starboard engine.

5. Hand bow and stern lines to a dockhand, or step off with the lines and secure them. Finish off with forward and after spring lines.

Slow-Speed Maneuvering

Stern-In—No Wind or Current Stern-in is a popular approach to a slip. It usually affords easier access for crew and gear and may be the only practical option if the finger pier is shorter than the boat. In the absence of wind or current, backing in can be done with some degree of ease, but it takes some practice.

Typically, you will approach your slip from the right or left and turn before backing in.

1. Deploy fenders and have your docklines ready.

2. Proceed perpendicularly to the slip, leaving sufficient room to swing the stern around the forward pivot point.

3. As the bow comes even with the slip, execute a sharp but slow-speed turn away from the slip.

4. When you are aligned with the slip, shift to reverse gear at idle speed and power in. Switch between reverse and neutral to slow your advance, using equal power in both engines to avoid turning the boat. (With twins, there is no prop walk since the two engines cancel each other—provided that both are turning at the same rpm and in the same gear.)

5. Twin inboard engines give you the ability to steer while going in reverse. If you need to make an adjustment, shift one of the drives to neutral to allow the other drive to turn the boat. If you need the power from both drives, use slightly more power in one drive to execute a slow turn.

6. As you near the inner end of the slip, apply light power in forward gear to halt your progress. Use both engines in forward to cancel the prop walk. Or you may prefer to use a little more throttle on the starboard engine, since that will walk the boat toward the side dock.

7. Have a dockhand tie either the bow or stern to secure the boat. If using a crew member, have him wait until he can step from the stern with a line in hand.

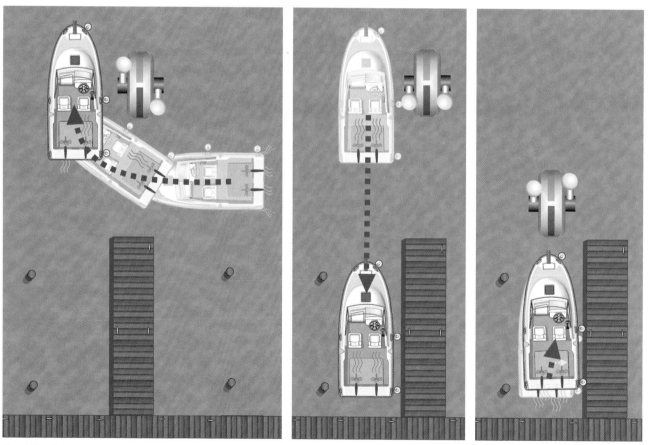

Backing into a slip with no wind. *Approach the slip perpendicularly, then turn away until your stern is aligned with the entrance. Back in using both drives, shifting between reverse at idle speed and neutral to slow your advance. Finish with a bit of forward gear, giving a little more throttle to the inside drive to walk the boat to the dock.*

Wind or Current into the Slip. If wind or current is driving you into the slip, you'll want to get a forward spring line in place as soon as possible so your boat is not driven into the main pier.

1. Enter the slip normally (see above), but with a forward spring line at the ready. Prior to backing in, attach the forward spring line from your boat's midships cleat, and tie a loop on the free end of the line.

2. Upon entering the slip, use a boat hook to place the loop over the dock's outboard cleat or a piling.

3. Make sure the spring line is short enough to keep you from hitting the main pier behind you. As you near your destination, the spring line will halt your progress, and the combination of wind and power will hold you tight against the side pier.

4. Tie up and cut the engines.

Wind or Current out of the Slip. If wind or current is driving out of the slip, you'll want to get an after bow spring line in place so that your boat is not driven from the slip. Timing is less critical than with the wind into the slip, however.

1. Enter the slip normally (see above), but keep an after spring line at the ready. Prior to backing in, attach the spring line to your boat's midships cleat and tie a loop on the free end of the line.

2. Upon entering the slip, use a boat hook to place the loop of the spring line over the cleat at the inside end of the slip or a piling. This line will prevent the boat from being blown or swept away and help keep it close to the side pier.

3. Tie up and cut the engines.

Wind or Current off the Finger Pier Crosswinds or currents can be either a help or a hindrance, depending upon the direction of the

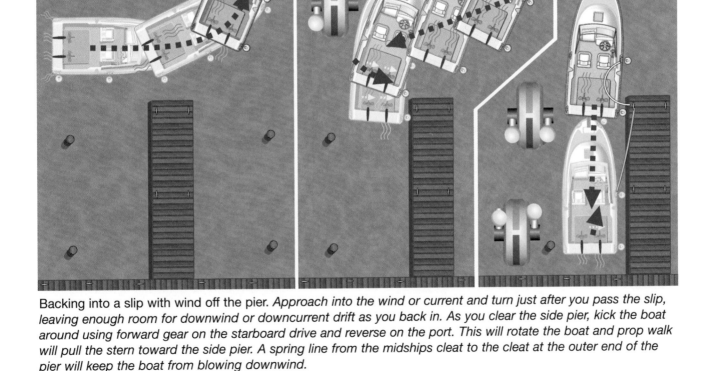

Backing into a slip with wind off the pier. *Approach into the wind or current and turn just after you pass the slip, leaving enough room for downwind or downcurrent drift as you back in. As you clear the side pier, kick the boat around using forward gear on the starboard drive and reverse on the port. This will rotate the boat and prop walk will pull the stern toward the side pier. A spring line from the midships cleat to the cleat at the outer end of the pier will keep the boat from blowing downwind.*

driving force—toward the finger pier or away from it. If the force is toward the pier, all you have to do is enter the slip, leave a little room, and let nature take its course. If, however, the driving force is off the pier, you have a challenge on your hands.

The best approach is to begin with your bow into the wind or current and turn partially away from the slip. The theory is that the wind or current will straighten the bow as you back into the slip.

1. Powering into the wind or current, move past the slip to allow room for the boat to drift downwind or downcurrent while you are backing into the slip.

2. Bring your boat around so that its stern is facing the slip at an angle, with the bow distinctly aimed into the wind or current. Your objective will be to just clear the corner of the side pier as you back toward your slip.

3. Shift into reverse with both engines and back as straight as you can. There will be no prop walk, but the current or wind will push you off the dock.

4. Clear the side pier and place the starboard drive in forward gear to bring the bow around nearly parallel with the side pier. Meanwhile, the prop walk from both drives will push the stern toward the dock.

5. In many cases, the wind or current will be blocked within the slip by other boats, structures, or land; however, if the wind or current *is* strong within the slip, place a forward spring line, attached to your midships cleat, over a cleat or piling at the outer end of the slip.

6. With both drives in reverse gear, power directly but slowly into the slip.

7. Slow down, if you need to, by shifting the drives into forward gear briefly to halt your progress into the slip. If you apply more power to the starboard drive than the port drive, the resulting prop walk will help pull the stern toward the dock.

8. Apply light power to the starboard drive in reverse to pull the boat in against the spring line (if you deployed one).

9. Step off the boat with bow and stern lines to hold the boat to the dock, and add a second spring line.

ADDITIONAL HANDLING SKILLS

Departing and docking are not limited to docks and piers; you may need to launch a boat from a boat ramp, tie up at a mooring, or beach your boat for lunch and a swim. (Anchoring will be discussed in Chapter 11. See also Station Keeping on page 167.) With these skills under your belt, you'll have more options for enjoying your boat and a greater mastery in powerboat handling.

Moorings

DEPARTING A MOORING

Departing from a mooring is the easiest of all departure tasks. Your boat will naturally point into the current or wind—whichever is dominant. If the current is strong, be prepared to counter it, especially if there are boats astern of you.

1. Untie the mooring line and toss it from the bow, making sure the line is far enough away that it won't foul the propeller. It's easiest if a member of your crew does this, because you may need to apply some power in forward gear to maintain your position. If you have to do this yourself, get to the helm quickly to take control. Do not apply propulsion and leave the helm to go to the bow.

2. Once you're free of the mooring, drift backward until you have clearance.

3. Apply light forward throttle while also turning to go around rather than over the mooring line.

4. Once you've moved to the side of the mooring, power away.

APPROACHING A MOORING

Approaching and tying to a mooring is also quite easy. Your biggest challenges will be avoiding other boats and gauging how to stop the boat over the mooring.

1. Approach the mooring from a direction that puts you into the wind or current, whichever is stronger. The other boats in the mooring field will provide a good indicator of wind or current direction: they'll be pointing into the dominant element. This means you'll approach your mooring parallel to other moored boats.

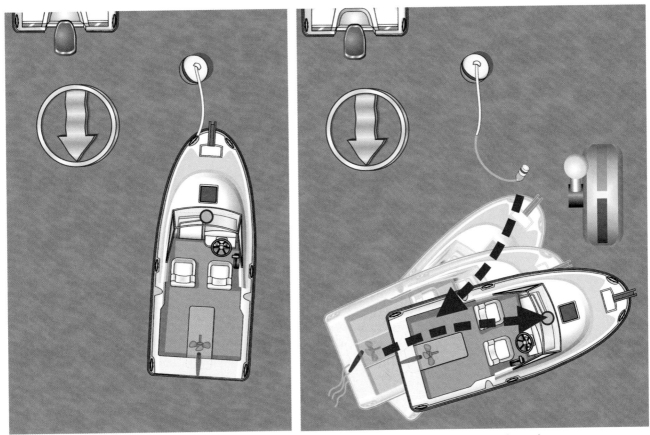

The biggest challenges in departing from a mooring are to avoid striking other boats and running over your mooring gear. It's best to turn the boat a bit after releasing the mooring so you can motor around your line.

2. If you have a crew member, she should be in the bow with a boat hook to snag the mooring pennant. She can also provide you with hand signals to indicate direction and distance from your bow to the pendant. (Often, you cannot see the mooring over your bow as you draw near.)

3. Carefully maneuver between other moored boats until you approach your mooring. To maintain slow headway, alternate between forward gear and neutral.

4. Place the engine in neutral when you are about a half boat length from the mooring, and drift up to the pendant. If the boat begins to drift backward, briefly shift into gear to hold position.

5. Have your crew member retrieve the pendant and tie the mooring line to your bow cleat. Once she signals that the line is secure, cut your engine.

If you are single-handed, you have a couple of choices: 1) You can perform the same approach described above but drift slightly farther forward,

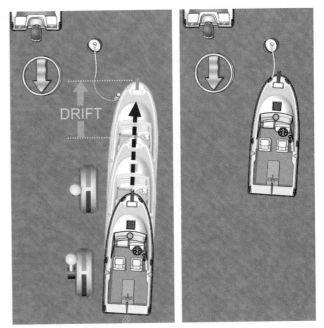

Select the side from which you will approach the mooring and plan to put the engine into neutral about a half boat length away. Ideally, your boat will temporarily halt with the mooring pendant directly off the bow. Retrieve it with a boat hook and attach it to the bow cleat.

put the engine in neutral, and go to the bow your-self to retrieve the pendant; or 2) You can rig a line from your bow to your cockpit and power along-side the mooring. Retrieve the pendant and attach it to the bow line and release. Now, with the engine in neutral, go to the bow, pull in the line, and attach the mooring line directly to your bow cleat.

Boat Ramps

Using a trailer at a boat ramp is a common skill required of boaters who launch and pull their own boats. Hang around any busy boat ramp for a few hours, and you'll likely witness at least one instance of pandemonium. Ramp skills are worth learning.

LAUNCHING AND DEPARTING FROM A RAMP

Given that many boaters will want to use the same ramp, your first challenge may be just getting to it. Put your wait time to good use by checking that your boat is ready to launch. Is all the gear aboard, drain plug in place, and a line tied to a bow cleat and ready for use? Now is a good time to untie the tie-downs, but be sure to leave the bow eye line attached to the winch.

When it's your turn, follow these steps:

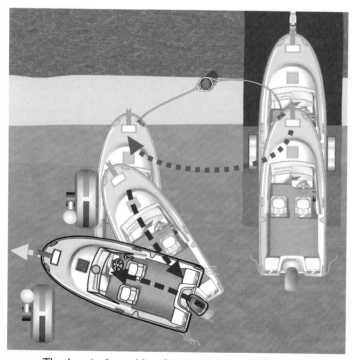

The key to launching from a ramp is maintaining control over the boat when it floats off the trailer. Make sure you have a line to the bow so you can walk it away from the ramp and tie it up or beach it.

1. Double-check that all your safety gear is aboard.

2. If you have a flat-bunk trailer (i.e., one with car-peted longitudinal beds to support the boat), back down the ramp slowly until the boat can float free of the trailer. If your trailer bunks have rollers, back down until the boat begins to float at the stern.

3. Place chocks under your car wheels. Let the winch line out slowly while pushing the boat into the water. When it floats free, grab one hand of the cleated bow line and unhook the winch cable.

4. Have a crew member move the boat via the bow line to a nearby dock or beach. Tie the line to a fixed object to keep the boat from drifting away. If no fixed object is available, use an anchor.

5. Clear the boat ramp as quickly as you can to make room for the next in line. Park and secure your vehicle and trailer.

6. Next, load your passengers aboard. If neces-sary, push the boat into deeper water. Ensure that the drive is submerged so cooling water will be drawn in when you start the engine. Before you start it, make sure you have ade-quate depth around the engine to avoid drawing in sand or debris with the cooling water. Also, run the blowers and/or check for fuel vapors before starting the engine.

7. Start and warm the engine.

8. Retrieve the bow line and carefully apply power in reverse until you have a clear path, then shift to forward gear and power away.

RETRIEVING A BOAT AT A RAMP

The ramp may have a dock for temporary staging, or you may need to beach the boat while you retrieve the tow vehicle. Then follow these steps:

1. Back the trailer down the ramp and into the water. How far into the water will depend on the type of bunks on your trailer. Padded or car-peted fixed bunks generate considerable fric-tion and must be at least partially submerged so you can float the boat onto them. Roller bunks generate very little friction: you may be able to winch the boat onto the trailer with just the

lower part of the first set of rollers in the water. This may enable you to keep your trailer's wheel hubs out of the water, which is worth doing if possible. Chock your car's wheels.

2. Approach the trailer in your boat. Make sure it is centered and aligned with the trailer, and level side-to-side. You may need to shift your weight to the center to ensure this. Approach the trailer in neutral with just enough momentum to glide up onto the bunks. (It's a bad idea to power the boat onto the trailer. The prop wash tends to erode the ramp, and sand is likely to be sucked into the engine cooling system.) If this does not work, back the trailer farther into the water and try again.

3. Once you've gotten the bow nestled between the bunks, you can attach the winch cable, then cut and raise the engine. Winch the boat up onto the trailer until the bow is securely positioned against the trailer's bow ramp, next to the winch. Winching can be very risky if the strain is too great or the cable is in poor condition. A cable that breaks under stress is capable of flying apart at great speed, injuring bystanders or damaging boats and tow vehicles. If there is too much tension, back the trailer deeper into the water, remove the boat, and start over.

4. Be courteous to other boaters. Remove the chocks and pull your rig away from the ramp as soon as you've securely winched the boat onto the trailer.

5. Tow the trailer and boat to a parking area. Remove the drain plug, drain the bilge, stow and secure the gear, and apply the tie-downs before departing. Also make sure that you are not carrying any aquatic debris as you leave.

Beaching

Many boaters visit beaches while they are out on the water. A beach is a good place to stop and let the crew off or to serve as your temporary dockage for the day. But before you just drive up onto the beach, get to know the area. Is it (hopefully) a sandy beach? Is the area free of dangerous rocks that can damage the hull? What is the tide cycle?

The first place to look is on your charts. Even if your chart isn't highly detailed, rocky areas are generally marked. If rocks are present, seek another

spot to beach. In the absence of a chart, slowly patrol unfamiliar waters while looking at the bottom. Station someone on the bow to serve as a lookout. (Make sure your lookout is safely secured to the boat; you don't want him falling out if the boat hits an object.) Proceed cautiously and be prepared to shift into reverse gear if your lookout spots trouble.

If the area is tidal, you need to know the tide cycle and the tidal range. You will need sufficient water under the hull when you're ready to depart. If the tide is near high water, beach the boat temporarily to let off crew and supplies, then immediately back off to deeper water to avoid being stranded until the next high tide.

To beach your boat:

1. Approach the beach at right angles at a very slow speed—alternate between idle and forward gear.

2. Make sure the propeller is in sufficient depth of water so that it does not kick up sand or mud.

3. The engine rules, so if the water is too shallow, do not go farther. If the slope of the beach is steep enough to accommodate the propeller, stop when the boat makes initial contact. Driving the boat up onto the beach will wear away the hull or bottom paint.

4. Tie a line from the bow to some fixed object on or near the beach such as a tree, or carry your anchor onto the beach and embed it in the sand.

5. If there is any cross current or wind, the boat is likely to swing and come to rest sideways along the beach. To avoid this and keep the boat perpendicular to the beach, deploy a second anchor off the stern. Use this anchor to help you depart when you are ready.

6. If the slope is gradual enough, wade out and drop the anchor at a comfortable distance off the beach. Otherwise, back the boat off the beach and drop the anchor off the stern, then pay out line carefully to ensure the line does not get wrapped around the propeller while you power back to the beach.

Often, it is better to anchor the boat slightly offshore, especially if there is a falling tide. Keep an eye on the boat as the tide drops to make sure the boat will not be high and dry when you want to leave. Readjust the anchor lines as needed.

PART III

BOAT HANDLING BEYOND THE HARBOR

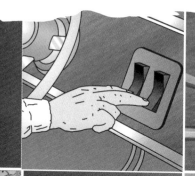

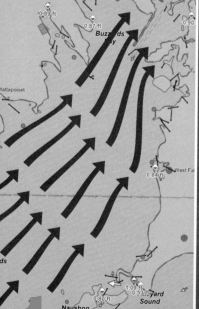

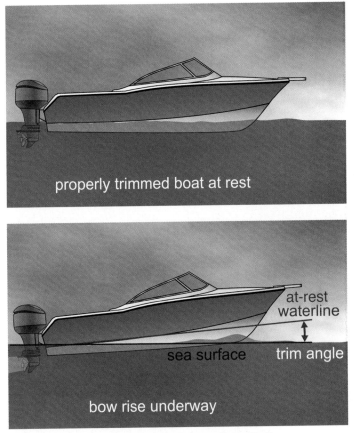

CHAPTER 7

Underway on Calm Seas

This chapter takes your boat out to open water, where you can accelerate beyond no-wake speed. To get the most out of your boat underway, you'll need to be able to adjust the boat's trim to the conditions, as well as turn and stop at cruising speed.

BOAT TRIM AND PERFORMANCE

Trim is the attitude of your boat in the water: bow down, bow up, or canted to port or starboard. In Chapter 1, we talked about static trim with the boat at rest. Now that we are going to sea, and the boat is under power, several elements in addition to weight distribution will affect trim underway: hull shape, drive trim, and special devices such as trim tabs. The result is called dynamic trim. By understanding and using trim appropriately, you can improve planing efficiency, keep your boat balanced, and improve the comfort and safety of your ride.

The fore-and-aft trim angle of a properly loaded boat at rest, should be zero—that is, level with the water. As a planing hull moves from displacement speeds to planing speeds, the trim angle increases until the boat is planing, then levels out. The actual angles depend upon the boat's shape, its loading, and the sea conditions. Many planing-hull powerboats have trim tabs that allow you to adjust the trim angle to achieve the optimum trim for your

The boat at rest rides somewhat parallel with the surface of the water (top). As soon as propulsion is applied, a bow wave begins to form and the bow rises slightly (above). The difference between these two attitudes is the trim angle.

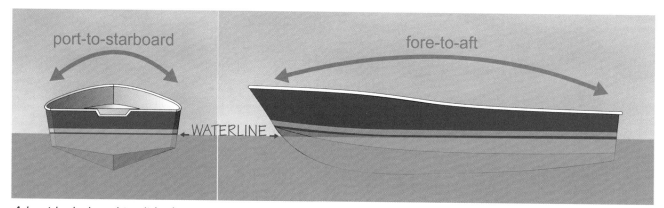

A boat is designed to sit in the water "on its lines," both port to starboard and fore to aft.

speed and the load you're carrying. In addition, an outboard or sterndrive engine also gives you the ability to adjust trim by trimming the propeller in or out. Too much or too little trim angle will affect your boat's performance, as we'll see later.

Generally speaking, a boat operates most efficiently when it is riding very slightly bow-up and level side-to-side.

Boat Attitude Underway

While underway, a boat's attitude affects its efficiency, steering, and how it takes the seas, which, in turn, impacts comfort and speed. For example, you can often achieve more speed by getting the bow up, which reduces the amount of hull in the water—thus reducing frictional drag. If the seas become choppy, on the other hand, getting the bow

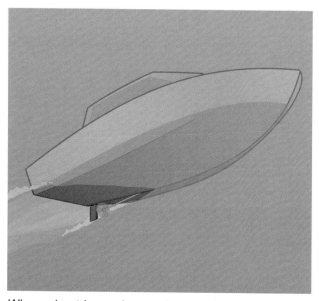

When a boat is on plane, only a small amount of the hull remains in the water.

down may help cut through the waves rather than taking them on the flatter hull sections farther aft.

Each boat responds differently depending upon its hull design, how it is loaded, and the prevailing conditions. Learning your boat's unique characteristics takes time; however, some basic principles apply.

BOW UP

Let's say you're out for a cruise and you want to open her up. Due to the hull shape, the bow will naturally rise a bit. By elevating the bow, you can increase your boat's speed; however, the compromise is that the ride, steering, and fuel efficiency may suffer. There are several reasons why this happens. First, with the bow out of the water, it is no longer cleanly parting the waves. Instead, the flatter sections aft are taking the seas, which may result in pounding, even in moderate waves. In addition, if the bow is elevated enough, much of the sharper part of the keel that helps keep the boat on track will be out of the water. The boat may wallow, and you may have more difficulty steering.

Too much bow-up configuration can also cause your boat to *porpoise*, which is a repeated, rapid rising and falling of the bow that can become unsafe. Typically, this is viewed as a design flaw, but it is heavily influenced by the operator's choices, such as the use of excessive speed for the prevailing conditions or incorrect trimming. You can correct porpoising by slowing the boat, adjusting the trim tabs, or carefully trimming the outboard or I/O drives (which we'll cover later).

While a slight bow-up attitude is generally a good thing, too much bow out of the water can cause other problems as well. If your boat has too much bow out of the water at low speeds, it will

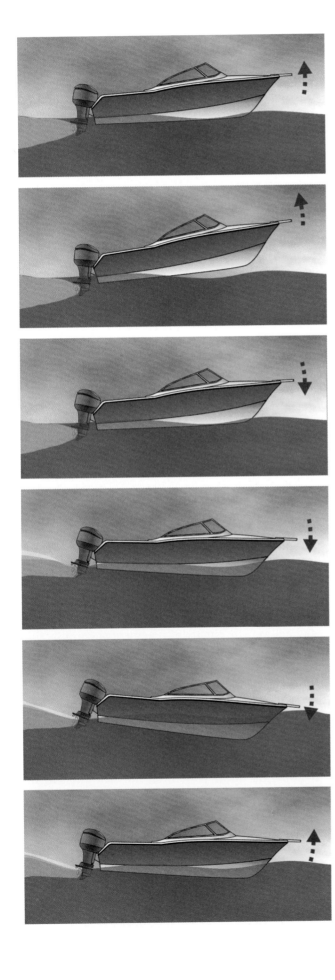

Porpoising is the repetitive dipping and rising of the bow. Here's what happens: The bow is forced up by too much trim until well out of the water. Then the weight of the bow begins to force the bow back down again, and momentum pushes the bow deep into the water. The buoyancy of the bow and the drive trim then bring the bow back out of the water with a strong upward force. The cycle repeats itself, vastly reducing control. The porpoising can become more severe unless trim is adjusted.

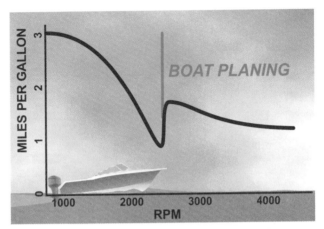

A good measure of the efficiency of a hull in the water is the boat's fuel consumption, indicated here by miles per gallon. At slow speeds fuel efficiency is quite good. However, it drops rapidly as the boat tries to achieve a plane. As you increase the rpms, your boat will climb its bow wave and level out. At this point, your miles per gallon will increase. If you continue to increase the rpms, the mpg will decrease somewhat.

require more power to get on a plane. A bow-up attitude will literally pit your boat in an uphill battle as it tries to climb its bow wave. This can lead to an uncomfortable ride, poor visibility forward, considerable fuel consumption, and a sensation of going nowhere.

Trim Options

Planing entails getting your boat up onto its own bow wave. How is this best accomplished? More power can help, but more power means a larger engine, which would weigh the stern down even more. By applying the appropriate trim you can lift the stern, which makes it easier for the boat to get onto plane.

So how do you control trim? There are four options: boat trim, drive trim, trim tabs, and interceptors.

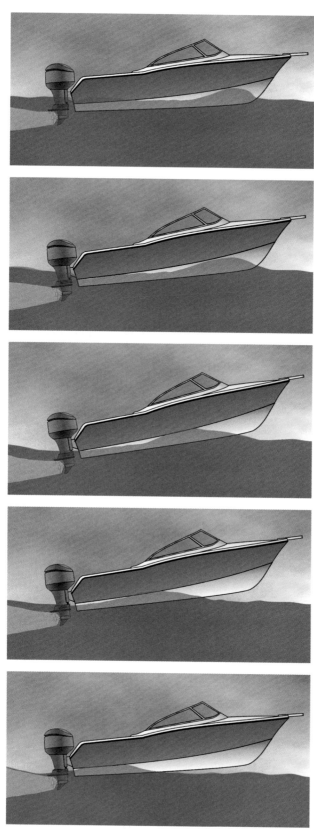

Planing: a refresher course. *At slow speeds, a planing-hull boat is in displacement mode. As it accelerates, it creates an increasingly larger bow wave and begins to climb up onto the bow wave. Finally the boat achieves plane and levels out.*

BOAT TRIM

Boat trim depends largely on the weight distribution in the boat. Where are people and gear situated? Ideally, you want the load distributed such that when the boat sits in the water at rest, its waterline is parallel to the water.

Once underway, hull dynamics add another dimension. Most boats experience a bit of bow rise related to hull shape—how much rise depends on the design. While you can adjust the trim to some degree by shifting weight on the boat, most boats require additional help.

DRIVE TRIM

If you have an outboard or I/O engine, you can use the engine to help trim the boat by adjusting the drive's angle relative to the transom. If the drive is *trimmed in*, the propeller will be discharging slightly downward, which helps lift the stern of the boat and keep the bow down. If the drive is *trimmed out*, the propeller thrust will be directed upward, forcing the stern down and the bow up.

When you are attempting to get a boat up on plane, trim the drive all the way in to lift the stern out of the water. This will counteract the natural bow-up attitude as the boat works to lift itself onto its bow wave.

As soon as the boat begins to plane, you will feel a sudden change in boat attitude and speed. Some of the bow rise subsides, and the boat will settle to a more neutral position. Also, the boat's speed will increase substantially, as if it has been freed of a great burden—which it has. At this point, ease back on the throttle to achieve a comfortable speed while maintaining plane.

After the boat is planing, adjust the trim again. At this point, if you keep the drive trimmed in, you may depress the bow too much, causing it to dig into oncoming waves and slow the boat. It also increases the wetted surface area or the hull, which will slow the boat. How much to trim out depends upon your boat and the prevailing conditions.

If you trim too far out, the bow will rise and begin to obscure your forward visibility. This attitude will expose the flatter aft sections of the hull, which are less able to cut through the onrushing waves or chop, leading to pounding. Also, your steering may become mushy, and the boat may wallow rather than tracking smoothly. If you elevate

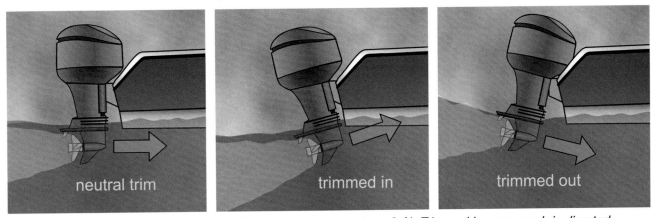

Neutral trim: the prop is level and even with the bottom of the boat (left). Trimmed in: prop wash is directed downward, which will raise the stern and depress the bow (center). Trimmed out: propeller depth, or draft, *is reduced slightly and prop wash is directed upward; this will depress the stern and elevate the bow (right).*

the propeller(s) to a point too close to the water's surface, it will begin to lose its grip as the water becomes aerated. If this happens, the rpm will rise and boat performance will degrade.

Your best trim setting will be where you achieve the maximum speed for the throttle setting. If you subsequently change the throttle setting, the bow will rise or fall, changing the boat's trim, and you will have to readjust the drive trim.

One method for determining the optimum trim setting involves the use of a GPS and tachometer. A GPS will provide an accurate measure of your speed, while the tachometer measures engine rpm. You will find that as you trim out, the rpm will go up and your speed will increase. As you continue to trim out, the speed will rise to a maximum and then begin to decline, but your rpm may continue to rise. Your most efficient setting is likely to be where you have maximum speed for a given throttle setting. A fuel flow meter can give you a more refined indication.

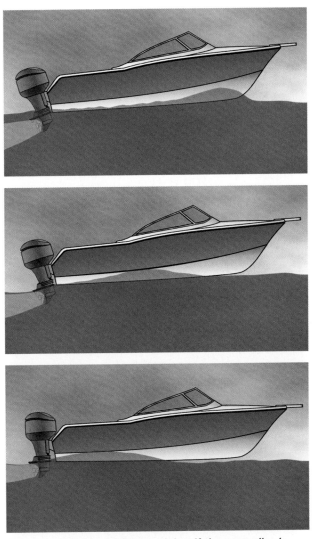

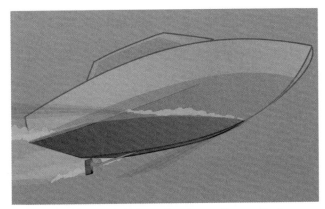

With the bow trimmed too far down, the wetted surface looks like this.

A boat will achieve plane quicker if the propeller is trimmed in to elevate the stern. The stern is lifted as the boat climbs up on its bow wave (top). The boat quickly achieves plane and levels out (center). Once leveled out, the propeller is trimmed out to a neutral position (above).

Boat Handling beyond the Harbor

TRIM TABS

Trim tabs are hydraulically adjusted plates that are mounted on both sides of the transom and aligned with the bottom of the boat. They are relatively small—about a square foot or so in area—and work by diverting the flow of water from under the hull as you tilt them up or down.

The two trim tabs are controlled by individual switches, which allows you to adjust for any starboard-to-port imbalance. If you lower a trim tab, it will elevate the stern on that side and lower the bow on the opposite side. If you lower both tabs equally, they will elevate the whole stern and, as mentioned earlier, help get your boat onto a plane.

Trim tabs are adjustable metal plates that are mounted flush with the bottom of the boat on both sides of the transom. They are adjusted independently using rocker switches at the helm.

If you lower them too far, they operate like drag chutes, slowing the boat.

Getting the right setting is a matter of experience. A good practice is to lower the tabs all the way as you begin to accelerate, then progressively raise them until you find a good mix of stern lift and sufficient speed to get up and stay on a plane.

PUTTING TRIM TABS TO WORK

Trim tabs have several applications. You can use them to compensate for a shift in people or gear from one side to the other, or if a crosswind is tilting the boat. (Generally, a boat will tilt *toward* a crosswind.) In both cases, adjust the trim tab down on the affected side to level your ride.

Trim tabs also can help you stay on plane at a lower speed. When deployed in the down position, they provide lift to the stern, which improves planing. At the same time, though, they will increase drag.

If the seas turn choppy, you can use trim tabs to slow down yet still stay on plane, saving wear and tear on your boat and crew. Trim down until you will feel the boat begin to slow. Continue trimming down until the boat starts to come off plane and the stern begins to sink. Then immediately trim up until you just reach plane again and can maintain it. At this slower speed, you will take less pounding while still taking advantage of the efficiency of planing. Although fuel consumption may rise, your ride will be a great deal more comfortable.

Keep in mind whenever you make a trim tab adjustment that there is a distinct time lag while the

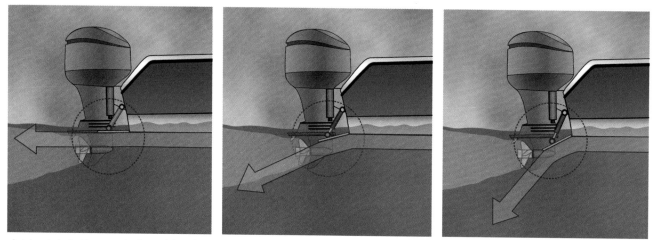

A trim tab in the neutral position is level with the bottom of the boat and has no effect on the water flow under the boat (left). When slightly depressed, a trim tab directs the water flow downward (center). When fully depressed, a trim tab directs the flow sharply downward (right).

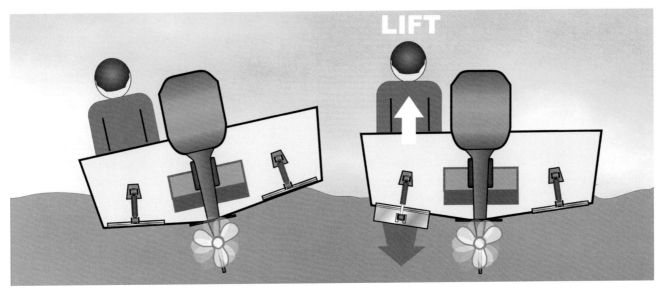

Uneven loading on a boat can be corrected by deploying the trim tab on the depressed side, thus elevating that side.

hull dynamics settle down. Wait a minute until the correction takes place or you could easily overcompensate.

INTERCEPTORS

Interceptors are an alternative to trim tabs that accomplish much the same task. Interceptors use vertical blades located on either side of the hull at the transom. Lowering one or both of these blades an inch or two into the flow of water coming from under the hull creates lift. Interceptor blades are relatively short and a bit wider than comparable trim tabs.

Interceptors are typically found on larger boats, but they are becoming more popular.

Appropriate Use of Trim

While trim has several advantages, you have to know how to use it appropriately. For example, raising the bow while on plane increases speed, but if you have the bow trimmed too high, you may also have a difficult time maintaining your heading and seeing where you are going. You are also exposing the flatter aft sections of the hull to oncoming chop, creating a rougher ride. These issues are not just matters of comfort or convenience: they can lead to loss of control.

Once a boat is on plane, therefore, it's important to bring the bow down so that the boat rides more nearly level. This may slow the boat a bit, but it will also improve tracking and forward visibility and

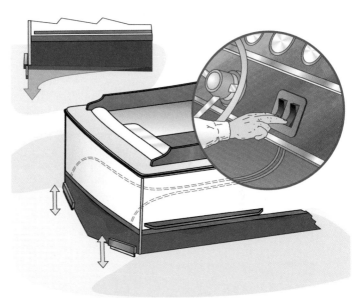

The interceptor drops vertically in front of the water flow. This redirects the flow of water downward, which creates upward force on the hull.

eliminate porpoising. And by placing the sharper bow in line with the oncoming waves, it will better cut through the waves and smooth your ride, reducing pounding and increasing everyone's comfort.

On the flip side, be careful not to trim the bow too far down. Aside from making it difficult or impossible to remain on plane, you run the risk of taking water over the bow and, in the extreme, having the bow dig into oncoming waves.

Bow up and bow down can be achieved by using either the drive trim or the trim tabs. Trim

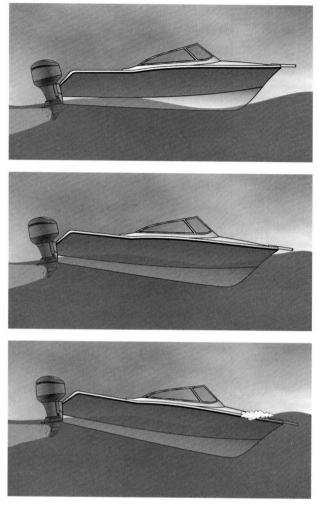

Trimming in too much will force the bow down too far, causing the boat to drop off plane (top). The bow will push into oncoming waves (center). Higher seas may break over the bow (bottom).

tabs are more effective in lifting the stern, which makes them very useful for helping get the boat on a plane. Many owners of outboard-driven boats choose trim tabs over drive trim for this purpose. Once underway, they lift up the trim tabs and use the drive trim for fine adjustments. Because trim tabs create drag as well as lift, drive trim is the better choice for finer adjustments.

Finally, under no circumstances should you lower the trim tabs in a following sea (i.e., when you are traveling in the same direction as the waves). Going into the waves, the lowered tabs generate stern lift. With a following sea, the lowered tabs can actually serve to lower the stern, thus exposing the transom to flooding by an overtaking wave. This can make a dangerous situation even worse, as you will see in Chapter 9.

TURNING IN CALM SEAS

Turning a boat underway is a relatively simple maneuver in calm seas. As we saw in Chapter 3, a boat turns about a pivot point, and the pivot point changes to coincide with the amount of hull in the water or the waterline length.

When you are in forward gear and still in displacement mode, the pivot point typically lies along the centerline about one-quarter to one-third of the boat's waterline length aft of the bow. However, when your boat is on a plane, the waterline length (the amount of the hull in the water) will be reduced to a small aft section of the hull. Now the pivot

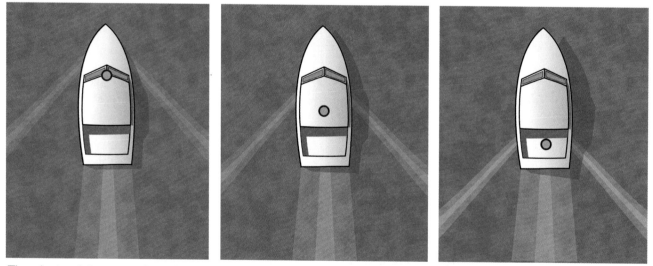

The pivot point moves aft as the boat goes up on a plane. During displacement mode the pivot point is near the bow (left). As you start to plane the pivot point will move to midships (center). When you are fully planing the pivot point will be near the stern (right).

point will be located about one-third of the way back from that small portion of the hull in the water. In other words, your boat may pivot about a point aft of midships.

To execute a turn, follow these steps:

1. Be sure the path is clear ahead, and you will not be moving into the path of another boat.

2. Turn the wheel in the desired direction of the turn, beginning the turn gently. The boat will heel, and the keel will help carve the turn. The more keel in the water, the sharper the turn you can execute.

3. Be aware that your boat will slip sideways somewhat. If you are planing on the flatter aft section of the hull, the boat will slip more.

4. Sharpen your turn as you proceed. The boat will heel more, and the turn and slip will become more pronounced.

5. If you begin the turn with the boat planing, try to keep it on a plane. The process of turning naturally reduces boat speed through the water, increasing the chance of coming off a plane.

6. As you approach your new desired heading, reduce the turn gradually so that your boat will settle in on the new course and not oversteer.

As we saw in Chapter 3, a boat has less of a grip on the water than a car has on the road. The friction that holds the car in place isn't available to a boat on the water. Therefore a boat will tend to slip in a turn, similar to a car skidding on sand or ice. How well a boat tracks through a turn is highly dependent upon the hull design. If the boat stays on a plane, it may skid considerably. This is often the case with modified-V hulls, because when on plane, their sharper, better-tracking forward sections are out of the water.

A Word of Caution

If you suddenly reduce throttle while entering a turn or turn too sharply, your boat may come off plane, possibly initiating an undesirable chain of events:

1. As your boat comes off plane, the pivot point will move rapidly from aft of midships toward the bow.

Boats are designed so that they naturally lean into a turn. This allows the hull to carve the turn and maintain better control.

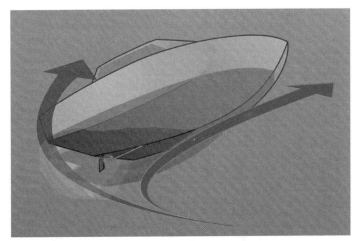

Even though the keel will carve a path through the water, the boat will skid considerably as it turns. The flatter aft portions of the hull are particularly vulnerable to skidding.

2. This shift will cause your boat to spin around the new pivot point. This is called *bow steering*.

3. The boat will slow suddenly and sit lower in the water, especially the stern.

4. You now face the possibility of being swamped. Your boat has slowed substantially, but your boat wake will continue moving forward. If the wake catches up with your stern, you could be deluged with water. You may even be broadsided by your wake if your boat spun out in the turn.

To avoid this situation, turn only as sharply as the plane can sustain, or enter the turn at displacement speed. If you choose to stay on plane, do not reduce the throttle too much before entering

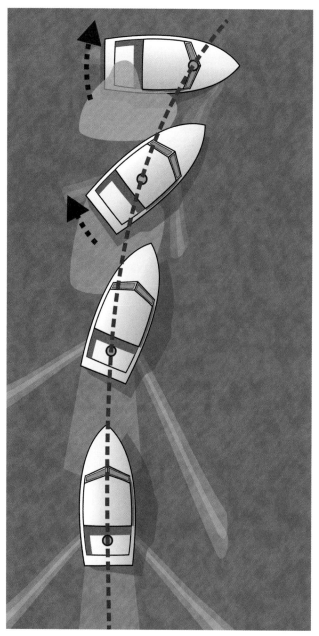

There is always the risk that the boat will come off plane in a sharp turn. If this happens, the pivot point will shift rapidly from near the stern toward the bow. This means that all of the momentum of the boat is converted into pushing the stern out in a skid. You also risk being swamped by your own wake as it catches up.

the turn. During the process of turning, your boat's speed through the water naturally decreases as your boat's momentum is diverted into the turn. You can continue to plane throughout the turn by setting a wide enough turn radius. If you feel the boat dropping off plane, straighten the wheel a bit and add some throttle—assuming you have the space to do so safely.

If you must come off plane, try to slow down as gradually as possible to minimize your wake. You need to allow time for your wake to dissipate somewhat before it catches up with you. This is true whether you are going straight or negotiating a turn. If you drop off a plane too rapidly, your stern will drop at the very time your wave overtakes the boat. Your cockpit could be swamped by a wall of water.

Stopping abruptly is not a good idea. When coming off a plane your stern will drop. If there's a large wake coming up behind you, you could be swamped. To avoid this, slow your boat gradually, giving the wave an opportunity to dissipate.

CHAPTER 8

Understanding Waves

Now that you've left the confines of a harbor and you're out on the open water, it's time to face the inevitable. Sooner or later, you're going to have to deal with waves. Before we address the techniques and maneuvers that will help you negotiate waves (Chapter 9), let's take a moment to see how they work.

HOW WAVES ARE FORMED

Wind blowing over the water creates friction. The friction causes the water to be pushed by the wind, forming ripples. As the wind continues to blow—over time and over distance—the ripples develop into waves, which will continue to build and move with the direction of the wind that formed them.

WAVE TERMINOLOGY

- Crest—the peak of a wave
- Trough—the hollow between crests
- Wavelength—the distance from one crest to another

- Wave height—the height from the trough to the crest
- Wave period—the length of time between passing crests

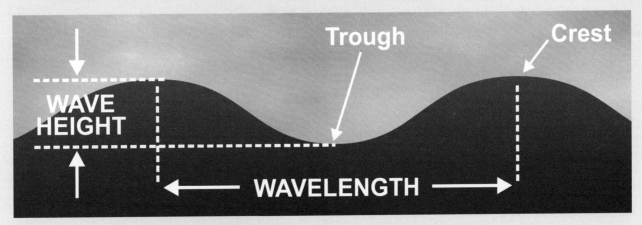

Boat Handling beyond the Harbor

The fundamental characteristics of waves—their height, speed, and wavelength—depend on three factors:

1. Strength of the wind
2. *Fetch*—the distance over which the wind is making contact with the water
3. Amount of time the wind has been blowing

Life Cycle of Waves

Near their point of origin, waves are closely bunched by the wind that created them. The farther downwind you travel across windswept water, the higher the waves become. This is because the fetch progressively increases. For example: on a windy day, the downwind (leeward) end of a bay will have bigger waves than the upwind (windward) end. The longer the wind blows, the larger the waves will become.

Just as time is a factor in building waves, it also takes time for waves to subside after the wind abates. (This why seas are sometimes rough the day after a storm.) As waves move out and away from the wind, they spread farther apart, their height diminishes, and they tend to settle into regular, smooth shapes called swells, which can travel hundreds or even thousands of miles.

Swells will dissipate over time. If, however, swells reach shore before they have a chance to dissipate, the waves will begin to change shape once again. As the water becomes shallower, the waves will grow in height, and become more tightly bunched and steeper, and eventually they'll break.

Wave Shapes

Wave shapes fall into two categories: cycloidal waves and trochoidal waves.

CYCLOIDAL WAVES

When the wind kicks up and waves begin forming, their shape is *cycloidal*. The wind forms a gradual slope on the windward side of the wave, while the

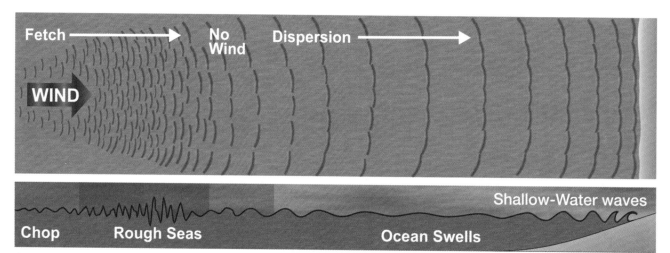

Local winds produce choppy, tightly spaced waves; downwind, the increasing fetch causes these waves to become steeper and more dense, creating rough seas. Farther away, as the wind abates, the waves spread out and become more regular in shape; they then disperse across the ocean as swells.

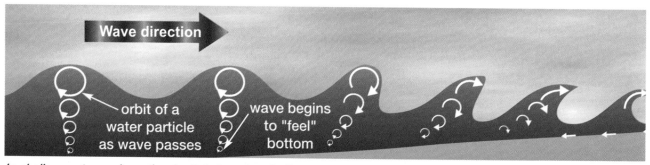

In shallow waters, where the depth is less than half a wavelength, waves begin to bunch together, and the crests begin to overtake the troughs. This causes breaking waves.

lee side has a steeper slope. As the wind grows and the waves build, sharp crests form. This is called *chop*. As the wind continues to increase, these crests eventually become so thin that they are blown along as white, foamy, aerated water. These are called *whitecaps*. If the crest becomes too steep, it will fall forward as a breaking sea. Thus a cycloidal wave takes on progressive characteristics from chop to whitecap to breaking sea. Cycloidal waves have wavelengths of less than 100 feet between crests. A cycloidal wave is more dangerous than a trochoidal wave because its sharp face presents a wall of water to any boat it strikes. These waves can become even more dangerous if they break over a boat. When traveling with the wind, the back of a cycloidal wave can be deceptive; it can seem smooth until the unwary boater finds his boat going over the crest and into the void on the steep front face.

Trochoidal Waves

As the wind abates, the waves will take on a trochoidal shape. Trochoidal waves are long and rounded, with wavelengths up to 1,000 feet. They can be quite large (ten- to twenty-foot swells are common), but they're well-spaced and easy to deal with. In deep water, swells will retain a regular and smooth shape. Thus, your motion afloat will be a regular pattern of rising and falling. As these waves approach the shallow waters of the coast, however, friction with the seabed transforms them into cycloidal waves again.

Although trochoidal waves travel long distances, the individual water molecules within the waves do not. In other words, a trochoidal wave is similar to "the wave" created by an audience at a sporting event. As the members of the audience raise and lower their hands or cards, the "wave" passes by; the individual audience members never leave their seats, but the wave progresses around the stadium.

Trochoidal waves. Trochoidal is from the Greek trochos, meaning wheel.

ROGUE WAVES

Rogue waves—abnormally large waves that appear without warning—have caused marine accidents both at sea and along exposed coastlines. While rare, they have been reported during all sorts of weather, including calm seas.

It is believed that rogue waves (also called *freak waves*) form when several waves traveling in different directions end up at the same location at the same time and combine into a single wave or group of waves. Heights up to 100 feet have been recorded, although their lifespan is short—mere minutes.

Because of their unpredictability, you can only remain vigilant, keep a good lookout, and be prepared. If you see an unusually large wave approaching, immediately don life jackets, close hatches, and point your boat into the wave.

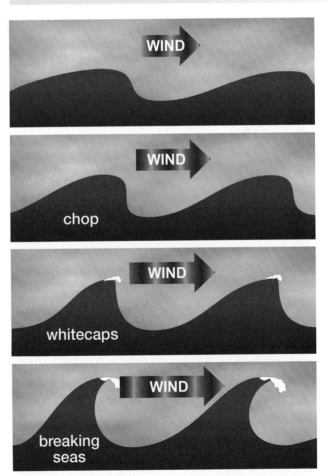

Cycloidal waves. These waves begin as chop, develop into whitecaps, and eventually form breaking seas.

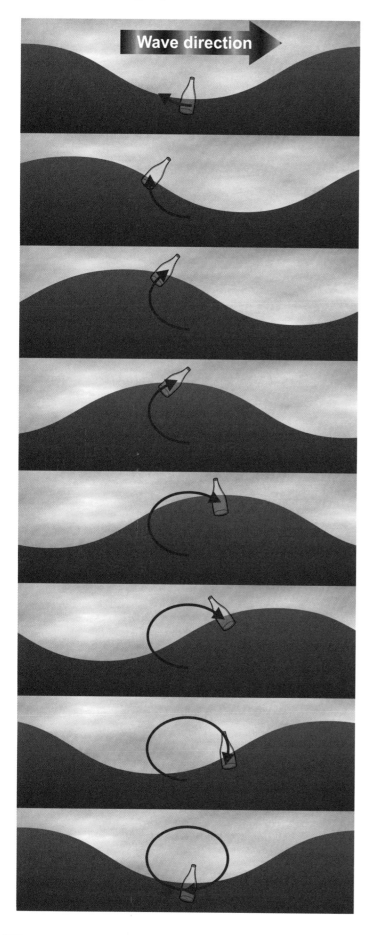

Wave direction

Within a trochoidal wave, the individual water molecules follow a circular path, which creates the wheel-like shape of the wave. Aside from that circular motion, however, the individual water molecules will not travel with the wave. This phenomenon can be demonstrated by watching the path of a bottle floating in the water as a wave passes—note that the bottle does not travel with the wave. For that reason alone, trochoidal waves are easier to deal with in a powerboat.

HOW WAVES INTERACT
Wave Reflections

When a wave contacts a steep shoreline, the kinetic energy of the wave rebounds out to sea, causing *reflected waves.* This results in a composite of incoming and outgoing waves near shore. When an incoming wave crest meets an outgoing wave crest, the resulting crests can be as much as twice the height of the incoming wave. When a trough coincides with a crest, the incoming wave will be reduced.

When a wave approaches a steep shoreline at an angle, however, it is reflected back much like a ball striking a floor, at an equal and opposite angle. Now, incoming waves meet the outgoing waves at an angle. Crests along one incoming wave front will meet outgoing crests only at points of intersection, not along the entire line. This results in waves that build like pyramids.

Shorelines are rarely straight, so reflected waves typically come from multiple directions at once, with the likelihood and severity of pyramidal waves becoming even more pronounced. This leads to confused seas near shore. Pyramidal waves can be particularly difficult to maneuver through.

The degree to which waves will reflect is directly related to the shape of the shoreline itself. A vertical wall, such as a cliff, is an excellent reflector. Almost all of the wave energy that strikes a cliff will be reflected back out. A gently sloping beach, on the other hand, will dissipate much of a wave's energy, generating little or no reflected wave

Wave Refraction

When waves approach a gently sloping shoreline at an angle, the part of each wavefront nearer to shore will be traveling in shallower water than the rest of

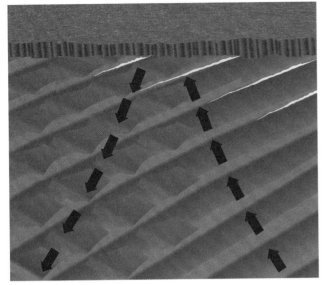

As waves approach shore they are reflected back out to sea. The amount of reflection depends upon the steepness of the shoreline. A vertical bluff will reflect almost all of the wave energy, while a shallow beach will absorb much of it).

Pyramidal waves are formed when incoming and outgoing waves meet at an angle. The resultant peaks can be quite steep.

the wave front. As a result, the shallower part will be slowed, while the rest of the wave advances unabated. This difference in speed will cause the wave to turn, and thus to approach and break more parallel with the shore. This is why someone on a beach around the corner from a point may find waves approaching nearly head-on, even though the wave originated from an entirely different direction.

These are known as *refracted waves.*

These effects can be felt some distance from shore, and reflections from an irregular shoreline only serve to further confuse the seas. For instance, you may encounter significantly rough water in the lee of a small island. This happens when waves are refracted around both sides of an island and rejoin on the lee side from opposing directions. When the two wave trains come together at an angle, they can form steep pyramidal waves.

Wave Trains

The interaction of various waves and reflections can cause patterns, called *wave trains,* to form. These patterns are difficult to detect, and without prolonged observation, may seem like random, totally confused wave action.

Wave trains are groups consisting of seven to ten waves. These groups tend to have a repeating

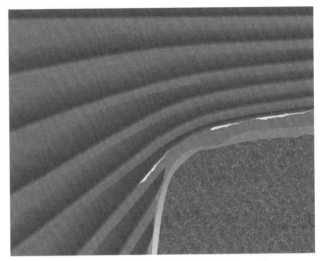

As waves approach a bend in the shoreline, those near the point are slowed while those farther out are not. The result is that the waves wrap around the point.

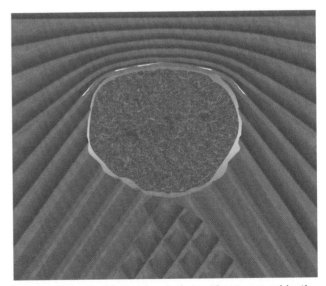

When waves pass an island, they refract around both sides and rejoin on the lee side. The interaction there can cause rough seas with pyramidal peaks.

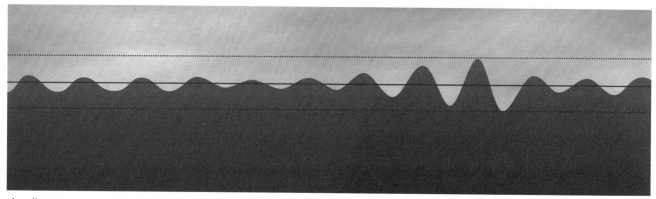

As direct waves and multiple wave reflections interact, they generate irregular patterns. Often, groups of three large waves will form within a sequence of 10 waves. (The numbers, of course, will vary with conditions.) Try to plan your maneuvers within the calmer segments of the pattern.

Powerful and dangerous, these pyramidal waves are formed by the interaction of crossing wave patterns. By all means maneuver around them. (Courtesy Dag Pike)

pattern: out of the ten or so waves within each group, some will be significantly higher than the rest. Often these higher waves bunch together in groups of three, with the third wave of each group tending to be the largest. Quite often, the waves following the tallest of the three are the shortest. Your job as helmsman is to learn to read these waves. Clearly, you will want to execute your maneuvers over the shortest waves, but you'll likely have to take other waves into account at the same time. Be prepared to adapt your plan if pyramidal waves form.

Current–Wave Interaction

Waves are created by winds, but they can be amplified by currents. When the wind and the current are opposed, the current slows the forward motion of the base of the wave, making the wave steeper and causing it to break earlier. This often results in

closely spaced, steep standing waves of great height that represent a real danger to boaters. You'll see this effect especially in harbors, channels, and bays where tidal currents are prevalent.

Standing waves are waves that don't appear to be moving. Their steep peaks seem to stay in one spot, followed by deep troughs, forming a "roller coaster" surface for the approaching boater. Often, trains of standing waves will form, which can cause particularly treacherous conditions in inlets and narrow channels (see Chapter 10).

Effects of Land

The shape and characteristics of shorelines can have a profound effect on wind and waves. For example, shorelines often will funnel wind, increasing its speed. This can focus waves in an unexpected direction or build waves to dangerous heights in a progressively constricting passage. A good example of this can be found in Buzzards Bay between the southeast coast of mainland Massachusetts and Cape Cod. The prevailing winds come from the southwest during the summer months. Winds are accelerated by the constricting bay in the approaches to the southern end of the Cape Cod Canal. The faster winds add to the increasing fetch in the upper bay, leading to some really choppy seas, particularly in late afternoon after the winds have been blowing all day.

Land can also provide a false sense of security. Winds may be deceptively calm in the lee of land, but a short trip away from the shore could expose your boat to unexpected winds and waves. It is not uncommon to find wind conditions much more severe at sea than on nearby land, so you should rely

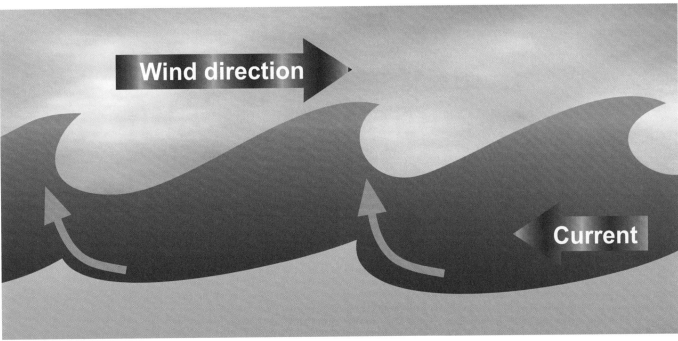

When winds oppose currents, the waves tend to steepen. Underwater irregularities can cause these waves to build far beyond what you might expect.

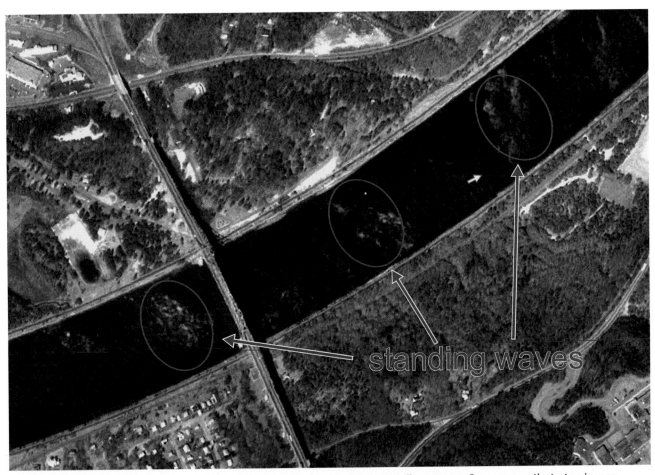

The additive forces of opposing winds and currents tend to form standing waves (i.e., waves that stay in one place). Standing waves are often found in inlets, narrow channels, and canals (this example is the Cape Cod Canal), and they can be very dangerous if closely spaced. (Courtesy Maptech)

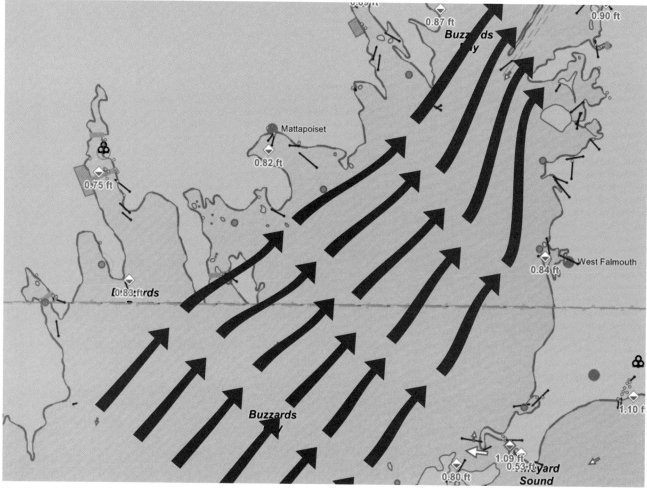

A narrowing bay will cause winds to accelerate.

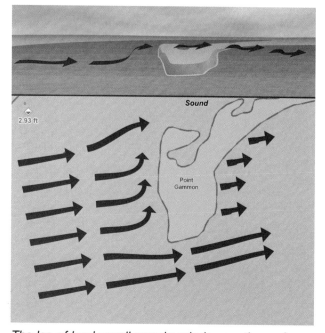

The lee of land usually masks winds near the surface. Winds may be sent aloft by interaction with the land or slowed by friction.

upon marine forecasts over local weather reports. Local knowledge can also be invaluable—keep your ears open and ask questions at your marina.

SEA STATE
Beaufort Scale

In 1806, Sir Francis Beaufort, an admiral in the British Navy, created the Beaufort Wind Force Scale to describe the sea in all its various states. Initially, the scale listed a set of qualitative, observable conditions and described how a naval vessel would respond under those conditions. The observable conditions, numbered from 0 to 12, ranged from "just sufficient to give steerage" to "that which no canvas could withstand." In 1946, the International Meteorological Committee revised the Beaufort Scale to become the Beaufort Wind Speed Scale, defining the values according to wind speed and providing a more quantitative measure.

THE BEAUFORT WIND SPEED SCALE

FORCE	WIND SPEED (KNOTS)	WAVE HEIGHT (FEET)	DESCRIPTION	OBSERVABLE CONDITIONS
0	< 1	–	Calm	Sea like a mirror.
1	1–3	¼	Light air	Ripples with the appearance of scales, but without foam crest.
2	4–6	½–1	Light breeze	Small wavelets, still short but more pronounced; crests have a glassy appearance and do not break.
3	7–10	2–3	Gentle breeze	Large wavelets; crests begin to break; have foamy or glassy appearance; perhaps, scattered white horses (whitecaps).
4	11–16	3½–5	Moderate breeze	Small waves becoming longer; fairly frequent white horses.
5	17–21	6–8½	Fresh breeze	Moderate waves taking a more pronounced long form; many white horses are formed, chance of some spray.
6	22–27	9½–13	Strong breeze	Large waves begin to form; the white foam crests are more extensive everywhere, probably some spray.
7	28–33	13½–19	Near gale	Sea heaps up and white foam from breaking waves begins to be blown in streaks along the direction of the wind.
8	34–40	18–25	Gale	Moderately high waves of greater length; edges of crests begin to break into the spindrift; the foam is blown in well-marked streaks along the direction of the wind.
9	41–47	23–32	Strong gale	High waves; dense streaks of foam along the direction of the wind; crests of waves begin to topple, tumble and roll over; spray may affect visibility.
10	48–55	29–41	Storm	Very high waves with long overhanging crests; the resulting foam in great patches is blown in dense white streaks along the direction of the wind; on the whole, the surface of the sea takes a white appearance, the tumbling of the sea becomes heavy and shock-like; visibility affected.
11	55–63	37–52	Violent storm	Exceptionally high waves (small- and medium-sized ships might be lost to view behind the waves); the sea is completely covered with long white patches of foam lying along the direction of the wind; everywhere the edges of the wave crests are blown into froth; visibility affected.
12	63–71	45+	Hurricane	The air is filled with foam and spray, and the sea is completely white; visibility is extremely affected.

In the United States, small craft advisories are issued for anticipated winds of force 6 or 7. Gale warnings are issued for winds of force 8 or 9, and storm warnings for force 10 or 11. (A tropical storm warning is issued for winds from force 8 to 11 if they are related to a hurricane or other tropical cyclone.) Anything stronger results in a hurricane warning.

PIERSON–MOSKOWITZ SEA SPECTRUM (SEA STATE TABLE)

WIND SPEED (KTS)	SEA STATE	SIGNIFICANT WAVE (FT)	SIGNIFICANT RANGE OF PERIODS (SEC)	AVERAGE PERIOD (SEC)	AVERAGE LENGTH OF WAVES (FT)
3	0	<.5	<.5–1	0.5	1.5
4	0	<.5	.5–1	1	2
5	1	0.5	1–2.5	1.5	9.5
7	1	1	1–3.5	2	13
8	1	1	1–4	2	16
9	2	1.5	1.5–4	2.5	20
10	2	2	1.5–5	3	26
11	2.5	2.5	1.5–5.5	3	33
13	2.5	3	2–6	3.5	39.5
14	3	3.5	2–6.5	3.5	46
15	3	4	2–7	4	52.5
16	3.5	4.5	2.5–7	4	59
17	3.5	5	2.5–7.5	4.5	65.5
18	4	6	2.5–8.5	5	79
19	4	7	3–9	5	92
20	4	7.5	3–9.5	5.5	99
21	5	8	3–10	5.5	105
22	5	9	3.5–10.5	6	118
23	5	10	3.5–11	6	131.5
25	5	12	4–12	7	157.5
27	6	14	4–13	7.5	184
29	6	16	4.5–13.5	8	210
31	6	18	4.5–14.5	8.5	236.5
33	6	20	5–15.5	9	262.5
37	7	25	5.5–17	10	328.5
40	7	30	6–19	11	394
43	7	35	6.5–21	12	460
46	7	40	7–22	12.5	525.5
49	8	45	7.5–23	13	591
52	8	50	7.5–24	14	566
54	8	55	8–25.5	14.5	722.5
57	8	60	8.5–26.5	15	788
61	9	70	9–28.5	16.5	920
65	9	80	10–30.5	17.5	1099
69	9	90	10.5–32.5	18.5	1182

Source: U.S. Army Transportation Center, Fort Eustis, Virginia.

Pierson—Moskowitz Sea Spectrum

Oceanographers have long sought to understand the relationship between wind and wave conditions. Perhaps the simplest model was proposed by Willard J. Pierson and Lionel Moskowitz in 1964. Pierson and Moskowitz worked on the assumption that if the wind blew steadily for a long time over a large area, the waves would eventually come into a state of equilibrium with the wind. They defined this as a fully developed sea.

The table opposite shows the relationship between wind speed and sea state in an ocean setting, including wave heights and lengths and the time intervals between waves.

CHAPTER 9

Underway in Waves

It is a wise boater who understands that heavy seas are better observed from shore than from a tossing boat. Nonetheless, there may be times when you won't have that option. You may depart on a calm, sunny day, only to have a strong wind come up unexpectedly, or you may be caught in a storm during an extended offshore cruise.

Even sea conditions that most boaters would classify as moderate can impact boat handling. A one- to two-foot chop may present little more than speed bumps to a 40-foot cruiser, but it'll seem like high seas to a dinghy. Depending upon the size of the waves, how you are approaching them, and what type of boat you have, your experience could range anywhere from uncomfortable to dangerous. As seas build to whitecaps, most boaters should take note. When waves begin to break in open water, everyone should take evasive action.

QUICK TIP

Use trim tabs (down on the windward side; up on leeward) to help maintain an even keel. Boats with twin drives can use differential power settings to help hold course.

DEALING WITH WAVES
Taking Waves Head-On

The wind smoothes the windward side of a wave and causes the lee side to be sharper as the crest is bent over. Waves generally break when the angle at the wave peak falls below about 120°. If you are driving into the wind in these conditions, and if the waves are high enough, you may find yourself driving your boat into a wall of water. Depending upon the shape of your hull, your bow may cut through the waves, or it may be pounded by the waves.

For the smoothest ride possible, maneuver your bow so it cuts through the waves rather than rides over them (thus exposing the flatter aft sections to the full force of the waves). Ideally your bow will cut through the wave fronts and clear a path for the rest of the boat.

If you are operating with your drive trimmed out for speed, you'll want to trim it in a bit to lower the bow. If you trim in too far, however, you run the risk of submerging the bow. You should also go slowly because you are, in effect, colliding with the waves. Take it easy.

As the waves become higher, your strategies will change a bit. You'll want the bow to go over— not through—the larger waves, and you'll want to do so as smoothly as possible.

Meeting waves head-on can cause severe pitching. This is not only uncomfortable but could be dangerous, too.

If you crest a sharp wave with too much speed, your bow will be exposed to the full force of the wind. If the wind is strong enough it could push the bow aside.

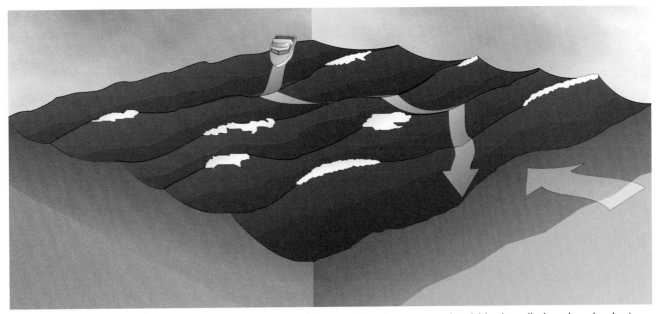

Since waves vary in size, and wave fronts are irregular along their faces, you should look well ahead and select your path to take advantage of the most favorable seas.

As your bow rides high over the oncoming wave, watch out for two situations—neither of which is particularly good. First, your exposed bow presents a lot of windage to the same force that's creating the waves. This makes your bow susceptible to being pushed aside. Second, your boat will very likely drop sharply into the trough on the backside of the wave, and the bow could dig into the next wave. (Again, the severity will depend on the height of the wave.) We'll discuss strategies for each of the situations below.

Through all of this, your mission is to keep the boat as close to level as you can under the prevailing conditions.

Taking Waves at an Angle

Locally generated waves can have short wavelengths, meaning you will go quickly from one wave crest to the next. To make matters worse, as you move toward the waves, the waves are also moving toward you, thus increasing the speed of impact with the steep wavefronts. Obviously, you will want to slow down.

Rather than take these waves head-on, it is bet-

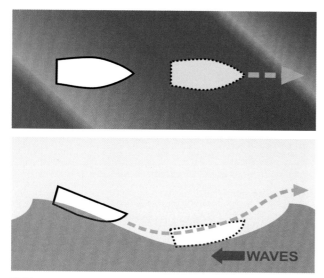

Taking waves at an angle rather than head-on effectively spreads out the distance between crests. This also lessens the apparent slope of the oncoming wave.

Throttle management is a full-time job in rough seas. As you approach an oncoming wave, throttle back to minimize the impact. As you make contact, increase the throttle to help lift the bow over the wave. As you crest the wave, cut the throttle back to prevent over-revving the engines and avoid going airborne. On the windward side, keep the throttle down to avoid pushing the bow into the trough. As soon as the bow bottoms out, add throttle to raise the bow and make progress toward the next wave.

ter to meet them at an angle. This tactic effectively increases the time and distance between crests and reduces the apparent slope as you approach each wave.

WHAT IS THE RIGHT ANGLE?

While the specific angle depends on the boat, a good starting point is about 30°–45° from the head-on approach. At an angle of 45°, you will have increased the effective spacing between wave crests by about 40%. Be aware, however, that as you approach on an angle, the wave's tendency will be to push your bow and turn the boat parallel with the wave crest. If this were to happen with large seas, you could be rolled over by broadside waves. Strive to maintain firm control over the bow.

Your strategy should be as follows:

1. Gradually adjust your course angle away from the wavefronts until you feel the crests prying at your bow and compromising your control.

2. At this point, turn more directly into the waves until you feel you again have positive control of the helm.

3. Your path needn't be a straight line. Steer at an angle through each trough and up each wavefront, then turn toward the wind as you reach the crest and come down the backside. When you reach the trough, steer at an angle once again.

4. Use your throttle. Speed up to help the bow up and over the wavefront, then immediately throttle back as the bow crests the wave so you don't go down the back side too fast.

5. Your path will be dictated by the waves. If your destination is directly into the wind, tack back and forth across the waves, much as you would in a sailboat beating into the wind. This will lengthen your trip, but will be safer and more comfortable than pounding directly into the wave fronts.

Losing control of your bow is your biggest danger, for it can quickly lead to a broach and capsize. In heavy conditions, where even a 15° approach would expose too much of the boat to the wind or waves, steer quickly to address the waves head-on. Slow down as you approach oncoming waves to reduce the impact, to give the bow a chance to rise up over it, and to minimize exposing the bottom of the boat to the wind. On some boats it is helpful to briefly apply power *just* before impact, as this will help lift the bow up and over the wave. As soon as you have done that, reduce power again so that your propeller(s) are not running free in foam or air as the stern is lifted by the wave crest. When the stern is back in solid water, apply power to provide steerage for your next maneuver. Although quick throttle changes are necessary, try to make them smooth as well.

This process may be repeated hundreds of times in an hour. It's very stressful and tiring. That's why you need to rotate helmsmen, if possible. As the storm builds, you may want to save your best helmsman for the worst conditions. In any event, this is not a time for an inexperienced helmsman or someone not familiar with how your boat handles.

Running Parallel to the Waves

When you are running parallel to the waves, you are in a *beam sea*. At this angle, you will roll with the waves, and the amount of roll can be considerable. In moderate seas, the rolling motion can be uncomfortable. If the waves become steep, however, the roll can become quite dangerous. Capsizing is a distinct possibility. Some boats, such as round-bottomed trawlers, will begin to develop a roll pattern, which, as it is reinforced by each successive wave, will eventually result in a capsizing.

If a beam sea rears up while you're en route to a destination, don't despair. There are some techniques to help you avoid the rolling effects of a beam sea while still pursuing your destination. Essentially, you'll zig-zag your way there by heading into the waves and then turning with the waves. We'll begin this example by turning into the waves.

1. Turn the wheel hard toward the oncoming wave and give the throttle a quick burst of power. Ideally, you should take the wave at a 45° angle.

2. Add a little more throttle until you rise over the wave.

3. You should crest one or two additional waves on this same course. Seek out the low spot on each wave and steer for it.

4. After zigging into a few waves, you'll want to zag with a following sea. Don't attempt this turn

The narrower the boat's beam, the more susceptible it is to being rolled when running parallel to the waves.

until you encounter a relatively low wave. As soon as you've cleared the low wave and your stern is sitting in the solid water, turn sharply toward the retreating low wave, add a brief burst of power to come about, and take the wave at an angle. (Under any other circumstances you would avoid going over a wave crest in a following sea, because it's difficult to know how far or how steeply the wavefront drops. In this case, however, you'll know what the wavefront looks like because you've just traversed it.)

5. Advance most of the way up the backside of the next downwind wave, then turn sharply into the oncoming waves again, and repeat the process. By taking two or three waves into the wind and only one downwind, you will maintain a nearly parallel course.

Running with the Waves

Running with the waves may seem to be a better, more benign choice because you are moving with the wind and waves instead of into them. But this apparent calm can be deceiving.

Boat Handling beyond the Harbor

You will now be riding on the smooth side of the wave. If you advance up and over the back of a wave crest, you drop down the steep downhill slope of the wavefront and into the trough. If the wave is large enough, your bow may dig into the trough, allowing the wave you've just crossed to catch up. There are several risks involved with this situation:

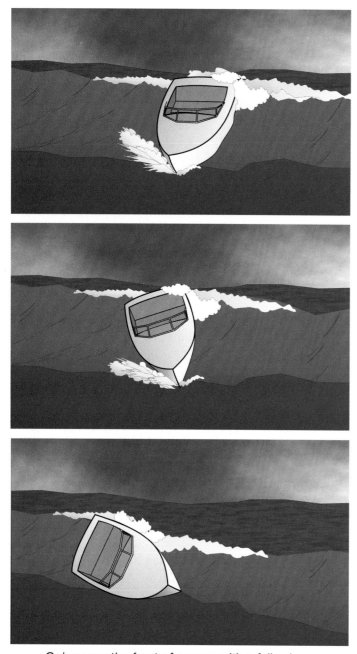

Going over the front of a wave with a following sea can be dangerous. This sequence shows how a broach can occur: the bow digs in after reaching the bottom of the wave (top); the wave just crossed pushes your quarter aside (center); and the wave rolls the boat (bottom). Keep the stern square to the following seas to prevent this.

- As the wave catches up to the stern, it could spill over the transom and fill the cockpit.

- If the wave strikes the aft quarter on either side, the boat could be pushed sideways. If you're pushed so far that your beam faces the wave, you could capsize.

- The approaching wave could even catch the stern and flip it over the bow in a disaster called *pitchpoling*. This is the most dangerous capsize, but usually only happens in the most extreme sea conditions.

All of these situations are extremely dangerous; any one of them could sink the boat and seriously injure its passengers. Thus running with the waves can be even more dangerous than heading into them.

Your best strategy for running with the waves is to position yourself on the back of a wave and stay there.

- As the seas build, waves tend to become irregular rather than continuous fronts. Some waves will converge to form larger sets of waves. Pick an area of smaller waves to ride on.

- Use your throttle to match your speed to the waves.

(continued on page 136)

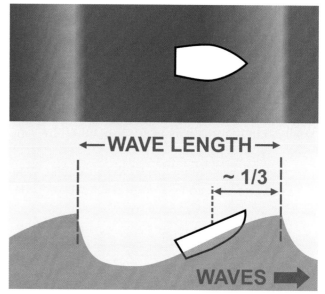

The safest spot in a following sea is about one-third of the way back from the crest. Adjusting your speed to ride the wave at that position gives you the best chance of staying perpendicular to the wave.

134

HANDLING BOAT WAKES

Boat wakes can produce extremely sharp waves. Fortunately, you will only have to cross one or two of them, and they usually dissipate quickly as they move away from the boat that created them.

If the boat creating the wake is coming toward you on an opposite course, the angle of its wake will likely be too sharp to take without a course adjustment. Follow the steps below to minimize the impact of the wake on your boat.

1. Position yourself as far away from the path of the other boat as is safely possible. This alone minimizes the impact.

2. Turn into the wake just before you reach it, take it at a 45° angle, and reduce throttle. (This means your turn will be executed after the other boat has passed.)

3. Once you've crossed the wake, turn back to your original course.

4. Remember that you are creating a wake as you pass by, so your wake presents a problem for the other boat as well. Reduce your speed near other boats to minimize your wake.

If you are following a boat that is creating a large wake, overtaking can be a challenge. If you are outside the wake, your task will be simpler. Simply accelerate enough to stay ahead of the wake while observing the rules of the road as the give-way vessel.

If you are within the cone of the other boat's wake, you will need to cross out of it:

1. Turn out and away from the other boat's path at about 45°. The water within the cone will be flatter than the surrounding seas, but it may be somewhat aerated. This will reduce the effectiveness of your propeller(s).

2. Accelerate to reach the wake, reduce power a bit to cross, then resume course after you've crossed the wake.

3. Remember that as you overtake the vessel in front of you, your wake may cause problems for the other boat. Minimize the effects of your wake: keep your speed at the minimum needed to overtake the boat and position yourself as far away as practical from it.

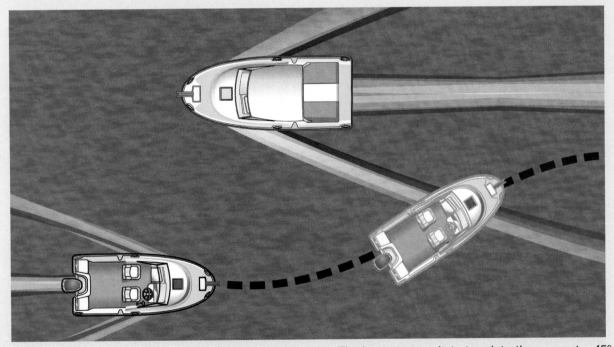

As another boat passes, you will be exposed to its wake. The best strategy is to turn into the wave at a 45° angle, then resume your course.

(continued from page 134)

- Find a reasonably stable wave and maneuver your boat about one-third of a wavelength back from the wave crest ahead. This position will keep you reasonably far from the wavefront behind you while also giving you some maneuvering room to make sure you don't go over the top of the wave in front. Continually adjust your throttle and wheel to maintain a favorable position.

- Make sure your trim tabs are fully up (not deployed). If they are deployed, the following sea can push the stern downward.

- Keep the stern square to the waves, especially if you must go over a wave. This will minimize the chance of being broached by the wave directly behind you.

HEAVY-WEATHER TACTICS

If you do enough boating, eventually you will encounter heavy weather. Prepare for this inevitability by knowing your boat and its limitations. To the extent possible, become familiar with how your boat responds to waves.

- What are the boat's heeling motions with seas from various angles?

- Does the bow lift over waves, slice through them, or dig in?

- Do waves from the bow quarter turn the boat from its course?

- Do waves from astern lift the stern, turn it around, or enter the aft cockpit?

- How responsive is your boat to your adjustments in steering and throttle?

The only way to know these things is to have experience in a wide variety of lesser conditions. Until you've gained that level of experience, your boating excursions should be confined to waters within easy reach of harbor.

Hedging Your Bets

Monitor weather radio to stay current on any developing storms or fronts. If a storm is reported, determine where it is, where it's going, and how quickly it's moving. Then do some plotting. If you have the ability to get to a safe harbor before the weather hits, do it.

Keep in mind, however, that the most dangerous conditions in a storm are generally found in the shallow water near shore. Here the shallow depths force waves to break; the wave troughs decrease the water depth, potentially exposing your boat to the bottom; and you run the risk of being grounded, then pounded by waves. If you must run an inlet or cross a bar to reach a safe harbor, do so only if you're certain you can do it safely. Otherwise, ride out the storm at sea.

Keep in mind that storms can bring major changes in wind direction. What may have been safe shelter in the lee of land can suddenly become dangerous water to windward of a lee shore on the backside of the storm. Always keep a weather eye and stay tuned to NOAA weather radio and other weather forecasts.

Be Prepared

If you can't get to shore in time, prepare yourself for heavy weather. You'll need to remain steadfastly at the helm even during the worst moments of the storm.

PLANING BOATS AND STORMS

Most coastal planing-hull boats are relatively small, light, and not designed for heavy seas. If they have cabins, the windows, ports, and hatches do not have reinforced fixtures and heavy glass to withstand pounding seas. They're also unlikely to have enough freeboard to prevent taking on water, or adequate scuppers (drains) to shed water once it's onboard. So, if you find yourself in one of these boats with a storm approaching, your only option may be to make a run for it.

At some point, however, worsening seas will force any planing boat to slow down and come off plane. In that case, the best response is to go as slowly as possible while maintaining steerage.

You can tell a great deal about approaching weather by staying alert to your surroundings. If you see a squall approaching, head for safety. (Courtesy NOAA)

Storm Preparation Checklist

- ☐ All crew must wear life jackets.
- ☐ Put on foul-weather gear.
- ☐ Anyone not below should wear a safety harness.
- ☐ Check the VHF radio and make sure at least one other crew member knows how to use it.
- ☐ Have a throwable PFD and/or other man-overboard recovery gear at the ready.
- ☐ Close and secure all hatches, and install protective covers if available.
- ☐ Lash down everything aboard, and stow everything below.
- ☐ Reduce the boat's windage by removing unnecessary canvas and objects abovedecks.
- ☐ Pump the bilges dry, and continue pumping as necessary.
- ☐ Prepare a sea anchor.
- ☐ If you carry a life raft, ensure that it is ready for deployment and that you have everything you need in your ditch bag.
- ☐ If the weather persists, develop a rotation of assignments at the helm.

Pull out your charts and find your location. Although it's often not feasible, it's certainly helpful to know the waters you'll be in when the storm hits. What kind of waves can you expect? Where are the wind funneling effects? Where are breaking seas most likely? Where are hazards such as bars, points, shoals, shallows, rocks, and wrecks?

Develop a plan of where to head. Try to get a handle on the larger picture of the region and visualize the advancing storm to determine your strategy. There is a good chance that at some point you will need to abandon your destination navigation in favor of avoidance navigation (i.e., steering the best course to deal with the waves). If you cannot make safe harbor, head for deep water. Check weather conditions regularly.

Check your fuel supply with an eye toward riding out the storm under power. If you are likely to run low, you will need to plan for survival with the boat headed into the wind, using a drogue or sea anchor (see below). Of course, a severe storm shouldn't coincide with low fuel in the first place: this predicament is almost always the result of poor planning or carelessness.

Heaving-To

As conditions deteriorate to the limits of your boat's seakeeping ability, you may attempt heaving-to. This is a maneuver more common to sailboats, but it can be adapted for use by powerboats.

A sailboat heaves-to by backing the jib and lashing the rudder in the opposite direction. The windage of the jib turns the boat in one direction, while the action of the rudder does the opposite. The net result is little forward propulsion and a slow sideways slip to leeward.

Whereas the sailboat maneuver is passive, the powerboat version requires constant adjustment and attention to the helm. Use minimal throttle—just enough to maintain a heading about 10° to 25°

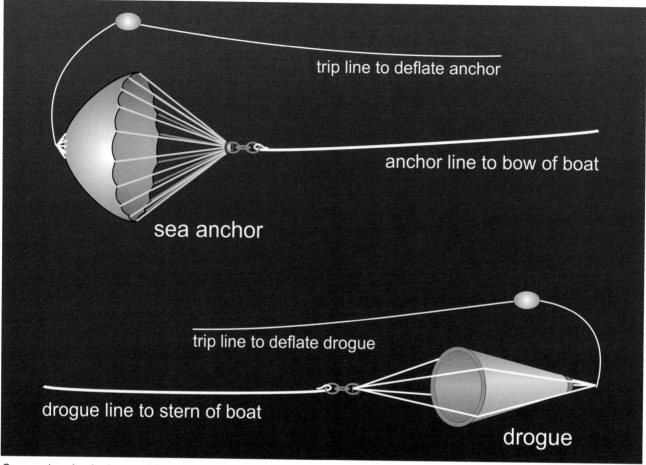

trip line to deflate anchor

anchor line to bow of boat

sea anchor

trip line to deflate drogue

drogue line to stern of boat

drogue

Sea anchor (top); drogue (above). The lines above each are release lines.

off the waves. (Slowing down also helps minimize the time that the propeller or rudder is out of the water when the boat is on a wave peak.) You are not trying to make forward progress; you are simply riding out the storm. Confirm that you have adequate room to leeward before attempting heaving-to, because you will be pushed downwind. Beware of wind gusts that may push your bow and be prepared to take immediate corrective action.

The last resort is lying ahull, which is just drifting. A typical sailboat has some amount of ballasted keel to help its stability, but a powerboat is more likely to be tossed around. To lie ahull, you need some help to keep the bow nominally heading into the wind, such as a sea anchor.

Using a Sea Anchor or Drogue

If you lose power, or power alone is not accomplishing the task, your only alternative is to deploy a sea anchor or drogue.

A sea anchor is basically an underwater drag chute. Deployed from the bow, the sea anchor fills with water and provides resistance as your boat is pushed backward by the wind. (If you don't have a sea anchor, a solid bucket tied to an anchor line might work in a pinch. If nothing else is available, tie anything you can to lines and deploy them from the bow.) Pay out the anchor line as far as possible, preferably more than 300 feet. Never deploy a sea anchor if you plan to attempt headway, since it will keep you from maneuvering, and you risk overrunning the line and fouling the propeller. You can recover the sea anchor by pulling on the release line attached to a float.

If you're powering with following seas but having trouble preventing your boat from going over the waves ahead, a drogue may help. Shaped like a funnel with a large opening toward the boat and a small hole at the other end, a drogue slows the boat and helps keep the bow facing downwind. Make sure the drogue line does not become fouled in your propeller.

CHAPTER 10

Transiting Inlets, Bars, and Narrow Passages

The vast majority of boaters spend their time in coastal waters. While these boaters are unlikely to experience the heavy seas that offshore cruisers sometimes face, most boaters will encounter perilous conditions that are unique to near-shore areas. Inlets, bars, and narrow passages are a challenging reality for the average coastal boater. The physical constraints of inlets and narrows cause the currents to accelerate through them, while also limiting space to maneuver. In tidal regions, large quantities of water transit these inlets and create strong currents and agitated water. These forces can also reshape the depth contours and form bars, rendering your charts unreliable.

To make matters worse, you may encounter wind in opposition to the current. This will cause waves to heighten and their spacing to shorten.

This chapter will provide you with a basic understanding of inlets, bars, and narrow passages and some essential tips to help you transit them. Nonetheless, when going through such conditions for the first time, it's a good idea to bring an experienced skipper along with you.

RUNNING AN INLET

Inlets provide boaters access to open water from sheltered bays, harbors, or rivers. Inlets are subject to tidal currents—often severe currents, particularly during maximum flood or ebb.

Sea breezes can compound the challenges of running an inlet. During the day, sea breezes can blow quite strongly through an inlet. The breezes abate at nightfall, then often reverse to land breezes

Tremendous amounts of tidal water course through narrow inlets. In this aerial photograph you can see significant currents and rough waters. (Courtesy Maptech)

Learn all you can about an inlet before you run it. Know which paths to take and which to avoid, and be well prepared to handle your boat in heavy seas. (Courtesy Maptech)

As a waterway narrows, the current flowing through it intensifies. This can have far-reaching effects. Note the lighter colored water flowing out of the inlet. This indicates a strong current. (Courtesy Maptech)

overnight. When sea breezes combine with incoming waves and meet an outgoing tide, large standing waves can form at the mouth of the inlet.

Know the Inlet

Before you enter or exit an inlet, especially an unfamiliar one, you'll need to learn all you can about the waterway and the present conditions. Ask yourself the following series of questions.

IS THE INLET TOO NARROW?

Narrow inlets tend to be more hazardous than wider ones. The narrower the inlet, the more constriction placed upon the water and the faster the water will flow. Also, a narrow inlet restricts your movement. If you can choose between a narrow inlet and a wider one, the wider will have a slower water flow as well as more maneuvering room.

WHAT IS THE PHASE OF THE TIDE?

Consult tide tables ahead of time, so you know what to expect and can plan your entry or exit for the best conditions. Onshore breezes prevail in the daytime. When combined with an outgoing tide, these breezes cause steep waves and shorter troughs. It might be better to wait for slack water when the current is at a minimum, or wait for an incoming tide so the current is flowing with the wind.

WHAT IS THE CURRENT LIKE?

Currents may not be evenly distributed throughout an inlet. Within a short distance, you could transit from relatively calm conditions to a fast flow. Currents may also flow in different directions. Eddies—areas where a current turns or even reverses itself—can pull you into a dangerous situation.

Local knowledge can help you make sense of an unfamiliar inlet. Talk with boaters who know the waters. Ask them what areas to avoid. Consult your charts as well. Look for any bottom contours that are likely to divert currents. In the accompanying photo chart, you can see where the currents have curved and carved channels through the sand below. You can expect the current to push you along these same paths.

WHAT ARE THE WAVE PATTERNS?

Are waves breaking or forming whitecaps? Where do they break? Are they breaking out into the channel, or is there a clear path? Is there a jetty?

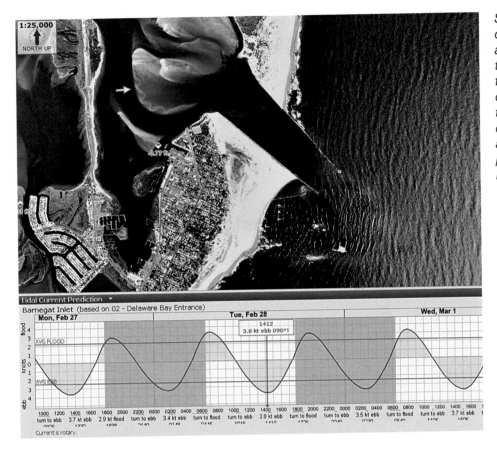

A jetty near an entrance can reflect waves across the inlet and cause interactions with larger waves, or standing waves (see Chapter 8). If the waves are too big, wait it out or find another inlet.

If you do choose to transit the inlet, seek out the most regular and widely spaced waves. Avoid confused seas if at all possible. To illustrate, let's look at the wave patterns in the accompanying photo chart (above). You can see the somewhat regular wave patterns approaching the shore. Note the bunching of waves right around the mouth of the inlet. This means you will be transiting steeper waves at very close intervals if you go that way. Also note the crossing wave patterns off the south end of the inlet. You should avoid wave patterns like these because crossing waves can reinforce each other, making them even steeper with pointed crests. Plus, with the wave fronts coming from multiple directions, maneuvering will be more difficult. Instead, seek out the most benign water. In the example in the photo chart, one would travel due west and power into the inlet hugging the north side of the entrance, then turn gradually northwest. This route will give the most favorable wave patterns—widely spaced and regular.

IS THERE A BAR?

Bars can cause breaking waves, and traversing them is tricky, if not downright dangerous. Be sure to read the section on bars later in this chapter.

HOW DEEP IS THE WATER?

Depth is a critical factor. You need to know the exact location of the channel, the stage of the tide, and how prevailing weather conditions affect the depth of the water. (For example, a strong offshore wind could potentially flush water from the area landward of a bar, reducing the available depth.)

WHAT ARE THE PREVAILING WEATHER CONDITIONS?

Even if you know the inlet, storms can alter or magnify the conditions. For example, strong winds can push water away from the lee side of a bar, leaving less available depth for navigation. Strong onshore winds minimize your control of the boat. Heavy rain or fog can obscure your vision. When entering an inlet or transiting a bar, you need excellent visibility. Heavy seas can make an already difficult situation downright dangerous.

Transiting the Inlet

WITH THE CURRENT, INTO THE WIND

Let's say you're departing an inlet for open waters and you're going with the current. The current will be pushing you toward the waves. As we covered in Chapter 3, going with the current reduces your ability to steer. Therefore, to gain steerage, you will need to accelerate your speed, which will increase your impact with oncoming waves. As a general rule of thumb, go as slowly as you can while still maintaining steerage.

Because inlets are generally narrow, you may be unable to take the waves at an angle as you would in open seas. Instead, you'll most likely have to take the oncoming waves head-on. Be especially careful with large cresting waves because they may toss your boat out of control. You have two options for handling them.

Option 1. If there is sufficient space and it is safe to do so, maneuver around large cresting waves.

1. Carefully observe the oncoming waves, looking for those that are about to break. Don't just look at the wave directly in front of you; keep an eye on the next several set of waves and try to anticipate their movement.

2. Identify the lowest part of each wavefront and steer toward it. (The lowest part of the wave will break last.)

Option 2. If there is not sufficient space to maneuver, follow these steps:

1. Proceed into the waves in a straight line. If a wave looks like it may break on your bow, shift into reverse gear and back down away from the wave. (This may be easier with an outboard or I/O drive, since you can maintain steerage.) Backing down may be a last resort, but it is preferable to taking a large breaking wave over the bow.

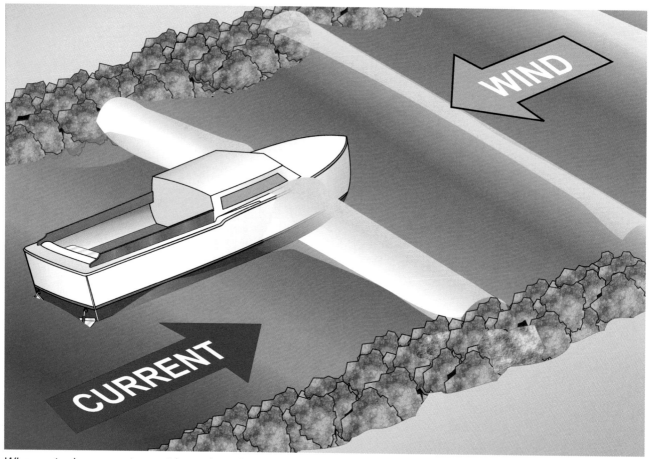

When outgoing currents meet incoming winds, waves will steepen. If the waves become too steep, turn around. Otherwise, maneuver to the lowest part of the wave whenever possible and use your throttle to avoid any waves that might break on your bow.

2. As soon as the wave crests and breaks, advance through the foam. Recognize that you may have less grip on this foamy water and add power carefully to avoid overspinning your prop. Keep in mind that the water may be substantially shallower in the trough.

With the Wind and Waves, and into the Current

If entering the inlet or entrance from open water, you will find yourself in following seas where conditions may seem more benign. However, as you get closer to a bar or the shoreline, the waves will heighten and the distance between them will be shortened by the shallower bottom and the wind. They will likely begin breaking.

With very short spaces between waves, and confused seas as you approach the inlet, it will be very difficult to ride on the back of an incoming wave. Plus, in order to give yourself ample reaction time to changing conditions, you'll need to slow down as you approach the inlet. This means the waves will overtake you. That said, you'll want those wavefronts to pass under the boat and not break directly behind you or into your cockpit.

On top of everything, the onrush of the opposing current will become more apparent as you approach the inlet.

How do you manage so many variables? Some guidelines:

- Important: before you commit to this passage, make sure you have adequate fuel, you and your crew are in life jackets, and all loose gear and lines are secured. If you lose power, you're in big trouble. You don't want to run out of fuel or foul your prop on a loose line halfway through your passage.

- If conditions permit, approach the inlet from the side rather than coming straight in. That said, avoid exposing your beam to the waves. A 45° approach angle is best because it allows you a better view of the conditions than if you come straight through them.

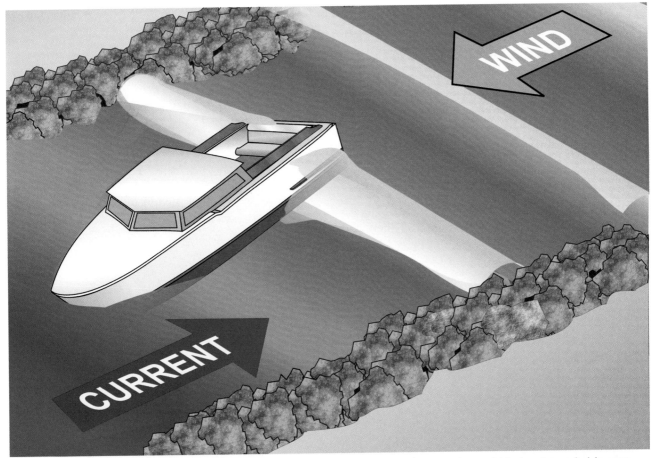

When traveling with the waves, be sure you keep your stern square to the seas to avoid being turned sideways. This boat will need to turn to starboard with some power to avoid being turned.

Boat Handling beyond the Harbor

- Look outward at the oncoming waves and the conditions forming at the mouth of the inlet to plan your approach.

- Despite having approached at an angle, you don't want to enter the inlet at an angle. Instead, turn so as to square your transom to the oncoming waves, facing the inlet for a straight-in final approach.

- As with all following seas, do your best to avoid going over a breaking wave ahead of you. If you do, you may be propelled forward like a surfer.

- If a wave in front breaks, back away by slowing your boat until the wave dissipates into foam and ripples. Then go forward carefully, keeping in mind that you may lose some grip on the foamy water.

- Carefully observe the wave patterns. Waves break where the water is shallow, so you will find few breaking waves in deep water. Deep water is where you want to be.

- Keep an eye on the waves coming from behind you. You don't want a following wave to pick up your stern and propel you forward, or worse, to push the stern into a broach. You may be forced to go over the wave ahead if faced with a large wave from behind. If you do, make sure you keep the stern square to the wave so your boat will not be pushed sideways. If necessary, briefly accelerate to get away from the trailing wavefront and ride up the back of the wave in front.

- Continually adjust your throttle to maintain the best position relative to the waves.

- Monitor wave patterns as you approach the inlet. Look for areas where waves peak consistently and avoid them. They may be standing waves.

- Keep in mind that incoming waves come in groups, with several typically larger than the rest. Before beginning your transit of the inlet, hang back and observe the wave patterns. Choose the best set of waves to transit with, and time it well.

Remember, once you have committed to running an inlet, you may not be able to change your mind. Stay sharp, tough it out, and have a safe passage.

WAVES, WIND, AND CURRENT COINCIDE

If the current and wind are moving in the same direction and you're going along with them, the process is much safer and less stressful. Under these conditions, the current helps spread the waves farther apart. If, on the other hand, you're moving against these combined forces, the task will be a little trickier. On the plus side, however, you will have plenty of steerage as the flow of water past the boat is increased by the current. Some guidelines:

- While the waves may be spread out, you will be facing the full force of both wind and current. Make sure you and your boat are prepared for this transit and the crew is wearing life jackets. Once you start, you are committed. If your engine stops, you will be in deep trouble with no route of recovery.

- Increase throttle to make headway, particularly within the narrowest part of the inlet where the current speed will be accelerated.

- Maintain continuous control over the throttle and wheel to stay square to the waves.

- As you approach an oncoming wave, slow down to lessen the impact. As you impact the wave, add throttle to help the bow lift and rise up over the wave, then throttle back as you cut through. Accelerate again until you reach the next wave crest.

What happens if you're entering an inlet with all the forces heading in your direction? Once again, you'll find yourself in following seas. This time, however, the waves will be farther apart and smoother than if the current were opposed to the wind.

With the longer back of the wave, you can ride the waves directly in rather than approach the inlet at an angle. Keep in mind that once you start, you are committed. The wind and current will force you to continue.

Some guidelines:

- With the current, your speed over the ground may substantially increase, but your steerage will diminish. You may need to give a few bursts of throttle to improve your steerage and control.

- Keep the boat square to the waves and stay on the back of a wave as long as you can.

- Monitor your lateral position and observe the direction of the waves relative to the inlet. If the waves approach at an angle, they can push you to one side. Anticipate this and steer a bit in the opposite direction to leave adequate room.

TRAVERSING BARS

As strong currents flow through inlets, the water tends to carve paths through the sea bed. Sand particles are swept up from the sea bed and suspended in the tumultuous water. When the fast-moving water exits the inlet and slows down, the sand particles settle to the bottom again. Over time these sand particles can accumulate into large shoals called *bars*.

Bars have an adverse affect on waves. As waves roll toward the bars, the shoaling water causes the waves to break before they reach shore. Traversing a bar means you may face breaking waves—a treacherous situation. To make matters worse, the water over sand bars is sometimes so shallow that you'll have to plane over them to avoid grounding. Also note that bars change shape over time and can be moved by large storms. As such, your chart may not be entirely accurate. Crossing bars is a challenge best left to experienced skippers.

Bar Fundamentals

Sandbars present several challenges. They cause currents to eddy, and with added winds, they can create significant standing waves. Incoming waves are likely to break as they approach a sandbar, resulting in reflected waves that travel out into the channels. Strong tidal flows tend to carve channels through bars. These channels are sometimes navigable, but the constant flow of currents can cause the channels to shift over time. (In fact, a channel can shift position within a single boating season.) The greatest challenge, however, will be breakers.

PREPARING FOR A BAR CROSSING

Specific locations develop reputations for their challenging bars. Before attempting to cross a bar, learn all you can about it.

- Talk with boaters who have transited the bar and ask their advice.

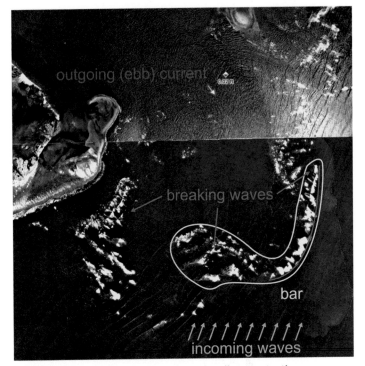

Sandbars and the shoaling water leading up to them cause waves to break. This aerial photo shows several bars. The bar within the yellow circle is preceded by shoals (the lighter area to the right of the bar). The white regions in the photo are breaking waves. Notice the regular pattern of incoming waves being distorted and bent by the bars. You also can see confused wave patterns near the current arrow as the bent wave fronts and reflections actually cross each other, forming closely spaced, complex waves. (Courtesy Maptech)

- Understand the local tidal conditions and timing. Local boaters will be able to tell you the best tidal conditions for crossing the bar. Recognize that you will likely have to cross the bar twice—once outbound and once inbound—so it's important to know the tidal conditions both ways.

- It's a very good idea to observe the bar and entrance from land before you take to the sea. Look for the darker water that indicates deeper water. Be particularly mindful of breaking waves and light water. Scope out standing waves and breakers and note the areas to avoid.

- Observe how other boaters are crossing the bar and the paths they take. Also note the sizes of their boats. If all the boats are larger than your own, don't attempt the crossing.

- Look for navigation aids.

Boat Handling beyond the Harbor

- Consult the latest charts. Navigation software sometimes comes with with photo charts. While these photos may have been taken years earlier, they'll still provide valuable insights.

- Inspect your boat before departing. Your engine, throttle, and steering will be crucial to a safe crossing; make sure they'll be in good working order. Also make sure that you and your crew are wearing life jackets, close all hatches, secure all loose gear, and confirm that your radio is operational.

During an outgoing tide, this inlet is blocked by waves breaking over bars. An incoming tide or slack water may diminish the size of the breakers. In situations like this, it's often better to wait. (Courtesy Maptech)

This Coast Guard lifeboat is battling steep breaking waves while departing over a bar. (Courtesy U.S. Coast Guard)

Crossing a Bar

OUTBOUND CROSSING

On the outbound crossing, you'll be powering into the waves. Follow these steps:

1. Observe the waves and try to avoid breakers. Follow the darker water.

2. Slow your boat as you approach the oncoming waves.

3. Take the waves head-on rather than at an angle. (You should turn no more than 10 to 15° off the wave.) You need to make forward progress past the bar as efficiently as possible and cannot take the risk of being turned sideways.

4. Look for patterns of lesser waves at the bars and speed up to transit them as they cross.

5. If no lulls occur, power up to the bar and, if possible, wait for a wave that already has broken. Accelerate through the broken water and attempt to get past the bar before the next wave begins to break.

6. If necessary, seek out a wave that is not too steep and has yet to break and approach it carefully. Throttle up and over, then throttle back as you clear the wave. Speed up to clear the bar before the next wave approaches.

7. Approach the next wave, heading for the lowest part, since this is the last part of the wave that will break. Again, back off on the throttle just before impact and gently power up and over.

8. Keep repeating this pattern until you are clear of the bars and any breaking water.

9. Once you begin transiting a bar, there's no turning back. Stay sharp and keep powering.

INBOUND CROSSING

On the inbound crossing, you'll be traveling with the waves and, most likely, a following sea. Your greatest challenge will be to see what lies ahead. Here are some tips:

- Plan for a favorable tide. An incoming tide or slack water is better than an outgoing tide. If the tide is unfavorable, consider waiting.

- Hang back and observe the wave pattern. Proceed when you see a set of lower waves.

This Coast Guard lifeboat has been broached. (Luckily, these boats are designed to right themselves even if capsized.) Your best strategy for avoiding this situation is to take the waves squarely, either directly into them or directly with them. (Courtesy U.S. Coast Guard)

■ As with any following sea, travel at the same speed as the waves and ride on the back of a wave. Stay ahead of any breakers behind you.

■ Approach directly—not at an angle—and keep the stern square with the waves.

■ After the wave ahead of you has broken, accelerate through the whitewater.

■ When you're clear of the bar, take a breath, then prepare for the inlet or harbor channel.

OPERATING IN NARROW PASSAGES AND RIVERS

Narrow channels and rivers, like inlets, tend to have accelerated currents. Before you start out, get good information about the waterway to help you navigate. And remember that traveling downstream will be more difficult because steerage is reduced. (This is why vessels heading downstream have the right-of-way over those heading upstream.)

Bank Effects

The banks of narrow channels provide additional challenges beyond currents. For starters, if your boat gets too close to the bank, the bow wave can cause a bank effect. As a boat pushes its bow wave forward, a pocket of lower water forms behind the wave. When you're in open water, this pocket is continuously backfilled by the surrounding water. When you travel close to a riverbank, however,

there is less available water to replace the depression; your hull, the bow wave, and the riverbank all serve to constrict the flow of water to the pocket. This void creates a suction that pulls the stern toward the bank. At the same time, the bow is being pushed away from the bank by the bow wave reflecting off the bank. These two forces turn the boat toward the center of the channel and into any oncoming boat traffic.

To counteract this effect, speed up a bit and steer slightly away from the bank. On a twin-engine boat, you may be able to correct by applying a bit more power to the engine away from the bank.

The magnitude of these bank effects is somewhat dependent upon the steepness of the bank. A steep bank or sheer vertical wall will have greater impact than a gradually sloping beach. If traversing a narrow channel with steep banks on both sides, slow down and proceed near the center of the channel.

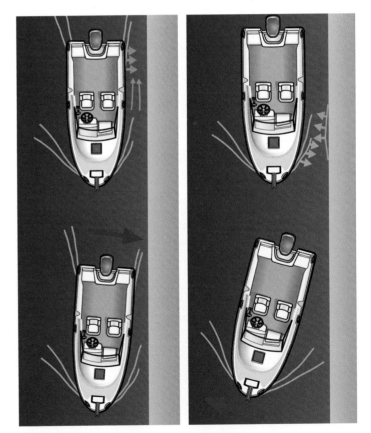

Boats moving close to a river or canal bank may encounter the bank effect: water drained away by t he bow wave causes a void that will suck the stern toward the bank (left), while the bow wave reflects back from the shore and pushes the bow out (right). The combination turns the boat away from the bank.

If you encounter another boat, and you are appropriately on the starboard side of the channel, apply a bit of right rudder to counteract the bank

effects until the other boat passes, then straighten after the other boat passes.

Currents flow to the outer side of a bend due to momentum and centrifugal force. This is where you'll find the deepest water. Shoaling often occurs downstream of a curve. Eddies can form in this region, too.

Turning a Bend

Sharp bends in narrow channels or rivers offer another set of challenges. Silt or sand carried downstream by the current is often deposited in the calmer water on the inside of the bend at its downstream end. This creates shoals there. Also note that the water on the inside of a bend may actually be drawn back upstream. These eddies can catch and turn your boat if you get too close.

When turning around a river bend, follow this strategy:

1. Before anything else, signal your approach to oncoming traffic.

2. Ease the boat toward the center of the channel, then carefully turn into the bend.

3. Do not turn too much, as the current pushing against your aft quarter will tend to rotate the boat farther.

4. By moving away from the near side of the channel, you will be more likely to avoid shallows and eddies, and you will gain earlier visibility around the bend.

5. Avoid getting pushed to the outer side of the bend, where bank effects could turn you.

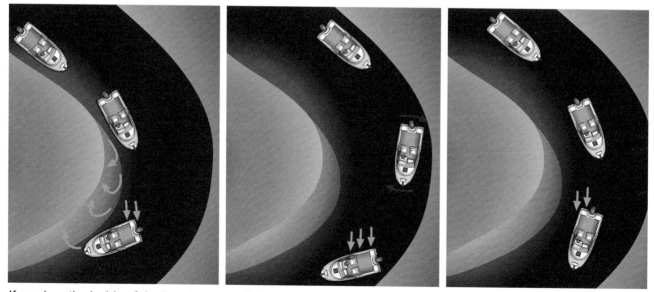

If you hug the inside of the bend, you are likely to get caught in eddies (left). If you follow the outside bank, you can encounter bank effects, plus you'll have the strongest currents on your quarter (center panel). The best strategy is to stay in the center, where you will have room to maneuver (right).

PART IV

SPECIAL SITUATIONS

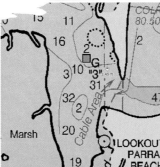

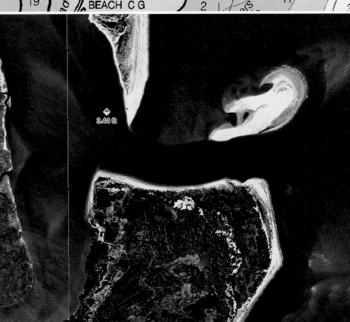

CHAPTER 11

Anchoring

Anchoring is a process of securing the boat to the bottom. When underway, you may choose to anchor for a brief snack, to stay overnight, or in an emergency to keep you from drifting into greater peril.

The anchor system comprises more than just the anchor. It also includes an anchor line (called a *rode*), and a collection of shackles to connect all the pieces.

ANCHORS

Like boats, anchors come in a number of different designs. Also like boats, there's no one perfect solution for all situations. Where do you start in choosing the right anchor for your boat? The first step is to determine your needs. Where do you plan to boat? What is the bottom like in that area? What do you intend to do when you get there? The answers will help you narrow down your choices.

It's prudent to carry at least two anchors at all times. Anchors can be lost (e.g., wedged on the bottom) and rodes have been known to break. In some situations, you'll need to use two anchors at the same time. Plus, you're likely to encounter a variety of bottom characteristics during your travels, so you'll want two different anchors to cover a wider range of possibilities.

In this chapter we'll cover three basic anchor designs, which are not only the most popular for recreational boats but also the most practical.

The anchor system consists of the anchor, the rode, and a collection of shackles to connect the pieces. Pictured here is a combination chain-and-rope rode. (Courtesy Danforth)

Fluke Anchor

The most popular anchor is the fluke, or light-weight, anchor. It folds flat, so it takes less stowage space than other types.

The fluke anchor works by laying flat on the bottom. When its rode is pulled, the flukes, which can swivel to either side of the shaft, burrow into the bottom.

These anchors work well in sand and mud, but, due to their lightweight designs, they have some difficulty digging into grassy bottoms.

Plow Anchor

Plow anchors hold better than lightweight anchors, especially in grassy bottoms. They are also effective in most other bottom types. Plow anchors are typically found on larger boats. They do not fold down and tend to be rather heavy. Thus, they are generally mounted on bow rollers for ease of deployment and retrieval.

When deployed, the plow section of the anchor digs into the bottom, much as a farmer's plow digs into the soil. If the pull direction changes, the plow comes out and resets in a new direction.

Claw Anchor

A claw anchor also offers a better hold than a light-weight anchor. The advantage of the claw anchor is its rounded blade. Because the blade rotates in place, it holds very well when the direction of pull changes, unlike a plow anchor. Claw anchors are effective in most types of bottoms.

RODE

The rode, which is a combination of a chain and rope or just chain, does more than simply tie the anchor to the boat.

The rode forms an arc between the anchor and the boat: it is nearly vertical at the boat and nearly horizontal at the anchor. The weight of the rode causes the arc, or catenary, which plays an essential role in the anchor's ability to hold ground. To be effective, an anchor's shaft must be nearly horizontal to the bottom, so the rode must pull along the bottom, not straight up. Also, the catenary acts as a shock absorber. If the boat is pushed by a boat wake or strong gust, the rode will stretch out momentarily, then settle back into

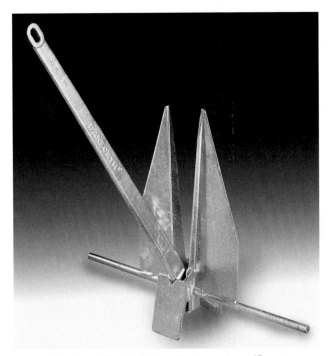

The ubiquitous Danforth is a fluke anchor. (Courtesy Danforth)

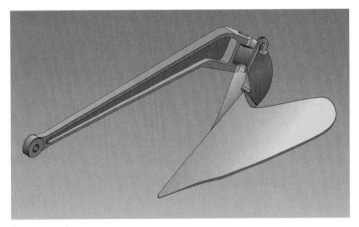

Plow anchor.

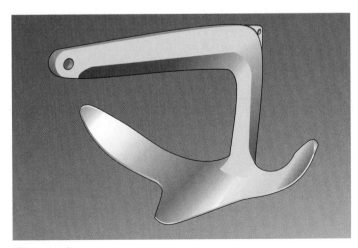

Claw anchor.

151

its arc. If the line were always taut, any sudden movement from the boat could yank the anchor free from the bottom.

Rodes are usually either a combination of rope and chain, or all chain. Chain is used at the anchor end for two purposes: 1) the chain's weight keeps the rode nearly horizontal at the bottom; and 2) the chain doesn't chafe against the bottom as rope would.

How much chain is needed? As much as possible is probably the best answer. However, boats have practical limitations for carrying and storing chain. A more practical answer is about 10% of the length of the total rode, although some would use as little as 5%.

Sizing Your Anchor and Rode

Most manufacturers have prepared tables of anchor sizes for their particular brand of anchor. These are usually based on the size of your boat. The table below offers a summary.

The table also provides sizes for the chain or rope used in the rode. It is important that your anchor system not have any weak links. That is, every component used in the rode should have a breaking strength greater than the holding power of the anchor. This is especially true for the shackles that interconnect the components.

SELECTING AN ANCHORAGE

When possible, select your anchorage so you'll have enough space between your boat and shorelines or obstructions, and between your boat and other boats. Remember that shifts in wind and current will swing the boat around the anchor. Make sure there's sufficient room on all sides.

The type of bottom may determine which anchor you use and your anchoring strategy. The sea bed may be layered with one type of material near the surface, and another a short distance below. The anchor must penetrate the surface layer and dig into the more substantial material below it.

Bottom Types

Charts may indicate the type of bottom, such as sand, mud, clay, gravel, cobbles, pebbles, stones, rocks, and shells. The next section provides a description of the most common types along with the abbreviation that would appear on the chart.

SAND (S)

Sand is common, particularly in coastal locations. Loose sand may not provide solid holding power for your anchor, but in most cases you will find packed sand below the loose sand. Packed sand usually provides good hold. Lightweight, plow, and claw anchors work well in sand.

CHOOSING THE PROPER ANCHOR SIZE

BOAT LENGTH	FLUKE ANCHOR			PLOW ANCHOR		CLAW ANCHOR	CHAIN	ROPE
	Galvanized	Hi-Tensile	Aluminum	Hinged	Fixed		Diameter	Diameter
(ft)	(lb)	(lb)	(lb)	(lb)	(lb)	(lb)	(in)	(in)
Up to 20	4–8	5	2.5–4	25	9	2.2–4.4	3/16	3/8
20–25	8	6	4–6	25–30	14	11–16.5	1/4	3/8
25–30	15	12–14	7	35	14	22	1/4	7/16
30–35	22	20	7–10	35–45	14	33	5/16	1/2
35–40	22	25–35	13	35–45	22	44	3/8	5/8
40–45	40	35–40	15	35–45	44	44	7/16	5/8
45–50	65	60	18–21	35–60	55	66	1/2	3/4
50–60	85	70	29–42	75	55	66–110	9/16	3/4

Mud (M)

Soft mud suffers from a lack of holding power, but deeper mud will usually produce a good hold. Your anchor will need to be large enough to get past any surface layer of peat or muck into a firmer bottom. Lightweight, plow, and blade anchors work well in mud.

Grass (Gr)

Grass presents a slippery surface that might be difficult for lightweight anchors to penetrate. Heavier anchors may be able to penetrate the grass, but the bottom must hold. Grass in a soft bottom may have only moderate holding power. To have good holding power, the anchor will need to penetrate below this layer. With grasses it is very important to carefully deploy, set, and check your holding power (discussed later). Plow and blade anchors are preferred for grass.

Gravel (G), Pebbles (P), or Stones (St)

Gravel is an uncertain bottom. Loose, small gravel is much like soft sand, while larger aggregate may hold better, particularly if it is mixed with firmer sand or mud. Most anchors will work in gravel.

Rocks (R)

It may be difficult for an anchor to find a purchase on rocks. The blade or flukes must be able to wedge around one or more rocks to set. Once wedged, the anchor may be difficult to retrieve.

Coral (C)

Many coral regions are protected, and anchorage may be prohibited. You should avoid anchoring in coral.

Shells (Sh)

Shells are similar to gravel—the surface layer may not hold well. You will need to get the anchor below the top layers into mud or sand to get a good purchase.

DEPLOYING THE ANCHOR

Set the anchor from the bow. When anchored, the bow should face into the wind so it can rise over waves, or part them so they don't rush into the boat. Do not anchor from the stern. Boats anchored stern-to have sunk because waves are more able to rush over the transom. Under certain conditions, you may choose to add a second anchor from the stern to keep the boat from swinging, but do not anchor in a position that allows waves to hit the beam or stern.

Dropping the Anchor

When you've reached the spot where you'd like to anchor, follow these steps:

1. Approach your anchorage either into the current or into the wind. (If a current is present, it will usually predominate.)

2. It is best that you hold your boat essentially motionless over the bottom as you lower the anchor. If not, the rode may start paying out rapidly as soon as the anchor sets, which may injure the person paying out the line.

3. Drop the anchor vertically—do not throw the anchor.

4. If the wind or current is too strong to maintain your position while anchoring, advance beyond your selected anchorage and drift backwards. Drop the anchor so that it will hit bottom at the proper location.

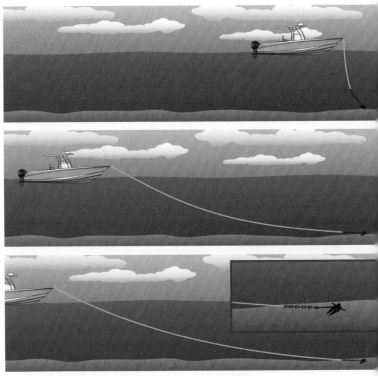

Drop the anchor straight down to its intended destination (top); power in reverse, paying out rode (center); and continue in reverse to set the anchor into the bottom (above).

Setting the Anchor

Once the anchor reaches the bottom, you want to set it:

1. Run the anchor line around a cleat so you can halt the payout at the appropriate time.

2. Make sure everyone's arms and legs are clear so they won't get caught in the line and pulled overboard.

3. Pay out the appropriate scope of anchor line as the boat drifts or is slowly powered backward. (See below for more on *scope*.) Resist tying off or restricting the payout of the line until you have paid out the planned amount.

4. At the appropriate rode length, cleat the anchor line and apply more power in reverse to set the anchor.

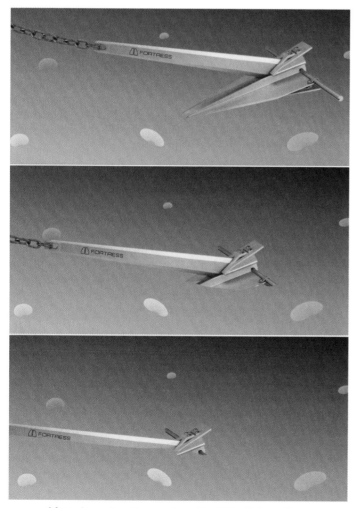

After dropping the anchor, it will lie flat on the bottom. As you power in reverse, the anchor's flukes will dig in until they are totally buried.

Scope

Scope is the ratio of the rode length to the depth to the seabed. Depth, in this case, is measured from the anchor roller or bow chock to the seabed. Scope is an integral part of anchoring successfully. As mentioned earlier, vertical pull on the anchor will dislodge it from the seabed, but horizontal pull will keep the anchor deeply set. As you pay out more rode, the boat floats farther from the anchor. This means that the rode will pull on the anchor from a low, horizontal angle.

How much scope you'll need depends upon the prevailing conditions. Under normal conditions (winds less than 20 knots), your scope should be 7:1. If you are just stopping for lunch in light airs and keep a good anchor watch, a scope of 5:1 should be sufficient. Under storm conditions (i.e., above 20 knots), you'll need a minimum of 10:1.

To convert scope to actual rode length takes a simple calculation. Let's say your anchor roller is 5 feet above the water and the depth to the seabed is 10 feet, making a total depth of 15 feet. To achieve a scope of 7:1, you will need to pay out 105 feet (15 × 7 = 105 feet). If you're looking at stormier conditions and need a scope of 10:1, you will need 150 feet (15 × 10 = 150).

When deciding how much rode to pay out, keep in mind that if you're anchored during a rising tide, the change in depth will shorten your scope. Pay out enough rode to handle the rising water.

Checking the Set

Once your anchor is set, you'll want to monitor your position and check that the anchor is holding:

1. Identify two objects on shore—preferably in line, but not dead ahead of your boat—and watch them.

2. Does their relative alignment change? If it does, your anchor may be dragging. (Keep in mind that the boat may swing around the anchor in response to changes in current or wind.)

3. If the anchor is dragging, first try motoring in reverse to set the anchor again. If this doesn't work, you may need to repeat the entire anchoring process—possibly at a different location.

Even if you're confident that your anchor is firmly set, it's still a good idea to maintain an

The right ratio of scope depends on the expected weather conditions: 5:1 is okay in light breezes, but 7:1 is best in normal conditions; 10:1 or longer is necessary in stormy conditions. When determining height of the bow above the bottom, use the highest tide level you'll encounter while anchored (blue) rather than the current tide (white).

anchor watch, which means you (or a crew member) check the anchor's position from time to time. Check your position against the same set of reference points. If your boat shifts direction due to winds or current, find another line of reference and repeat your checks. There is always the risk that the anchor will come free and not reset properly in the new position.

Alternatively, you can use the anchor watch function on your GPS. This is an alarm that will alert you if your boat drifts outside a set radius.

RETRIEVING THE ANCHOR

What goes down, hopefully, comes up. Anchors are expensive, so you will want yours back. Generally, anchors can be retrieved by pulling straight up on the rode.

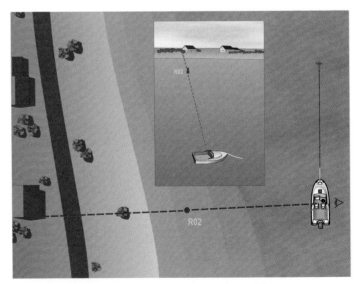

Find two land features in a row that align with your position, then periodically check to make sure you have not drifted.

To remove the anchor, move toward the anchor and haul in the rode. Continue until you are directly above the anchor. The anchor should break free when you pull straight up. If, however, it does not break free, tie off the rode, and power away in reverse in the opposite direction. The resultant leverage should free the anchor.

1. Pull the boat slowly up to where the anchor is set, stowing the rode in its locker as you go.

2. When you are directly over the anchor, pull the rode straight upward to break the anchor free.

3. If the anchor resists, cleat the line, bring the boat around (with the stern in the opposite direction), and briefly apply power to break the anchor free.

4. Once the anchor releases from the bottom, pull in the remainder of the rode.

5. When the anchor reaches the surface, dip it up and down to remove any mud or debris before pulling it aboard.

Some anchors, such as the plow or claw, can really dig in. On rare occasions, particularly in a rocky bottom, an anchor can become wedged so tightly that even pulling straight up may not help. If you expect to anchor in rocks, you may want to add a lighter, secondary line, called a *trip line*, to the anchor. Some anchors have a hole near the shaft, just above the plow or claw. Attach the trip line here and pay out the second line along with the rode when you set the anchor. If you are unable to retrieve the anchor using the rode, you may be able to pull out the anchor by hauling backward on the trip line.

ANCHORING IN NARROW OR TIGHT LOCATIONS

When you anchor in areas subject to tidal currents, your boat will swing in opposite directions, depending upon the current and your duration of stay. Consequently, you may find you do not have enough room to fully swing about your anchor without hitting obstructions or the shoreline. The solution is to deploy two anchors in opposite directions, called a Bahamian moor.

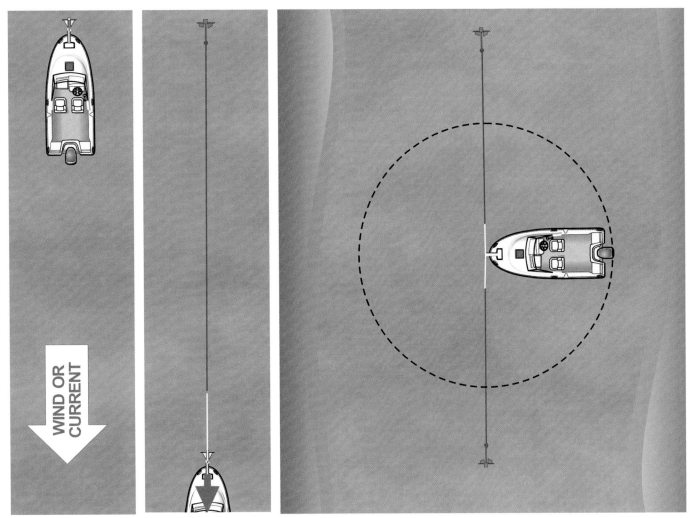

Drop the first anchor. Then motor in reverse, paying out two times the amount of rode you would need for the conditions. When the rode has paid, set the anchor, then drop a second anchor. Pay out the second rode while pulling in the first one until you get to the midpoint between the anchors. Your boat will rotate around a fixed point (right).

1. Drop your first anchor into the current as normal.

2. Back up with the wind or current, traveling twice as far as you normally would for the prevailing conditions, then set the anchor.

3. Drop your second anchor over the bow and pay out its rode as you power back to a point halfway between the two anchorages.

4. Cleat both anchor rodes.

5. Now your swing will be about a fixed point.

ANCHORING IN STORMS

If the weather deteriorates, one of the best ways to add security and holding power is to use two anchors deployed at an angle of approximately 45° from the bow.

1. Drop your first anchor, which should be off to the side of your final intended position.

2. Back away to set the anchor, moving somewhat toward the other side of your intended final position.

3. Power forward at a 45° angle to a location in line with the first anchor. Drop the second anchor and back away.

4. Deploy a 10:1 rode for each anchor.

5. Your final position should be downwind or downcurrent of the two anchors and halfway between them. In this configuration, your load is shared between both anchors, provided that the storm winds or current continue from the same direction.

6. In a severe tropical storm, your biggest concern

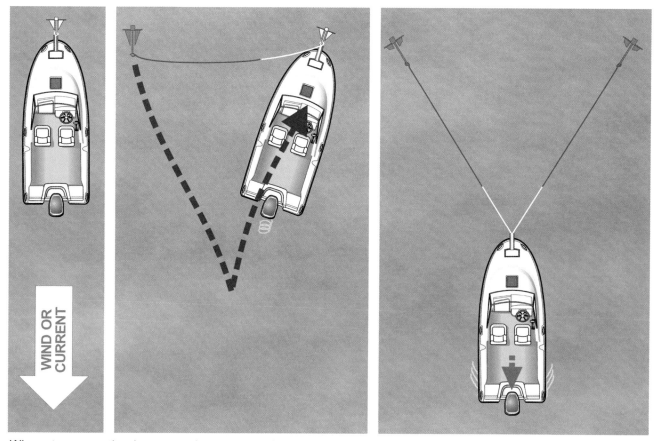

When strong weather is expected, use two anchors. Drop and set one anchor. Then power forward at a 45° angle and drop your second anchor. Power back to set the second anchor.

will be storm surge. Pay out as much scope as you can.

ANCHORING IN EMERGENCIES

Anchoring is often thought of as parking the boat in calm waters for a rest or overnight stay. However, one of the major reasons you need to develop anchoring skills is to deal with emergencies. Imagine that you lose engine power and find your boat drifting into a main shipping channel. To make matters worse, the seas are choppy.

You will need to deploy your anchor to secure your position until you can repair the problem or help arrives.

1. Make your way to the bow to release the anchor.

2. Because the boat is heaving and rolling, make sure you secure yourself to the boat to prevent falling overboard. You may find the safest way to the bow is via a hatch through the forward deck rather than working your way along the side deck.

3. Pay out as much scope as possible, then snub the line to set the anchor.

4. Use your GPS to set an anchor watch based on your position to check that the anchor is holding.

5. If you continue to drift, drop a second anchor to see if it will hold.

CHAPTER 12

Grounding

Grounding is the unfortunate act of placing your vessel on the bottom in such a way that it cannot continue its voyage. Depending upon the type of bottom and tidal conditions, this can either be an inconvenience or a perilous situation. Timely reaction is essential, but making a mistake can make matters much worse. Obviously, the best course of action is to plan ahead and know how you would handle a grounding beforehand.

COAST GUARD AND COMMERCIAL ASSISTANCE

If there is imminent risk to boat or crew, immediately contact the U.S. Coast Guard (USCG). If you cannot reach the Coast Guard, contact local authorities, such as the harbormaster or local marine patrol. They will come with an eye toward helping you keep the vessel afloat and removing any injured crew. Keep in mind, though, that their primary mission doesn't include towing recreational boats, unless they are in immediate peril. That job will usually fall to commercial towing companies.

Commercial towing services, including assistance with freeing a grounded boat, may be contracted on a subscription basis. For example, Sea/Tow and BoatU.S. offer subscription services, while many insurance companies offer policies or riders to cover towing. Otherwise, you will be at the

mercy of local tow services. Check cruising guides to find local services, or try recommendations from the local harbormaster or marina, both of which you can reach by radio. If you end up calling a tow

This boat missed the turn and landed on the rocks. A falling tide has left her high and dry. (Courtesy U.S. Coast Guard)

The Coast Guard uses lifeboats and helicopters in their search and rescue operations. While they won't be able to help you with minor groundings and similar inconveniences, they will come to your aid when a life is at stake. (Courtesy U.S. Coast Guard)

service, be sure you have a clear understanding of the terms and costs of these services before they attempt to free your boat.

Assessing the Situation

Help is not always immediately available when you need it, so you may be on your own for a while. Therefore, it pays to know what steps you should take to help yourself.

SeaTow is a membership organization providing free towing services to members. They have boats around the country, ready to render assistance upon a call.

Is Everyone OK?

Start with your crew and passengers first. Immediately ask everyone to put on life jackets and count noses to be sure everyone is still onboard. Then find out if anyone is injured and assign someone to attend to any injuries.

What's the Condition of the Boat?

At the same time, you need to assess the boat to see if you're taking on water. This is especially important if you're grounded on rocks. Check the bilges for water intrusion. If there is a leak, try to stop it by stuffing any material you can into the hole—clothes, bedding, spare life jackets, etc.

If the boat is literally sitting on the rocks, does it seem likely it will stay there? What are the chances that the boat will slip off the rocks and sink? Depending on how things look, you may not want to attempt to free the boat.

What Is the Tide Stage?

After assessing your people and your boat, you'll want to know the status of the tide. Is it rising or falling? The answer may take a little homework. If you have a chartplotter, you may have ready access to tide graphs, which are built into the included

The greatest risk of a grounded boat on a falling tide is that it will settle on its side, which would allow the seas to swamp the boat when the tide rises. (Courtesy U.S. Coast Guard)

cartography. Some GPS units include tide information. Try radioing nearby boaters to get tide information if you don't have tide tables handy.

If the hull integrity is still intact, then the rising tide may be all you need to escape the grounding. On the other hand, if the boat is holed, the rising tide will cause a bigger problem. You need to know the tidal range and whether or not the boat will be submerged by the rising waters.

If the tide is falling and the hull is solid, you need to act quickly, while you still have a chance of freeing the boat. Delay too long and you'll have to wait out a tide cycle before a rising tide can free you. Also, waiting through the low tide may be more hazardous, in many cases. For example, your boat may settle on its side at low tide; then when the tide returns it may swamp rather than float your boat. If this is a possibility, attempt to find ways to keep the boat upright.

This high-and-dry boat has been braced upright awaiting the next high tide to float it free. (Courtesy U.S. Coast Guard)

Any Wind or Currents?

The state of the wind and currents is particularly important, as either or both can compound your grounding problem by pushing you farther onto the shoal. In fact, a strong wind toward the mouth of a bay can actually lower the water level within the bay and cause a grounding where adequate water would otherwise have been available.

If the wind or current is pushing you farther onto the shoal, you'll need to take immediate corrective action. If possible, drop your anchor to hold the boat in place until you can figure out what to do.

Where Is the Deep Water?

It is essential to determine which direction will take you into deeper water. For starters, it's not always directly behind you. It's possible that you approached the shoal at an angle, and your grounding is more of a glancing blow. If you have grounded on a ridge or narrow bar and are sufficiently far advanced, it may be easier to reach the deeper water ahead rather than behind.

Observation is perhaps your best tool. Get up as high as you can—on a flybridge if possible—and look for darker water. Ripples, chop, and a lighter color are usually indicators of shallow water.

Here are some other methods:

- If you were using a fishfinder or charting sounder before you ran aground, look at the depth history to help determine what is behind you.

- Test the bottom around the boat. A boat hook can be very helpful. If you don't have a boat hook, use a *lead line* (a line with a weight on the end).

- Look at your charts. Locate your position on a chart and survey the region around the boat.

- If you have a chartplotter or GPS, you can pinpoint your position with precision. Look at the depth profiles and sounding to determine where you want to go.

- Set out in a dinghy and go looking for the deeper water.

What's on the Bottom?

While you have the chart out, look to see what the bottom is like. Are you dealing with rocks, either under the boat or nearby? The answer may limit your choices.

One way to test the bottom is using your boat hook. Is the bottom soft mud or sand, or something harder? Another option is to drag your anchor across the bottom and see what you bring up with it.

A soft bottom is less likely to cause damage to the hull, but it can create suction as it forms around the hull, which will make it harder to free the boat.

ROCKS OR REEF BOTTOM

Rocks present great risks. If you didn't hole your boat on the grounding, you might if you try moving your boat over rocks. This situation requires some expertise, and generally, you would be better off getting a professional to help. It also helps to have an external tow that can apply power in just the right spots.

If you are hung up on a reef, hull damage is just one of your worries. In most locations, reefs are protected by law. Get help fast so you can minimize any damage to boat and reef.

Is Your Propeller Stuck?

If your propeller and your rudder are free, you have a fighting chance of using your engine to get you off the bottom. Test the propeller at its lowest speed and look for any indication of prop wash. Try steering the rudder to see if it moves freely. If the propeller kicks up a lot of mud or sand, you need to be very careful to avoid costly damage.

If you have an outboard or sterndrive, it may help to trim out the engine or lower unit and lift the drive a bit. You have an advantage with these drives because you can see the propeller. Be very careful when running the engine, though, as you may suck up sand or debris into the cooling system and damage your impeller.

DEVELOP AND IMPLEMENT A STRATEGY

What are the chances that you can get the boat off by yourself? If it is risky or truly uncertain, you should seriously consider calling for help. If the bottom and conditions lead you to believe it's worth a try—go for it. This section will give you some guidelines.

Lighten the Load

The first task is to lighten the load on the boat. Pump the bilges dry and redistribute the load away from the portion of the hull that is on the ground. If the bow is stuck, simply placing the load aft may lift the bow enough to get you off. If you have a dinghy, put some of the crew and gear into it. Breaking free of the bottom may take no more than a few inches of lift, so moving just a few objects might do the trick.

Use Power

The quickest solution may be the use of power, but use it judiciously. It is possible to make matters worse. If you determine that the deeper water is

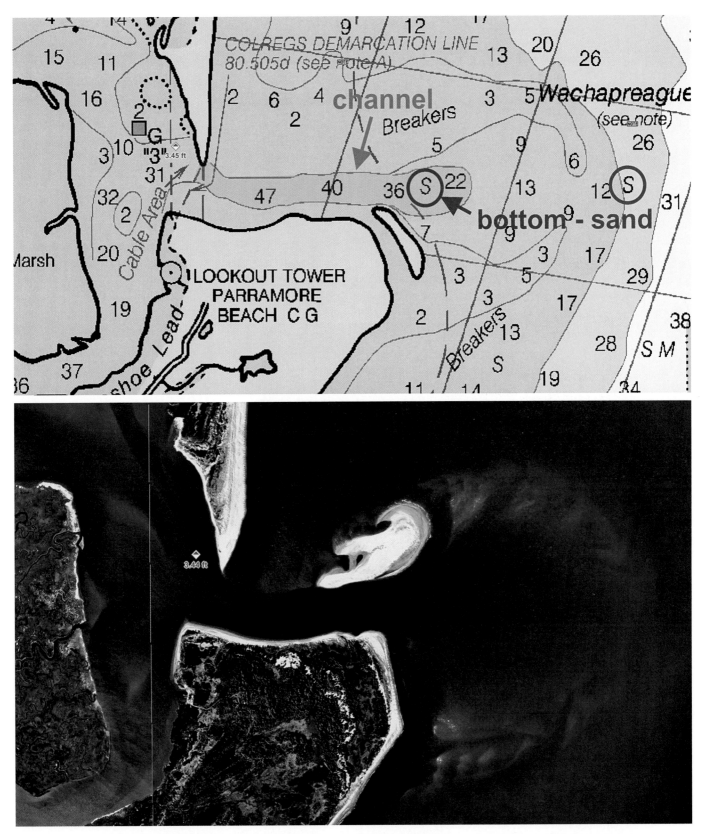

Paper charts provide not only depths and the locations of hazards, but the type of bottom as well. This chart shows the bottom to be sand and clearly shows the channel. In some ways, however, the paper chart does not provide the same level of detail as the photo chart. In the photo, you can see a distinct area of breakers (white area) north of the channel. Using both charts together can give you a clearer sense of your surroundings and help you avoid trouble. (Courtesy Maptech)

Special Situations

sternward, apply power slowly in reverse. There is a good chance that suction from the mud or sand against the hull is all that is holding you to the bottom. You may need to rock the boat to break this suction:

1. Apply power briefly while steering successively hard to port and hard to starboard. This will cause the rear of the boat to rock back and forth, potentially enlarging the boat's "footprint" on the sea bed. If you have an inboard, you'll need to do this with forward gear. Be careful to not push the boat farther onto the shoal.

2. When the boat begins to rock more freely, power in reverse and try to back up. Use steady power rather than strong bursts. (The latter will

kick up the bottom, which could pile up more bottom material around the hull. Also, you'll run the risk of damaging your impeller.)

3. Repeat the process from Step 1 until you're free.

4. If it seems like it's taking too long, check for progress by rocking the boat (see below). If the boat is still hard aground, you'll need to use another technique or get some help.

Kedging

Kedging is the process of deploying an anchor, then pulling on the anchor rode to help free the boat. Kedging is easier if you have a dinghy to take the anchor out to deeper water.

Aside from dropping the anchor in deeper

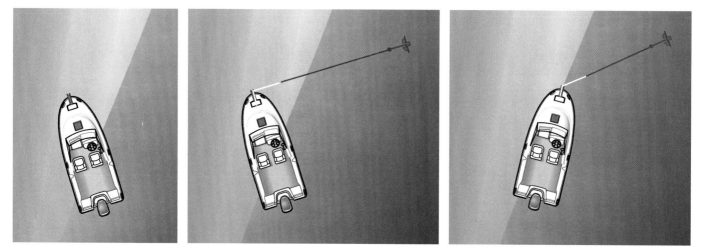

Kedging from the bow.

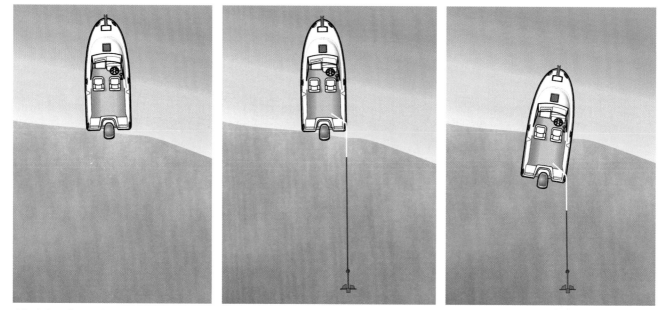

Kedging from the stern.

water, where exactly should you put it? Assess the boat's position to determine which part would be easiest to free. Often a kedge to the side of the bow can be used to swing the bow around and free it from the bottom. This works particularly well if the boat is grounded along the edge of a shoal rather than with the bow straight in. Or, if need be, you can kedge off the stern and attempt to back the boat. A winch or windlass can help. Using power and rocking the boat while pulling on the rode is often a successful combination. Just make sure that the anchor line does not foul the prop.

You can also try running the kedge rode up to a mast or other solid object high on the boat. Pulling from a high point above the boat will help tip the boat, which may effectively decrease its draft.

Rock the Boat

In concert with other steps, do whatever you can to rock the boat. This may be as simple as having the crew get the boat rocking by shifting their weight while on board, or getting off the boat and rocking it by pushing on the gunwale. (If the crew exits the boat, be sure that they work near the bow and nobody gets near the transom and propeller.)

Other methods to rock the boat include steering the boat in alternating directions and applying power, or if you have twin drives, alternating one drive with the other.

Get Help from Another Boat

If the crew of a nearby boat is willing, they can help in several ways. First they may be able to create a wake that can temporarily lift your boat. As the wake comes toward you, be ready to apply power. It may take several passes for this to work.

Another option is to extend a tow line to the other boat. By pulling on the line in the same manner as kedging, you may be able to free your boat toward deeper water. Generally, this works best to the side, either from the bow or the stern.

The third option is to use the line to turn your boat. Turning the boat can enlarge your boat's "footprint" on the bottom, which will help break the suction that holds the boat in place. Also, pivoting the boat rather than pulling straight ahead or astern applies more leverage and lowers the friction between the bottom and the boat.

If All Else Fails

If, after giving it your best, you are unable to free your boat, then you have a choice of waiting for a favorable tide or calling for professional help. Professionals will have the equipment and know-how to safely and effectively move your boat.

Remember, just about every boater runs aground from time to time, so you are not alone. Take it easy and patiently try each of the techniques described here—they are likely to help get you free.

Station Keeping

There are times when you will want to hold your boat in a single location for a period of time. For example, you may need to hold position until a drawbridge is opened or while meeting with another boat. This task is easy in still water, but wind or current can make it a challenge.

It's not possible to hold station in a broadside wind or current unless your boat is equipped with bow and stern thrusters, so let's concentrate on two conditions—into the wind or current (whichever dominates), and with the wind or current. When current is present, it usually dominates, but not always. Your boat's above-the-waterline surface area will determine how much effect you experience from wind.

INTO THE WIND OR CURRENT

Holding the bow into the wind or current is not as easy as it sounds. Remember, you control the boat from the stern, so the bow is free to do whatever it wants—and what it usually wants is to point downwind or downcurrent. Your job is to keep the stern to leeward or downcurrent of the bow. When the bow moves to port, therefore, you need to steer to starboard in forward gear to move the stern a like amount to port. By the time the stern is once again directly downwind or downcurrent of the bow, the entire boat will have shifted sideways to port, so you may need to oversteer to starboard to move back the other way. Now the bow swings to starboard, and the process repeats. A practiced skipper can minimize the resultant swings back and forth.

The other alternative is to make brief adjustments in reverse, thus moving the pivot point sternward so that you can swing the bow more quickly into realignment., Then shift back into forward gear. You will likely need both techniques to hold position. Thus, station keeping involves a succession of movements back and forth, and to some extent forward and backward, using throttle and wheel.

WITH THE WIND OR CURRENT

When wind or current is behind you, you can hold position simply by applying the appropriate power in reverse gear. The bow will naturally point downwind, which is where you want it.

If you have an outboard or I/O, you will be able to adjust your position toward port or starboard simply by turning the engine in the desired direction while staying in reverse. If you steer to port, for example, the directed reverse thrust from the propeller will ease the stern toward port. When you steer back amidships, the bow will fall in behind the stern, and the whole boat has moved toward port.

It's not quite as easy with an inboard, since you will have virtually no steerage from your rudder in reverse. You will need to shift into forward gear briefly and apply a burst of power with the wheel turned in order to kick the stern to one side or the other. Then shift back into reverse to regain and hold position.

Station keeping is a valuable and useful skill, and it will make you a more accomplished skipper in the harbor and around the docks.

Recommended Reading

Powerboat Handling Illustrated contains information that has been thoroughly researched and distilled to provide the essence of what you need to know to handle a powerboat. There are, however, other excellent books that provide expanded detail in some areas.

All About Powerboats: Understanding Design and Performance, Marshall, Roger. Camden, ME: International Marine, 2002.
Explains hull and boat design and selection.

Boat Docking: Close Quarters Maneuvering for Small Craft, Low, Charles T. Brockville, Ontario: Harvey Island Enterprises, 1997.
Covers a wide range of docking maneuvers.

Boat Handling Under Power: A Captain's Quick Guide, Sweet, Bob. Camden, ME: International Marine, 2005.
Waterproof, laminated guide to boat handling topics; meant to be taken aboard the boat.

Boatowner's Handbook, Vigor, John. Camden, ME: International Marine, 2000.
Provides summary data, tables, and descriptions on a wide range of topics including seamanship.

Complete Guide to Anchoring and Line Handling, Brown, David G. New York: Hearst Marine Books, 1996.
Presents detailed coverage of anchor and rode selection, and anchoring techniques.

Fast Powerboat Seamanship, Pike, Dag. Camden, ME: International Marine, 2004.
Written for those looking to handle a high-speed powerboat, but applicable to all forms of powerboating.

Getting Started in Powerboating, Third Edition, Armstrong, Bob. Camden, ME: International Marine, 2005.
Updated edition of a solid presentation of topics ranging from powerboat selection and handling to navigation and the rules of the road.

Heavy Weather Tactics: A Captain's Quick Guide, Rousmaniere, John. Camden, ME: International Marine, 2005.
Waterproof guide gives tips on dealing with severe weather and seas.

Knots, Bends, and Hitches for Mariners, United States Power Squadrons. Camden, ME: International Marine, 2006.
An excellent guide for the boater, with great illustrations and time-tested knots.

Modern Seamanship, Dodds, Don. New York: Lyons and Burford, 1995.
Another comprehensive guide loaded with technical information for recreational boaters.

On-Board Weather Forecasting: A Captain's Quick Guide, Sweet, Bob. Camden, ME: International Marine, 2005.
Waterproof guide covering the basics of weather and the onboard observations you can make.

Piloting, Seamanship and Small Boat Handling, 62nd Edition, Chapman, Charles F., with revisions by Elbert S. Maloney. New York: Motor Boating and Sailing, 1996.
A comprehensive guide to recreational boating.

The Propeller Handbook: The Complete Reference for Choosing, Installing, and Understanding Boat Propellers, Gerr, David. Camden, ME: International Marine, 2001.
A detailed handbook providing technical details on propellers and their applications.

Recommended Reading

RYA Motor Cruising Handbook, Jinks, Simon. Hampshire, United Kingdom: Royal Yachting Association, 2004.
An illustrated summary guide to topics for the cruising powerboat.

Small-Boat Seamanship Manual, Aarons, Richard N. Camden, ME: International Marine, 2006.
Based on the U.S. Coast Guard Boat Crew Seamanship Manual, with a wealth of information.

Sorensen's Guide to Powerboats, Sorensen, Eric W. Camden, ME: International Marine, 2002.
In-depth analysis of powerboat design and selection, including summary descriptions and specifications for a variety of boat models.

Stapleton's Powerboat Bible, Stapleton, Sid. Camden, ME: International Marine, 2002.
Broad coverage of topics of interest to a cruising powerboat operator including communications, weather, boat selection, and cruising.

Index